"When we first started working with incest, it seemed to be a terrible but rare occurrence; and then the dam burst, and the frightening reality of both its frequency and the damage done engulfed us. Now it's ritual abuse. Our first encounters seemed too frightening to be real, and yet now we hear unbelievable and similar stories much too frequently. Ryder's work is a welcome and sorely needed resource for therapists and survivors alike."

Pat Mellody, executive director of the Meadows,
Wickenburg, Arizona
Pia Mellody, author of *Breaking Free* and co-author of
*Facing Codependence: What It Is, Where It Comes From,
How It Sabotages Our Lives*

"As a mental health clinician with several years' experience treating child survivors of Satanic ritual abuse, I can recognize the real contribution Daniel Ryder's book will provide those of us who are working in this field. It takes courage to stand up and say, 'I believe that this type of abuse occurs.' It takes perseverance to compile a composite of treatment approaches and treatment issues pertinent to Satanic ritual abuse. There is no doubt in my mind that many of the children ritually abused today will turn to substances to blot out their painful memories tomorrow. It is time that clinicians combine their knowledge of the psychodynamic principles of post-traumatic stress disorder with the proven methods of the Twelve Step programs. We are all working together to heal people."

Pamela S. Hudson, M.S.S.W., A.C.S.W., L.C.S.W., author of *Ritual Child Abuse:
Discovery, Diagnosis, and Treatment*

"Anyone working with survivors of ritual abuse will find this book to be a wealth of information. *Breaking the Circle* abounds with helpful insights, no matter what your opinion of Satanism is. Ryder tells you what others are doing, what works for him, and lets you decide for yourself. I recommend this book highly.

The Reverend Dr. John L. Spangler, M.Div., D.S.T.
Green Bay, Wisconsin

"An excellent book—must reading for every psychotherapist and counselor. And if you are like me, hug your fear and read it anyway!"

Janet Hurley, M.A., licensed marriage and family therapist,
founder and co-director of TASK (Take a Stand for Kids),
Carmel Valley, California

"Many of the dynamics discussed in this book have not been disclosed in any previous forum on the subject. The unsettling 'reality' remains that there is a remarkable consistency in the victim/survivor experience as portrayed in this book and the independent findings of a wide range of professionals. I would strongly recommend this book to any professional or significant other who interacts with the victim/survivor."

Sgt. Jon Hinchliff, Minneapolis Police Department

SO-BZZ-606

"Breaking the silence and secrecy surrounding all types of abuse has historically been the key factor that has enabled survivors to seek and obtain professional help. This book is an important resource for professionals to help them identify and understand the signs and dynamics of this previously hidden type of abuse."

Ellen Luepker, M.S.W., licensed psychologist, co-author of
Psychotherapist Sexual Involvement with Clients:
Intervention and Prevention

"*Breaking the Circle of Satanic Ritual Abuse* is both a mind-blower and a mind-healer—it horrifies, yet heals. It offers tested techniques and Twelve tried-and-true Steps for recovery from abuse so terrifying and unthinkable that its shocked-for-life victims can't remember what evils ail them without this kind of help. One valuable component of the book is the author's compassionate and insightful sharing of his own Twelve Step recovery and that of others, as part of working through this extreme trauma."

Joe Klaas, M.A., author of <i>The 12 Steps to</i>
Happiness and Staying Clean

". . . can bring much-needed understanding to therapists, law enforcement officials, and anyone else who questions whether this really happens. I also advise survivors to read this very powerful book—which at times can be quite frightening—and bring out the hidden memories, dreams, and flashbacks to aid in the healing process and take back what was theirs in the first place—to be whole. Written by a survivor, this gives me hope that, after being abused throughout my life, I and others like me can mend, change, and build our rainbows for our future."

Tammy T., ritual abuse survivor

"For me, Ryder has sounded a new classroom bell. But this class is for teachers. We have much to learn in these pages. And the lesson may help us save a new generation of young people, some of whom don't even know they are crying out for our help."

A schoolteacher, California

"As president of Familes Of Crimes Of Silence, I would not hesitate to recommend this book to therapists who are new to the field of ritual abuses, as well as to parents who find that they have children who were abused in this manner."

Doreen Grace Kenney,
president of FOCOS (Families Of Crimes Of Silence)

BREAKING
THE
CIRCLE
OF
SATANIC
RITUAL ABUSE

RECOGNIZING
AND
RECOVERING
FROM THE
HIDDEN TRAUMA

DANIEL RYDER, C.C.D.C., L.S.W.

CompCare Publishers

2415 Annapolis Lane
Minneapolis, Minnesota 55441

Library of Congress Cataloging-in-Publication Data

Ryder, Daniel
    Breaking the circle of satanic ritual abuse/by Daniel Ryder
    p. cm.
    ISBN 0-89638-258-3
    1. Child abuse—United States. 2. Adult child abuse victims—
Counseling of—United States. 3. Cults—United States. 4.
Satanism—Controversial literature. I. Title.
HV6626.5.R93 1992   91-47929
362.7'6—dc20   CIP

Cover by Jeremy Gale

Inquiries, orders, and catalog requests should be addressed to:
CompCare Publishers
2415 Annapolis Lane
Minneapolis, Minnesota 55441
Call 612/559-4800 or
Toll free 800/328-3330

  6   5   4   3   2
97 96 95 94 93 92

This book is dedicated first of all to all those who have been victims of ritual abuse; to the ones who have died and to the ones courageously struggling to recover. It is also dedicated to the therapists, police, social service workers, cult researchers, and friends and families of the victims, who are just as courageously working to expose the abuse, fight back, and support the victims in their recovery.

Because of the sensitive nature of the material and the possible risks to some victims, most of the case example names in the text of this book have been changed. And to further protect their identities and honor client/therapist confidentiality, many of the examples have also been constructed as composites.

The first-person stories in the Appendix came to us directly from the survivors, although most have chosen not to use their own names.

Recognizing that ritual abuse recovery is just beginning to come into public awareness—and that it is constantly evolving as professionals document and survivors relate their experiences—CompCare Publishers does not endorse any particular ritual abuse therapies, recovery groups, or organizations.

Although the dynamics of Twelve Step recovery as it applies to ritual abuse are parts of this book, the book does not represent any one specific Twelve Step ritual abuse group, nor is it connected, except in theory, with the evolving Twelve Step ritual abuse movement.

NOTE: Some of the accounts of ritual abuse contained within are quite graphic and may trigger repressed memories and feelings. They may even cue some cult programming—suicide or self-mutilation, for example. It is highly advisable for ritual abuse survivors to develop a strong recovery network when dealing with these issues. Reader's who know or suspect they are ritual abuse survivors and are in therapy would do well to check with their therapists before reading it.

CONTENTS

CHAPTER 1
"What the Hell Was That?"

Fear of circles • Fear of being the center of attention • Vague memories of childhood • Overreaction to violent or "supernatural" films • Problems with sex • Exaggerated codependency characteristics • Fear of authority • Lack of trust • Problems with relationships • Fear of abandonment • Compulsivity • Use or avoidance of alcohol and other drugs • Survivor's guilt • Ritual abuse characteristics list • Codependency characteristics list

CHAPTER 2
Satanism

Opposition to traditional Judeo-Christian values • Rebellion against authority • Personal power • Transgenerational cults • Crime/abuse variations • Satanic holidays • Satanic symbols

ACKNOWLEDGMENTS

To God.

To Holly Hector for your support, as well as for your faith, courage, and commitment to helping satanic ritual abuse victims. You really make a difference.

To other professionals who have come forward to help survivors and also to fight back in any number of ways, including being interviewed for this book: Maggie Irwin, Pat Mellody, Pamela Hudson, Jack Roper, Ellen Luepker, Marita Keeling, M.D., Marty Smith, Myra Riddell, Bruce Leonard, M.D., Carolyn Grame, Ph.D., Janice and Dick Lord, Maureen Brugh, Sgt. Jon Hinchliff, and Linda Callaghan, M.D. And to all those others who are making a difference through their research, development of treatment techniques, and commitment within the broad context of ritual abuse.

I would also like to thank all those connected with the Los Angeles County Commission for Women's Ritual Abuse Task Force, Minnesota Awareness of Ritual Abuse Network, and Monarch Resources. In addition, I would like to thank Pam and all those connected with Cleveland's Twelve Step Ritual Abuse group for your cooperation. And also to the many survivors who have allowed parts of their stories to be used in this book—Faith Donaldson, Gina, Victoria, Jo G., Dan, and countless others—your courage is an inspiration.

I also want to acknowledge the staff at CompCare Publishers for taking the risk to stand up about all this, especially the editors for believing in the project initially.

Another note of special thanks to my agent, Mary Barr, of Sierra Literary Agency, for going "above and beyond" with this.

Daniel Ryder

EDITOR'S NOTE

This book, like recovery from ritual abuse itself, is a process. Symptoms recur. Experience is affirmed. Counseling techniques evolve. The Twelve Steps are worked and reworked. Like survivors themselves, struggling to reach their often-blocked memories of abuse, this book, too, gropes for truth behind the wall of secrecy and controversy that surrounds this topic.

Ritual abuse refers to practices or patterns of harming behaviors through which persons or groups seek to exert power over others. Ritual abuse is usually traumatic—physical or sexual, as well as mental, emotional, and spiritual. It is sometimes ceremonial, often centering around a commitment to an authority or "deified" leader, such as the Biblical satan.

Many groups throughout the world's history have been associated with traumatic physical or sexual abuse within ritualistic contexts. The theories and recovery techniques presented here may apply to survivors of a variety of ritual traumas.

Daniel Ryder, a counselor and journalist, as well as a ritual abuse survivor, has interviewed other survivors, therapists, representatives of human service agencies, and law enforcement officers from several parts of the country. What emerges is the first book to deal not only with what seems to be the increasingly visible phenomenon of traumatic ritual abuse—especially satanic ritual abuse—but also effective ways to recover from it.

We recognize that the subject of ritual abuse—involving criminal violence, sexual and emotional abuse, and the total disregard for personal boundaries and human worth—is not only controversial, but bizarre and horrible. Some readers, unless they have known survivors like these, will find some of this book very hard to believe. But whatever the degree of skepticism, we do know that there are people in our world who have been and are being ritually abused. We respect their pain and wish fervently for their healing.

FOREWORD

Breaking the Circle of Satanic Ritual Abuse is a powerful book that exposes the violent acts of satanic cults which have infiltrated the very core of our society. The content of the book is disturbing in that graphic details of victims' torture reflect such malevolence.

The author/survivor's search for truth led him to many places in the country to interview human service providers. The author not only unmasked the cult's modus operandi, but gave insightful ways of breaking free of cult abuse to begin the process of recovery.

The book gives a sense of unsettledness because the perpetrators appear like ordinary people, who go about doing normal activities by day and are often in positions of authority, thereby making it very easy to deny such evil exists.

For all of its horror, the book is about the courage of the survivors and the triumph of good over evil. It also gives us hope, in that the author, an excellent writer, who as a child was abused by a cult, has successfully broken through. This book is must reading for everyone, because this evil thrives in lies and denial. Awareness mitigates these.

Linda Y. Callaghan, M.D.

Board certified psychiatrist in private practice in Traverse City, Michigan; active staff member in psychiatry, Munson Medical Center; former assistant professor, Michigan StateUniversity Department of Psychiatry; member American Medical Association, American Psychiatric Association, Michigan Psychiatric Association; author of *Inrage, Healing the Hidden Rage of Child Sexual Abuse.*

AUTHOR'S PREFACE

An alarming phenomenon is surfacing with more and more frequency. A phenomenon so bizarre, so unlikely, it's hard for many
to believe. Yet it is frightening how often it seems to prove to be
true and to what extent it has happened—and is happening.

The phenomenon: people are reporting having been exposed to satanic cult ritual abuse while growing up. Growing up
in Los Angeles, in Minneapolis, in Cleveland—and in any number
of other metropolitan areas and rural towns. The reports include
stories even scare tacticians like author Stephen King would be
hard-pressed to match.

There are stories of children being buried alive, then being brought back as sons and daughters of satan; stories of child
sexual abuse, of orgies, of torture, of murder and sacrifice. There
are also stories of highly sophisticated brainwashing to ensure
compliance and silence. And even stories of children forced to be
accomplices in some of the killings.

As more of these stories surface, we will begin to understand much more about what's happened to many missing children and adults. We will know more about the past traumas of
some people afflicted with psychiatric disorders, such as severe
paranoia, schizophrenia, or multiple personalities. And we will
also know more about survivors of ritual horrors who, thus far,
may not have developed psychiatric disorders, yet are afflicted
with many codependency characteristics in the extreme.

While it is becoming clear that cult ritual abuse has been
going on for generations, the horrible tales are only now surfacing with steady frequency, simply because only recently has an
environment been created to support survivors getting in touch
with these kinds of memories. This environment is partially, if not
largely, attributable to improved counseling techniques, better
understanding of the psychological effects of trauma, and the

evolution of the Twelve Step self-help movement (begun by Alcoholics Anonymous) into areas of codependency, sexual abuse, and ritual abuse.

Codependency can be defined as a condition marked by an inordinate reliance on person(s), thing(s), or activities, for personal well-being and self-esteem. (For a complete list of codependency characteristics, see page 9.)

As a survivor of satanic cult rituals, I have experienced firsthand the abuse just outlined, while growing up in an upper-middle-class suburb in the Midwest. Not only have I experienced the abuse, but also the recovery—step by painful step—in my own personal therapy and through the Twelve Steps.

I'm also a counselor and have worked with people who display symptoms of having had satanic ritual abuse in their backgrounds as well. Often they come to therapy for other problems. I specialize in codependency counseling, for instance, and they come because their anxiety level is increasing, or they can't seem to shake their depression, or their, maybe, twelfth dysfunctional relationship is on the rocks.

Some would commit to recovery in therapy, and perhaps in a Twelve Step program as well. They would unearth the repressed feelings and memories connected to, say, Dad's drunken, raging physical or verbal episodes, or Mom's or Dad's more covert emotional manipulations, or even the compulsive behavior of a teacher or coach. Then some of these people would start to get significantly better.

However, a percentage of them didn't get significantly better, and had to continue to look back some more. As they probed deeper, more scarring levels of abuse began to surface. Now it might be sexual abuse by Dad or Mom, or a babysitter or neighbor. From anything as pronounced as forced sodomy to as subtle as Mom's occasional exhibitionism around the house, this abuse had left deep emotional scars. As these clients worked through these issues, many of them got significantly better as well.

But even with all this, there was a certain percentage of people still experiencing high anxiety, some deep depression, and any number of other problems. Some pretty extreme symptoms would continue to surface consistently.

For instance, some of these people would begin to have some of the most macabre dreams: dreams of black-robed figures; people levitating out of coffins with blood pouring out of their eyes; people being shot, stabbed; dreams about demons.

Also, the level of repressed feelings coming up now was...well, the word intense is an understatement: volcanic rage, convulsive fits of sobbing. Often they would have thoughts of suicide. And the fear about getting in touch with whatever memories were there would come in waves and was often at almost phobic levels. One client, for example, began to have flashbacks of a black-robed figure standing over him as a warning about remembering.

Also at this time, I was beginning to notice in some clients the beginnings of pronounced personality shifts during the sessions.

Given my personal recovery experience, these components were fairly easy to read as satanic cult ritual abuse symptomatology. Like many other counselors starting to cope with this, I attended seminars (now being conducted around the country) that were just beginning to deal with clinical methods for treating such survivors.

About this same time I referred these clients to a counselor with some experience working with satanic ritual abuse victims. And for the next year or so, I took time off from my counseling practice in order to spend part of the year interviewing satanic cult survivors and representatives from the fields of therapy, law enforcement, social services, and cult research from around the country for this book. Prior to being a counselor, I had been a journalist.

What has emerged is a multidimensional look at satanic cult ritual abuse and recovery.

This book illuminates the underlying dynamics of the highly sophisticated, transgenerational cults, as well as the more amateurish teen satanic cults—and explains how someone can be drawn, or forced, into each of these. It includes ways to diagnose ritual abuse, then provides a stage-by-stage look at the recovery process, from a Twelve Step recovery perspective and also from a general clinical perspective. Interviews are included with some leading therapists in ritual abuse pertaining to each stage of the clinical recovery process.

This book goes a step beyond personal and therapeutic issues to looking at how society is beginning to respond. I interviewed the chairperson of the Los Angeles County Task Force on Ritual Abuse, as well as a police sergeant in Minneapolis who has counseled countless cult survivors about personal security and also helped organize an innovative program to combat ritual abuse in that area.

Breaking the Circle of Satanic Ritual Abuse includes a scene from an emotion-charged Twelve Step ritual abuse meeting, and also outlines how to get one of these groups started. It features an interview with a representative from a group of satanic cult survivors in Colorado, who have banded together to start an outreach network across the country to provide referral information and treatment scholarships for fellow survivors.

Included in the Appendix are poignant personal stories, poems, and artwork by survivors.

The picture that has developed from this investigation is, on one hand, extremely scary and, on the other, optimistic. Scary in how heinous this type of activity is and how widespread it seems to be, and how well it has been protected by secrecy. Scary, too, because of who cult members are reported to be: parents, teachers, police officers, doctors, lawyers, priests, respected business owners—the list goes on. There is concern not only about what these people are doing behind closed doors, in basements or attics, or out in the woods at two o'clock in the morning, but about the evil stemming from these groups weaving itself into the fabric of society in broad daylight. This could take the form of such things as illegal insider stock trading, indiscriminate environmental polluting, kidnapping, illegal drug sales, political bribes, illegal pornography—evil never seems to exist in a vacuum.

The optimistic side is that people finally are starting to see some of this and fight back. Survivors are beginning to recover, and to speak out publicly. Therapists are committing to help by developing and refining new treatment methods for ritual abuse survivors, as well as often extending their sessions beyond the "standard hour" for these people. Law enforcement officials are now taking survivor depositions and attending seminars on ritual abuse. Task forces are forming.

And, while a lot of this has been going on in pockets all over the world, it is time to take the next step—networking to combine more forces, share even more information.

My hope is that this book will help.

I recently gave a seminar on satanic ritual abuse to some of the psychiatric and substance-abuse counselors at one of the country's leading hospitals. During the presentation, I outlined some of the more abominable forms of abuse, described common survivor symptoms, and outlined stages of the recovery process.

Because there is still debate about the credibility of this

issue, I expected at least some skepticism. I got none. Or at least none was voiced.

Instead, I got a number of informed questions about the recovery process, other possible symptoms, and what sources of help might be available for referrals locally. It turned out that one counselor in the audience had worked with several satanic cult ritual abuse victims. And the seminar left several other counselors wondering if they, too, had worked with some cult victims without realizing it.

Several months later, however, I did run into some skepticism during a radio talk show in Ohio. At one point, the host proposed that these reports were nothing more than the products of active—very active—imaginations. And besides, how could someone exposed to that much trauma not have any memories of it until recovery?

I found myself spending the first minute or so responding in rather clinical terminology about the psychological effects of such an experience, and how memories too horrible or frightening to deal with can be repressed in the unconscious. I tried to explain, too, how the unconscious can repress—or numb—a feeling, and then at some later point when it seems safer, release it. I then related, in less clinical terms, a therapy group episode involving a ritual abuse survivor.

During the group session, a woman was describing a flashback to an experience at age six. She had watched an infant being cut open during a cult ceremony, then was forced to put her hand inside the incision, while the cult members chanted to satan. She knew, even at age six, that it was not safe for her to rebel, to get sick, to get hysterical. She had to, in effect, go numb.

However, recounting this story in group, she began to shake, then to retch. When she couldn't handle the impact of the memory any longer, she left the group and went to an adjoining room. I sat beside her on the floor as she cried convulsively.

I then explained to this skeptical radio host that it is extremely difficult to fake feelings like this. And more than that, "Why would you want to?" I asked him.

He didn't know.

"WHAT THE HELL WAS THAT?"

It happened in Mark's senior year in high school during a football scrimmage.

Because of the informality of a scrimmage, the coaches were on the playing field. Mark played quarterback. The offensive coordinator gave him a play to call.

He knelt in the middle, the circular huddle closing in around him, the coaches leaning in as well.

"Slot right, forty-two . . . " Mark's muscles started to tighten. His stomach clutched. He began to get claustrophobic—really claustrophobic. What's happening to me? He groped for a reason. Almost in a panic, he blurted out the rest of the play, then broke the huddle in a hurry.

There were ten plays in the series, and the feelings repeated ten times.

Mark walked off the field in a daze, totally drained.

"What the hell was that?" He kept shaking his head. "WHAT THE HELL WAS THAT!?"

Fear of Circles

What that was, Mark was to find out years later, was a reaction to a well-hidden experience in his past—one some satanic cult ritual abuse victims have when they find themselves in a circle of people, or even worse, in the center of the circle.

During the cult ceremonies, human circles would be formed. Mark discovered later that as a child he had been abused physically and sexually in the center of those circles. He watched others physically and sexually abused—even killed—in the center of those circles.

For the longest time, human circles had scared Mark. He just never quite seemed to know why.

That is, until the experiences started breaking through into his conscious memory a few years ago. With this realization, he was finally able to begin to *break the circle*.

Fear of Being the Center of Attention

That is another thing about ritual abuse survivors: a lot of them don't like being the center of attention much—ever.

Hal, another satanic ritual abuse victim, reacted typically. For most of his life, Hal had a hard time trying to speak in public. His face would flush. His heart would seem to palpitate, sometimes race almost out of control. The words would come out shaky, and he always cut his talks short, that is, when he had the courage to speak at all.

And it wasn't as if he hadn't tried to change this. Public speaking courses. Power-of-positive-thinking books. Learning everything he could about his topics. While each of these helped somewhat, the fear remained obtrusive.

He would still have a hard time expressing himself at, say, a staff meeting at work, or in the codependency Twelve Step meetings he'd been attending for the past several years.

No matter what he was telling his conscious mind, Hal had this little child living inside him who was afraid, extremely afraid, for his life every time Hal became the center of attention. Because, again, when you were the center of attention in cult ceremonies, you were hurt, sometimes even killed.

In Hal's case, just doing self-talk affirmations about being poised, confident, and knowledgeable about his subject would never have been enough to reverse all of these deep-seated fears. He also would need to give himself—and his inner child—real messages about being safe now.

Now that Hal finally is in touch with his cult abuse memories, and is doing specific self-talk about his safety, this fear is subsiding measurably.

2

Hal was in codependency recovery and therapy almost five years before the ritual abuse memories started to break through. For some, it takes longer. For others, it happens sooner.

Generally, though, people seem to be in recovery in therapy and/or in Twelve Step self-help groups for other issues for a time before any satanic ritual abuse memories start to surface.

Vague Memories of Childhood

Another common trait among many ritual abuse survivors is that their memories of childhood in general are usually vague or almost nonexistent.

Oh, they may remember whom they took, or wanted to take, to the high school prom. And maybe they remember the name of their eighth grade math or English teacher, or even some minor things, like losing their milk money one day in second grade.

But other than these surface kinds of happenings for them, childhood is pretty much a blank.

One of my clients, who demonstrated several satanic ritual abuse symptoms, assigned perhaps the best metaphor I've heard to this phenomenon. "It's like the memories are a few staggered rocks jutting up near the shoreline of this otherwise huge ocean, blanketed in mist."

Overreaction to Violent or "Supernatural" Films

Most satanic ritual abuse survivors I have known have similar reactions to watching graphic depictions of violence or of evil supernatural phenomena, as in movies. One of the topics at a Twelve Step self-help ritual abuse survivors' meeting recently in Cleveland was reactions to these kinds of movies. Several who spoke said it was extremely difficult for them to watch violent or "supernatural" movies. And on the rare occasion when they did watch a film like *The Exorcist*, or a violent "slasher" film (in which knives or guns were used), they said they would become unnerved. This was not, they said, a "normal," short-term adrenaline rush of fear (the kind these movies are designed to evoke) but rather a fear often bordering on panic. The most frightening parts of the movie often continued to replay themselves in their minds for weeks or months afterwards.

Again, because some survivors have personally seen people knifed, shot, or dismembered, as well as what appeared to be supernatural phenomena, such as demonic possession, these movies to them are much more than external experiences to be set aside quickly.

Problems with Sex

Other common characteristics among cult victims are multifaceted problems with sex. They might seem a natural reaction to being exposed to the "kink" (offbeat sexual practices) of cult orgies, which often included their parents, neighbors, or other community members. Also, having been sexually abused physically in any number of different ways, and having had to watch other children exposed to the same abuses, a survivor's sexuality often becomes skewed.

Some survivors experience physical problems with sexual dysfunction, such as impotency and frigidity. Or they are unconsciously attracted to forms of sadomasochistic practices, exhibitionism, and voyeurism. Some also become addicted to sex.

Exaggerated Codependency Characteristics

Another dynamic that is becoming clearer as these experiences come to light and survivors seek therapy and support is that, besides the straight ritual abuse characteristics, these survivors also have most, if not all, of the widely accepted codependency characteristics in an exaggerated form. (See page 9.)

Fear of Authority

A codependent's typical fear of authority is magnified even more in a ritual abuse survivor because, again, there is the long-held, often unconscious belief that an authority figure, a boss, a teacher, or a leader of any kind could actually kill.

Lack of Trust

Another codependency characteristic seen often in ritual abuse survivors is difficulty with intimacy and, in general, difficulty with trusting.

This only stands to reason.

Here's a child, Johnny, whose parents go to church on Sundays. The father owns a reputable business in the community. The mother goes to PTA and volunteers at the local hospital as well. Then there's Mr. Smith up the street, who's Johnny's Little League coach. And what about Dr. Walker, a benevolent- appearing family physician, who's known the family for, well, almost as long as they've known St. Mark's Father Denzik and Patrolman Jones.

So, what happens to Johnny psychologically when he sees these same people late at night changing personas, donning black robes, calling out for satan, taking part in orgies, torturing, even killing?

Well, what happens to Johnny, to put it simply, is that his trust in people is significantly eroded, if not destroyed.

Problems with Relationships

Later in life, Johnny has difficulty establishing and maintaining relationships with women, with friends, with anyone. Unconsciously he's reluctant to initiate relationships because of the fear of being hurt again. As many codependents have a tendency to isolate themselves, the same is even more true of ritual abuse victims.

And if Johnny—now John, the adult—is in a relationship with someone, the first time this person makes a mistake, it will often push John into a black-and-white attitude about people either being all bad or all good.

John has a real struggle remaining in the relationship after his trust, even over a seemingly small incident, has been broken.

Fear of Abandonment

Many codependents characteristically fear abandonment. If

you've grown up with any kind of family dysfunction, you experience degrees of physical and emotional abandonment. If you're not able to express this fear—talk it out—it remains repressed and influences how much you're able to risk getting close to someone later in life.

For a cult victim growing up, fear of abandonment is so pervasive that it's almost impossible to try to relate substantively here. In watching killings, for instance, children fear that someday the parents might be killed as well, leaving them alone in the world. In cases where the parents seem to be possessed by demonic spirits, the children actually fear they may somehow lose their parents totally to the demon. In watching their parents in a sexual orgy with neighbors or others, children also experience severe forms of abandonment, worrying that one or both parents might someday leave to live with the neighbors or whomever.

Compulsivity

Another common codependency characteristic is being compulsive about things like work, shopping, sex, exercise, eating, religion, volunteering, gambling, and so on. These activities are often overused by codependents to avoid painful feelings and memories festering in the unconscious.

Wherever there are some unresolved issues, there is often some compulsion. If there are many unresolved issues, then there is usually a lot of compulsion. If you're an untreated ritual abuse victim, there's a good chance your life may revolve around compulsion.

Other codependency characteristics are included at the end of this chapter. And, again, most of these generally seem to be more severe in a ritual abuse victim.

Use or Avoidance of Alcohol and Other Drugs

Another dynamic for some ritual abuse survivors is the development of alcoholism/chemical dependency. Alcohol and drugs are consistently used to get over the pervasive fear that has developed in different areas of a survivor's life, or they are used as numbing agents for all the repressed pain just below the surface, or they are simply used as an escape.

Conversely, there are a lot of other survivors who won't touch any form of mood-altering drug. For one thing, they are unconsciously petrified about ever being "out of control" in any way—as they were during the abuse. For another, many ritual abuse victims were forced to take drugs during the ceremonies to make them more malleable in participating in such cult activities as torture, drinking blood, and sexual abuse. Consequently, an unconscious aversion to drugs, including alcohol, has developed.

Survivor's Guilt

The last characteristic I want to touch on here is the tendency to love those who can be pitied and rescued.

Because of having witnessed torture or killings, perhaps even having been forced to participate, ritual abuse survivors often experience survivor's guilt. And because this is so pervasive, survivors often look to people they can help in some way, unconsciously to atone for not being able to stop the killings, and also for their own guilt at surviving when others did not.

Ritual Abuse Characteristics List

Having some of the following characteristics may indicate ritual abuse in one's background:

1. Dreams with reoccurring images of blood, robed figures, demons, candles, satan, etc.

2. Vague, scattered, or almost nonexistent childhood memories.

3. Pronounced panic reactions to films like *The Exorcist*, *The Omen*, and violent "slasher" type movies or literature.

4. Self-mutilation. Cutting oneself, burning or hitting oneself, or having preoccupying thoughts of similar kinds of self-abuse.

5. An extremely passive nature. Inordinate fear of physical violence, knives, guns.

6. Hypersensitivity about being the center of attention. Being uncomfortable in, or around, human circles of any kind.

7. Sexual perversion or dysfunction. For example, sadomasochistic tendencies as a victim and/or perpetrator, or continual fantasies about sadomasochism.

8. A propensity for urinary problems, rectal symptoms, colitis, odd-shaped rashes (body memories) in the form of 6's, upside-down crosses, and other satanic symbols.

9. Hypersensitivity to unexpected touch and loud noises.

10. Extreme difficulty with trust.

11. Codependency characteristics in the extreme.

12. Extreme scrupulosity.

13. Phobia about snakes.

This is a compilation taken primarily from a list being used in Twelve Step ritual abuse groups. Characteristics 1, 7, and 8 were provided by Marita Jane Keeling, M.D., assistant clinical professor for the Health and Sciences Center in Denver, Colorado. Dr. Keeling presents seminars on the subject of adult survivors of ritual abuse. (See pages 67-72 for more behavioral, psychological, and physical indicators of ritual abuse.)

Codependency Characteristics List

Having any of the following may indicate a problem with codependency. The degree of the affliction depends primarily upon the amount of trauma one has experienced.

1. We became isolated, afraid, and/or defiant of people and authority figures.

2. We became approval seekers, and lost some of our identity in the process.

3. We often experience unmet potential in our relationships, work, etc.

4. We sometimes became alcoholics/chemical dependents, married them, or both. Or we tend to find other compulsive personalities, such as workaholics, to fulfill our unconscious abandonment needs.

5. We sometimes live life from the viewpoint of victims, and are attracted by that weakness in our friendship and career relationships.

6. We have an overdeveloped sense of responsibility. It is also easier for some of us to be concerned with others, rather than ourselves. (We also take what we do too seriously.)

7. We sometimes get guilt feelings when we stand up for ourselves. And we often give in to others.

8. We become addicted to excitement, although we have difficulty experiencing real fun.

9. We have difficulty with intimacy, confusing love with pity. And we have a tendency to "love" those we can pity and rescue.

10. We have often "stuffed" our feelings from childhood because of varying degrees of trauma experienced. And we have lost some of the ability to feel and express our feelings in the present. (Our being out of touch with our feelings is one of our basic denials.)

11. We have a tendency to judge ourselves harshly, and often have a low sense of self-esteem.

12. We've developed dependent personalities, afraid of abandonment. And we will sometimes do almost any-

thing to hold on to a relationship—no matter how dysfunctional the relationship is.

13. We are sometimes super-responsible, or super-irresponsible, but in each case we tend to be impulsive, looking for immediate, rather than delayed, gratification.

14. We often are reactors rather than actors, overreacting to things often beyond our control.

15. We are loyal, even when the loyalty is undeserved.

16. We guess at what "normal" is.

17. We have difficulty following through on projects.

18. We have compulsive natures.

19. We often seek approval, but even when it is offered, it is hard to accept.

20. We sometimes lie, even when it would be easier to tell the truth.

These characteristics develop in people who come from families suffering from dysfunctions. They are families in which one parent or both parents had been afflicted with alcoholism/chemical dependency, an eating disorder, compulsive gambling or spending, workaholism, chronic mental or physical disorders. Or from families in which there was extreme religiosity, incest, physical abuse, satanic ritual abuse . . . the list of dysfunctions goes on.

There is now a network of Twelve Step groups across the country to help people afflicted with these characteristics. Among these groups are Codependents Anonymous, Adult Children of Alcoholics (ACA and ACoA), Adult Children of Dysfunctional Families (ACDF), and Al-Anon. Some of these groups will be listed in your phone directory. Others, if they are relatively new in your area, may not be. If you cannot find a listing of meeting locations, contact a social service referral line or a local hospital with a chemical dependency treatment program.

The above list of codependency characteristics is a compilation of generally accepted lists being circulated in Twelve Step groups.

2

SATANISM

Satanism, for the most part, is all about power, as are witchcraft, Druidism, Santeria, and other practices sometimes associated with ritual abuse. (As the physical, sexual, and emotional abuse inflicted in these groups may be similar, the recovery dynamics for survivors are basically the same as well.) People involved with satanism call upon the powers of satan to be able to manipulate the world around them through prescribed ritual.

> Satan: A spiritual being, opposed to God, supremely evil. According to Christian tradition, an angelic being, once called Lucifer (Isaiah 14:12), created by God for good purposes, but who led a rebellion against God, and was cast out of heaven.
> Satan is believed to be the serpent in the Garden of Eden who tempted Eve to disobey God saying, "You shall be like God." (Genesis 3:5). Satan is also called the Father of Lies. . . . He is the ruler over demons and evil spirits who work to interfere with the relationship of God and man, by provoking man to evil.

This excerpt is taken from a *Ritual Abuse* booklet distributed by a task force for the Los Angeles County Commission for Women. (See chapter 22 for further information about this task force, and the ground-breaking booklet, which covers many aspects of ritual abuse.)

Opposition to Traditional Judeo-Christian Values

The heart of satanism supposedly is to oppose all the values of Judeo-Christian tradition, in what appear to be the most horrible and twisted of ways.

Colorado therapist Holly Hector, M.A., specializes in working with satanic cult ritual abuse survivors, and presents seminars nationally on the topic.

Along with what seems to be an insatiable quest for personal power, Ms. Hector said satanists have other primary goals. One is to try to completely shut the door to children ever choosing Christ as their God. Another is to try to make sure as many human souls as possible, simply put, go to hell. (Hell, to them, is construed as a desirable place to go.)

In satanic cults, children are systematically abused in order to turn them against the teachings of Jesus. They are told, said Ms. Hector, that Jesus died on the cross because he was a thief and a liar. Children may also be raped physically with crucifixes. Some of these are wooden crucifixes. Some are fashioned out of knife blades. Many have the figure of Christ on them.

"This is Jesus—and he is raping you!" cult members will often scream incessantly, as the child is being abused.

Other times cult members may dress as stereotypical depictions of Christ (in a white robe), said Ms. Hector, then either rape or torture the children.

Children may also be given replicas of Bibles, and will receive electric shocks every time they try to open them. They may be made to watch Bibles being desecrated with blood and excrement.

Ms. Hector also said some children and adults who have betrayed the cult are sometimes hung on crosses—even sacrificed on crosses—as part of the cult ceremonies.

"Some children are even forced to choose who will be sacrificed," she said.

Satanists find a rationale for these sacrifices beyond merely placating their sadistic impulses. As chronicled in the Old Testament, God would seem to call for animal sacrifices from his people. However, after Christ's ultimate sacrifice—death on the cross—sacrifices were no longer required.

However, satanists try to discount that Christ was the final sacrifice by continuing to sacrifice to satan, according to Ms. Hector.

She added that the more pain and torment cult members can inflict on a victim, and the more fear they are able to instill, the more power they feel they gain internally. They also are reported to practice cannibalism, believing the "eating of flesh" adds to their personal power—because flesh is "of the world," said Ms. Hector, "and they believe satan to be the prince of this world. Christians, on the other hand, believe that the power comes from the spirit."

Another way satanic philosophies become the antithesis of Judeo-Christian values is through opposition to the Ten Commandments. The overriding theme of the Ten Commandments is reasonable self-restraint. Some versions of satanism's "Ten Commandments" read almost exactly the opposite: the pervasive theme is self-indulgence.

Some satanic doctrine can be found in the *Satanic Bible,* written by Anton LaVey, the organizational head of the Church of Satan. Another publicized satanic organization is the Temple of Set.

Both organizations are reported to worship openly in "churches." And both have issued disclaimers over the years asserting that they are not in any way associated with ritual abuse of children, or in the sacrifice of animals and humans.

The groups that do reportedly participate in the abuse and killing are—and this goes without saying—anything but open.

Rebellion against Authority

Director for the Christian Apologetic and Research Information Services (CARIS) based in Milwaukee, Wisconsin, Jack Roper has extensively researched both satanism and the occult. Roper has also served as a consultant to law enforcement agencies across the country on the subject and was used as a consultant on cult dynamics for "The Oprah Winfrey Show."

One of the main underlying themes of satanism is rebellion against any authority, said Roper, accounting for the reversals of the commandments, as well as killings and grave desecrations.

Personal Power

Another main theme is attainment of personal power. For teens, this translates into power over parents and other authority, as well as sexual power. For adults in transgenerational cults, it's also power over authority, sexual power, and financial power. That is, a midwestern satanist farmer may offer a sacrifice for a good crop, or a stockbroker may offer homage and sacrifice to satan for wise investments, a business owner for the success of his enterprise.

Roper said it is his opinion that one major reason the transgenerational cults haven't been exposed is because of who these cult members are in the community—from Jane Smith who owns the realty office on Main Street to John Doe who volunteers at the local church.

Roper also cites the lack of tangible evidence cult survivors are able to produce once they start having memories. Roper said these cults are highly sophisticated at hiding evidence. With infant sacrifices, for instance, he talks of reports of cannibalism with the flesh of the victim, then feeding the bones to dogs, or looking for a grave that perhaps had been dug the night before, and sneaking in and burying the baby a few feet below the level that's been dug. The next day it is cemented over and the coffin is put in place. No one ever knows.

Transgenerational Cults

Transgenerational cults are those perpetuated through family generations. They are not exclusive to satanism, but may be based on other forms of religious tradition. Children brought up in such environments often view cult activities as the norm. Power, heritage, and programming keep the transgenerational cults flourishing. Some of these cults engage in prayer ritual, mind control, sexual orgies, child sexual abuse, torture, murder/sacrifice. And while cult activity is hard to quantify at this point, many of the therapists, researchers, and law enforcement officials interviewed for this book indicated that it is a lot more prevalent than almost anyone would imagine.

Sgt. Jon Hinchliff, a twenty-three-year veteran of the Minneapolis Police Department, is one of the people who holds this belief. Hinchliff has been actively investigating satanic and other ritual abuse crimes over the past five years.

From the data he's gathered, Hinchliff said he believes transgenerational cults are strongly rooted and may have evolved from the "old country." That is, various forms of occult practices, including satanism, were brought to America from European countries, Africa, and Australia.

Sometimes working in concert with a cult survivor's therapist, Hinchliff will advise the person to do a complete family tree, tracing back as far as possible in search of historical clues. (This is more a psychological help than anything else because if some somewhat solid connections are made, it makes the reality of the abuse much more credible to victims programmed to think they were making it up.)

Within the context of most transgenerational cult beliefs, blood lineage is extremely important. Because cult members believe that, as power is acquired through practicing the rituals, the most effective way to pass it on is literally through the family blood. Again, satanists believe power is stored in the blood.

For transgenerational cult groups, this, too, translates into power over authority, power in sexual conquest, power over relationships, power that blesses them with, again, good crops, other business successes, prestige—power they feel will last eternally.

In past centuries, among cult groups and cult families there was a lot of intermarrying just for the purpose of carrying on the power, said Hinchliff. Today this goes on covertly.

Some cult victims, said Hinchliff, are starting to find evidence later in life that their real father or mother may actually have been a cult-involved uncle, aunt, or grandparent.

Hinchliff has worked with a large number of professionals—therapists, law enforcement officials, lawyers, and social service workers—around the cult issue. He is also the co-founder of MINNARA, Minnesota Awareness of Ritual Abuse, a group that has formed to link people dealing with this issue at any level throughout the state. (See page 196 for an explanation of the goals and evolution of this organization.)

Also, within transgenerational cults, Hinchliff has learned that certain children are earmarked for certain roles. For instance, if a child seems to demonstrate some psychic ability (telepathy, telekinesis, or other paranormal abilities), she or he is groomed for channeling roles (as a conduit to the "spirit" world, for instance). Some children are groomed to be high priests or priestesses, some to be recruiters. Some are designated to be entrusted with the more sensitive secrets, such as where and how to dispose of victims' remains.

The children who learn about cleaning up the remains, for instance, learn they can't make errors. There's no room. The continued existence of the cult depends on it, said Hinchliff. For even minor mistakes, victims report severe punishment, such as isolation, bondage, or being placed in cages with snakes.

Like Roper, Hinchliff believes it is this attention to detail, combined with highly sophisticated mind-control techniques, and the identity facade of who the cult members appear to be, that may account for these types of cults going undetected for so long.

As an example of precautions taken as a cult ceremony is going on, some cult members are designated to monitor police scanner frequencies. Others, said Hinchliff, are stationed as perimeter security, establishing one, and sometimes even two, perimeters.

The sergeant said that, from the reports he's gathered so far, a lot of the ceremonies take place in remote rural settings. However, a significant number of ceremonies are also reported to be in urban and suburban areas.

According to Hinchliff, disposal of physical evidence is very thorough. He has heard reports of cannibalism as well. Reports of grinding the victim's bones to mix with farm animal feed. Reports of dismembered victims being cremated in homemade, stone grills and other types of "cookers."

Sometimes, said Hinchliff, a victim may be buried in an isolated spot on private property in a rural setting.

Hinchliff also said reports indicate the transgenerational cults are also highly organized on other levels as well. There are reports of women designated as breeders for baby sacrifices (the births never being recorded).

There are also reports, said Hinchliff, of a sophisticated network for kidnapping. That is, a child may be abducted from the Midwest and taken to a cult on the West Coast for sacrifice. While this causes a stir in the town the child is abducted from, it doesn't draw any attention to the town in which the cult is located. Or, if a child from the cult's general neighborhood is killed by the cult, after the evidence is disposed of, the child can merely be reported as kidnapped.

Again, Hinchliff agrees with Roper's belief that another

factor in keeping the cult activity hidden is the status of cult members in society. Hinchliff said victim reports show some of the members are doctors, lawyers, respected business people, PTA mothers, regular church attendees, clergypersons, law enforcement officials.

"They seem to have all the bases covered," he said.

Besides their mantle, or rather facade, of respectability, by being strategically placed, these people can make highly calculated countermoves before any disclosure makes cult activity public.

Say a victim starts having memories, goes to a police department, and files a complaint. If there is a cult member on the force, that information is relayed back to the cult.

Shortly afterward, the cult starts to mount a harassment campaign to scare the person and trigger the old code-of-silence programming: harassing phone calls, letters, threats of harm to the victim or family members. (In Cleveland, an informal "safe" network of police has formed for people reporting cult-related crimes.) The victim's therapist may begin to be threatened as well. Another cult response may be to rally family members to see that the victim is incarcerated in a psychiatric unit. Because of the extreme forms of abuse victims are exposed to in the cult, these campaigns are often successful in intimidating them. Victims tend to believe nothing can be done to stop the cult.

One of Hinchliff's functions is to work with victims on security issues. He advises victims to record telephone calls and save threatening letters as evidence. Because he gets calls from across the country, he advises victims to go to as many law enforcement agencies (police departments, sheriff's departments, FBI) as possible in their area to give depositions with specific lists of names, and then, if possible, to see that this information is relayed to the people doing the harassment.

According to Hinchliff, the cult's biggest fears revolve around being exposed, and sometimes this is enough to get them to back off.

Also, because much of the intensity of the victim's fear is based in the past, Hinchliff noted that a good therapist who is able, over time, to empower the victim psychologically can help reduce some of the fear.

Another reason this has not attracted more public attention, Hinchliff believes, is the prevailing climate of the judicial system. He notes that ritual abuse is where child sexual abuse was some fifteen years ago—that is, sporadic reports in the judicial system viewed with much skepticism. Hinchliff also said that, in a number of child sexual abuse cases that have now been prosecuted, the child will also talk about satanic cult abuse to lawyers and social service workers; but cult abuse sometimes will be left out of the court testimony because the lawyer feels that bringing up this issue may jeopardize the rest of the case. Again, usually there is no tangible evidence.

Hinchliff said it is imperative at this point for more and more professionals from different disciplines to keep coming together to share information, and to mount united efforts in starting to deal with cult abuse.

Crime/Abuse Variations

The intensity and extent of ritual abuse vary among the various satanic cults survivors have been exposed to. This is beginning to be validated consistently by law enforcement officials and therapists.

Carolyn Grame, Ph.D., is a therapist and researcher at the Menninger Foundation Psychiatric Hospital in Topeka, Kansas. At the time of the interview for this book, she had four patients in her case load reporting satanic ritual abuse.

Based on these patients' memory retrieval, she was seeing graduated distinction in the types of cults they had been exposed to.

One patient reported being exposed to what Dr. Grame refers to as a "high orthodox" transgenerational cult—a cult that carried on ceremonies in an elaborate underground tunnel system. She said that the patient reported often witnessing human sacrifice. This patient also reported a heavy emphasis on prostitution and the production of pornography, including "snuff films." Snuff films, said to show people literally being tortured and killed, are sold though covert networks as part of the pornography industry.

Another of Dr. Grame's patients was drawn into a satanic cult comprising a mix of teens and adults. This was a relatively new group, not transgenerational. Most of this patient's memories revolve around cult members self-mutilating, generating child pornographic material, and the sale of illegal drugs. This patient had memories of this cult carrying on animal sacrifices primarily, although one human killing was witnessed. Also, a focus of this particular cult was the desecration of figures and symbols relating to Catholicism. The person left this specific cult, then became involved first with the Ku Klux Klan, later with the Neo-Nazis, and eventually with yet another satanic cult before finally getting into therapy.

Satanic Holidays

Satanists and other occult groups are reported to share certain "holidays" when there is a marked increase in ceremonial activity. Of specific note are Jan. 17 and Feb. 2 (satanic revels); Mar. 21 (Spring Equinox); Apr. 21-26 (preparation for sacrifice) and Apr. 26-May 1 (Grand Climax); June 21 (Summer Solstice); July 1 (demon revels); Sept. 7 (Marriage to the Beast Satan); Oct. 13 (Halloween backward); Oct. 29-Nov. 1 (All Hallow Eve, Halloween); and Dec. 22 (Winter Solstice). Satanists often perform matching ceremonies opposite Christian "holy times," such as particular saints' days, Easter, Christmas, and Halloween (the day before All Saints' Day). There is also reportedly increased cult activity around full-moon nights and all Friday the thirteenths.

Satanic Symbols

The following list of symbols are associated with various forms of satanism. They may be used to one degree or another by transgerational cults or teen satanic cults. They may be used also as "shock-factor" graffiti by adolescents either "dabbling" in satanism or as an indication of acting out some other type of rebellion. In the case of adolescents, the use of these symbols needs to be assessed carefully by teachers, parents, and others concerned. "Dabbling" should be taken seriously.

Lightning bolts are sometimes called the Satanic S. Lightning bolts were also Nazi symbols under Hitler.

The *double-bladed axe* or *anti-justice symbol* used in the death ritual. When inverted, it relates to anti-justice.

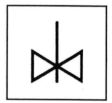

The *black mass indicators* show that a black mass has been or will be performed in this area.

The *blood ritual* represents animal and human sacrifice.

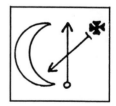

The *crescent moon/star symbol* (also known as *Diana and Lucifer)* represents the moon goddess Diana and the morning star of Lucifer. This symbol may be found both in witchcraft and in satanism. When the moon faces inside, it is primarily satanic.

The *circle* has many different meanings. One relates to eternity. More often the circle is used for protection from evil without and to contain power within.

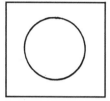

The *Church of Satan* symbolizes the Church of Satan in San Francisco. It can be found in the *Satanic Bible* above the "nine Satanic Statements." Adolescents sometimes use this as graffiti or in self-made tattoos.

The *goat's head* within a pentagram is the symbol for the Church of Satan.

The *triangle* represents fire or male virility when pointing upward, water or female sex when pointing downward. It also symbolizes the place a conjured-up demon would appear (and to confine the demon).

The *upside-down cross* is often used to mock the cross of Christ, and is found at ritual sites where sacrifices are purported have taken place.

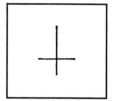

The *cross of confusion* includes the cross and an upside down question mark, questioning the deity or existence of Christ and Christianity.

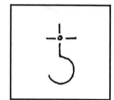

The *inverted cross of satanic justice* may be carved into a victim's chest as an indication that the victim is a traitor. It's also used as a backdrop near a "baphomet" for rituals.

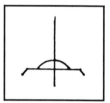

The *cross of Nero* or *peace symbol* represents the upside down cross with the arms broken downward in direction, supposedly signifying the defeat of Christianity by satanists/occultists. But the most common non-occult use of this symbol, prevalent in the 1960s but still used, is as a peace symbol.

The *ankh,* symbolizing life, has Egyptian origins. The lower part indicates the male, the upper part the female.

The *anarchy symbol* usually represents the abolition of all law. It has been used by some punk rockers and heavy metal music people. The symbol also can represent animal or human sacrifice and may be found on rocks or trees, or on the victim. The apex may point either up or down.

The *swastika* or *broken cross* originally represented the four winds, four seasons, and four points of the compass. At that time, its arms were 90-degree angles turned the opposite way as depicted here. If turned in a clockwise direction, it shows harmony with nature. The swastika shown here presents the elements or forces turned against nature and out of harmony. Nazi and occult groups use it in this manner.

The *horned hand, Devil's triad,* or *Satanic salute* is the sign of recognition between those in the occult. It may or may not be innocently used by those who identify with heavy metal music.

The *baphomet* was said to be at one time worshipped by the Knights Templar and later by those taking part in the black mass. Today it may be seen as a deity, a goat-headed god with angelic wings, the breasts of a female, and an illuminated torch between its horns.

The *upside-down pentagram* is often called the *baphomet.* It is satanic in nature and represents the goat's head.

666, the mark of the beast or the anti-Christ/ son of satan, is found in the Book of Revelation 13:16-18.

The *hexagram* or *seal of Solomon* is the most powerful symbol used in the occult. This symbol should not be confused with the Star of David.

The *pentagram* or *pentacle* may or may not include the circle. It is used in both black and white magic. Generally, the top point represents the spirit and the other points represent wind, fire, earth, and water.

The *UDJAT* is also described as the all-seeing eye.

The *scarab* is a design based on the dung beetle, the ancient Egyptian reincarnation symbol. The symbol has ties to Beelzebub, lord of the flies.

The *amulet* or *talisman* is an object, such as a disc, inscribed with a god's name, with writings or drawings, or an image of a supernatural power.

Trailmarkers may be a variety of symbols providing directions to where the occult activity is taking place, describing the activity and the terrain.

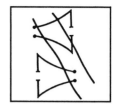

Unicorn horn or *Italian horn* was worn as a talisman by Druids and is now always worn as jewelry. It represents a financial plea to the forces of nature or chance.

The *altar* may be any flat object, usually a nine-foot circle, where implements of the ritual are placed. The pentagram in the center is etched into the slab. Human or animal blood is poured into the etching. Other symbols may be carved into the altar.

The *sun symbol* is a phallic symbol.

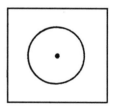

The *pyramid and the evil eye* symbolize the *eye of Lucifer* watching over the finances of the world. It is one of the most powerful of spiritism or divination symbols. It is also known as the all-seeing eye of the Illuminati. This symbol is on the back of the American dollar bill, but was not placed there by an occultist. Its meaning has been distorted through generations of occultism.

These symbols and explanations, gathered from several sources, were adapted by permission from *Exposing and Confronting Satan and Associates* by Wendell Amstutz. A copy of this book may be obtained by writing the National Counseling Resource Center, P. O. Box 87, Rochester, MN 55903. Phone: 507/281-8800.

RECRUITMENT

I had a conversation with a man who unknowingly may have ventured into the early stages of satanism in Sacramento, California.

He'd known a woman at work for a couple of years. The relationship evolved into a romance. After several what could be described as regular dates, she began to confide in him things that seemed, well, somewhat bizarre, yet also somehow intriguing to him.

She told him, for instance, one night, that she was Jesus reincarnated, then held out her wrists. There were no apparent cuts, yet both wrists were bleeding.

Another night, reportedly through a series of chantings, she somehow telepathically sent an orgasmic type of feeling into him that he reported lasting almost twenty-four hours. Then, as quickly as it had been sent, she supposedly shut it off while in his presence. As she was doing this, he said, she flashed what appeared to be a cold—very cold—sinister look. This sinister aspect of her personality he'd never seen before.

And while he was concerned, the orgasmic feeling he reportedly had experienced really hooked him, and he continued to see her.

One day he found a book on witchcraft in her apartment, and took it to a friend, who, at one time, had been involved in the practice of white witchcraft. After looking at the book, and hearing some of the stories, his friend advised him he was possibly being lured gradually toward satanism, and that he should be extremely careful.

Shortly after that, he ended the relationship.

"The whole thing got to really scare me after a while," he said. "And what was even odder was, I had known her for almost two years and in no way suspected she was into any of this."

The man is now in Twelve Step recovery for his codependency issues, and is exploring the dynamics around why he was unconsciously drawn toward this type of person in the first place.

On a societal plane, there are different levels of satanism, and different ways people are drawn into it.

As a cult researcher, Jack Roper said he looks at satanism as the "hub" of much of the occult movement. And according to Roper, there are any number of outside spin-off groups that may desensitize and then draw people toward satanism.

Among influences that may begin to pull some young people toward satanism, Roper cites the game "Dungeons and Dragons," which introduces them to the concept of demons and occult imagery. He also said there are any number of other fantasy role-playing games out now that include occult imagery and terminology.

As a follow-up to the interview with Roper, I went to a store in the Los Angeles area that sells these types of games. Other names of games I came across were "The Restless Dead" and "Death on the Rock." The game covers displayed demons, dragons, snakes, and, well, so much horrifying imagery that I actually felt . . . I don't want to say overwhelmed, but definitely uncomfortable, just being in the store with all these images staring down from the shelves.

Roper said many of the games, designed to be highly interesting, actually can become addictive for a significant number of people. At the same time, they also begin to desensitize people.

At a three-day seminar in Indiana on ritual abuse crime, Roper said a police officer from Albany, New York, presented a case study of a nineteen-year-old who was brutally killed by a satanist. The officer displayed some of the murder and torture weapons confiscated from the satanist. They included various types of daggers, guns, and electroshock equipment. All these are things, Roper noted, that magazines that report on the horror film industry don't hesitate to display prominently each month.

The pornography industry also desensitizes people to satanic practices, said Roper. This includes, along a continuum, anything from hard-core "snuff" films (actual torture and murder), to child pornography, to sadomasochistic "porn," to even more soft-core porn that depicts threesome sex scenes. (Sexual orgies are reported to be a part of some satanic cult ceremonies.)

Another influence, especially on youth, according to Roper's research, is heavy metal music. Some bands sing about hate, death, and social destruction. Some bands prominently display images and symbols that are also sometimes used in connection with satanic cults. These may include lightning bolts, demons, swords piercing hearts, skulls, and Nazi swastikas.

And there's another, more hidden, psychological dynamic to heavy metal attraction as well. If a kid has grown up in a dysfunctional family, especially in a highly dysfunctional one, he or she learns to function in—and actually is drawn to—chaos. This chaos may be represented by music that features erratic, raucous sounds and hard-pounding beats. In adulthood, the same person may be attracted to a crisis-oriented job or stormy relationships.

"Heavy metal speaks to the pain I've been through," Roper said a teen he was working with once told him. The youth was trying to get out of a satanic cult he had been drawn into.

Getting pulled into a satanic cult is often a methodical, well-calculated, and very insidious process. That is, unless you've been raised in a transgenerational cult, and already are programmed.

Roper described what he views as a typical process. The first stage, said Roper, may be an invitation to a party where alcohol and "light" drugs are being used. Invitations come from people designated by the cult as recruiters.

The next step often is to introduce sex into the equation. A prospect is then "fixed up" with another cult member in a sexual liaison. Maybe this happens several times. Then, stronger drugs are often brought in, purportedly to enhance the sexual experience.

Then the recruiter will start to turn the prospect on to occult literature detailing spells and other types of incantations, so the prospect, in essence, can develop the power to win over any woman/man. At this time, the prospect also is introduced to other areas of occult study.

In addition, by befriending the prospect, the recruiter will have been able to determine to what degree someone has experienced life trauma, such as being from a dysfunctional family, and they will proportionately "love bomb" the prospect, as some other cults do, said Roper. This essentially entails creating a caring facade, spending a lot of "quality time" with the candidate.

Eventually the prospect may be allowed into the "inner circle," where he or she is exposed to satanism and the ceremonies. And with this, there are generally initiation rites—rites of passage, so to speak.

In the cults made up mostly of younger people, prospects have to "prove their worth" through actions like animal sacrifice. Sporadically in teen cults, humans are also killed.

Another initiation rite, said Roper, is grave-robbing. And initiates are often specifically instructed to take the skull, because the skull is the container for the brain, which satanists believe contains spirit powers. Besides, the skull is also a symbol of death, and death is the ultimate victory for satanists because in death they expect to be with their lord, satan, for all of eternity. Again, they look at hell as desirable.

In 1989, in a somewhat rural town about forty miles west of Cleveland, Ohio, three young men—two aged eighteen and one aged twenty—were indicted for breaking into a cemetery. Excerpts from the *Cleveland Plain Dealer* newspaper at the time read:

> Three Norwalk area residents charged with opening two graves, beheading the corpses and stealing the skulls, were part of a cult that had recently gotten instructions on how to sacrifice babies to satan, Norwalk police said yesterday. "We're taking this very seriously," he [Police Chief Gary Dewalt] said. "They admitted sacrificing small animals to satan. They said they smashed their heads and drank the blood. One of them has mutilated himself with a knife. These aren't just kids fooling around."

Leaving the Cults

Some survivors get out of the cult (also see chapter 22) when they move out of the house, go away to college, get married, or change locales for whatever reason. However, according to Holly Hector, the survivors who go away to school, for instance, will often become reinvolved when they come home for the summer or other vacations. And some will move back to the same town after completing college.

It's important to note, said therapist Holly Hector, that it is most often some of the alter personalities in survivors with multiple personality disorder (MPD) that get reinvolved with the cult, or a cult in another city, without the "birth person's" conscious knowledge. Survivor reports indicate victims are often programmed to come back later in life to the original cult, or to get involved with another.

Sometimes the original cult may no longer be in existence, because of company transfers or cult members dying out. However, because of incomplete survivor memories, not enough data about cult evolution, including disbanding, there is little we can do other than hypothesize at this point.

In recent years there have been a number of avenues created to help people break away from satanic cults, including survivors' groups and other networks.

(See chapter 22. For a list of support network referrals, see pages 260-264.)

Some referrals may include "safe houses" that have been established, as well as "safe" law enforcement officials to contact. Also, there are now some Twelve Step ritual abuse groups where victims can go for support as well, although the openness of Twelve Step meetings can make them vulnerable to infiltration by cult members.

4

WHAT THERAPISTS ARE SEEING

In Addictions/Codependency Treatment

Increasing numbers of ritual abuse victims have been getting in touch and dealing with memories of ritual horrors in inpatient addictions/codependency treatment programs.

Professionals at the Meadows, a treatment center in Wickenburg, Arizona, first started seeing this phenomenon around 1987, according to Executive Director Pat Mellody. The Meadows specializes in such addiction and compulsion problems as alcoholism/chemical dependency, eating disorders, sex addiction and love addiction, compulsive gambling, and post-traumatic stress disorder. The center also deals extensively with codependents. The program is open-ended, with an average stay of five to six weeks, according to Mellody.

The intensive concentration of group and individual therapy in treatment programs like those at the Meadows is often very effective in helping people break through layers of denial around specific disorders and build a solid foundation of strategies and tools to use in ongoing recovery.

This type of therapy-intensive setting will also often provide a safe atmosphere for long-repressed feelings and memories to surface—memories of parents' drunken rages, of incest and other kinds of sexual abuse, and ritual abuse, such as satanic ritual abuse.

"This issue seems to be a lot bigger thing than anyone

would imagine," said Mellody. And he projects that centers like the Meadows will see increasing numbers of satanic abuse survivors as time goes on.

At the time of this interview, in a client census of fifty, seven satanic abuse survivors were being treated at the Meadows, with three others exhibiting similar abuse symptoms without as yet having any memories, according to counselor Maggie Irwin.

One of Maggie Irwin's special areas of expertise is working with satanic abuse victims. Ms. Irwin, who has had twenty-four years of counseling experience, reports that many people who come to the Meadows have had significant degrees of recovery in such Twelve Step programs as AA, Codependents Anonymous, Adult Children of Alcoholics (and other dysfunctional families), Sex and Love Addicts Anonymous, and Incest Survivors Anonymous. She said that many satanic abuse survivors have been experiencing fragmented flashbacks to cult abuse prior to coming to the center. "For example, they are repeatedly seeing things like daggers, or maybe hooded figures," said Ms. Irwin. Others, she said, might not be experiencing bits of memories yet, but are starting to have overwhelming panic attacks, with no concrete situations to attribute them to. Or they may be re-experiencing pronounced pain in the form of body memories, often anally or vaginally in connection with sexual abuse.

Also, some ritual abuse survivors come to the center in the midst of working on other incest/sexual abuse issues, and sequentially begin having ritual abuse memories while in the therapy-intensive setting. A significant number of ritual abuse survivors, said Ms. Irwin, have some of the memories prior to coming to the Meadows, but believe they are nothing more than the most bizarre delusions.

An initial procedure at the Meadows is the administration of a battery of psychometric tests, including the Minnesota Multiphasic Personality Inventory (MMPI), to develop as extensive a picture of the patient as possible. As part of these tests, a patient draws pictures of the childhood family (family of origin) and pictures of the same family now. Ms. Irwin said this is often quite telling, and sometimes this will be the first point at which suspicion of ritual abuse arises. Recently, she was presented with one patient's drawing of some family members sitting around a table dressed normally, with an uncle and other family members in the background as sinister skeletons with swords raised in their hands. (This wasn't a symbolic depiction of the death of these people, since they were all still very much alive.)

Ms. Irwin couldn't surmise satanic abuse just from the drawing, but based on this she would watch more closely for other symptoms of satanic abuse in this person.

Other symptoms, she said, can come in dreams. Some satanic abuse victims dream of people being knifed, of having to drink blood, of robed figures. Often in individual sessions they share some of the dreams or fragments of flashbacks they've been having—then wait tentatively for a response.

Ms. Irwin feels it is extremely important that survivors perceive they are being believed at this stage. This assurance opens them up to pursue, as well as to share, their increasingly more horrible memories.

As therapeutic rapport builds, survivors sometimes spontaneously go into age regressions during group and individual sessions. Ms. Irwin describes these regressions: "boundaries, time, and space fail, and the person goes back to experience the memory as if it were happening in the present." She said it is not uncommon for a satanic abuse survivor to end up on the floor in a corner of her office in one of these regressions, screaming, "GET THEM AWAY! GET THEM AWAY!" while telling her about being forced by cult members to eat part of a sacrificed baby, or being forced to help kill a cat, or being physically or sexually abused.

During these moments, Ms. Irwin tries to get as much data as possible about what is being remembered, and then, as calmly as she can, talks the person back into the present.

Ms. Irwin estimates that at least 90 percent of ritual abuse survivors emerge from the trauma with such extreme "shame-bound" internal identities that they actually experience many of the codependents' characteristics on a life-threatening level. She compares the internal sense of guilt they feel with that of some war veterans. However this guilt is often even worse for ritual abuse survivors because they started to experience it as children, with no mature, rational perspective whatsoever.

Other extreme codependent manifestations in such survivors may include unconsciously and repeatedly putting themselves in circumstances in which they could be raped or badly beaten; pursuing with abandon dangerous driving or sports; indiscriminately and heavily using drugs; constant compulsive overeating, or, at the other extreme, starving through anorexia.

Ms. Irwin's task is to help these survivors start to see these connections.

In addition, during this phase of treatment, she is often able to help patients explain any quirkish phobias they may have been plagued with throughout their lives. For example, one survivor felt she could never leave the house unless everything was clean and exactly in place. As the memories started to surface, she was able to see the connection; if she had left anything even slightly out of place after a ceremony she would have been beaten, tortured.

Maggie Irwin also helps patients construct some psychological boundaries between themselves and the past, so they don't become so overwhelmed when experiencing the memories. In addition, she tries to promote memory retrieval through more drawing, and through having survivors pose questions to themselves about the abuse and then "journal" with the nondominant hand. This latter is a method recommended by many therapists as a way of gaining quicker access to the unconscious.

Ms. Irwin believes it is imperative that ritual abuse survivors spend a lot of time focusing on codependency recovery. A primary area is restoration of choice. Her work with these survivors indicates to her that typically the primary intention of the cult is to take away any kind of choice-making process for victims, so essentially they become nothing more than pawns of the cult—much as some POWs' spirits are broken. Even when satanic abuse victims were allowed to make choices during ceremonies, said Ms. Irwin, the consequences were usually so horrendous (they may have been forced to decide who was to be sacrificed) that this could only lead to decision-making paralysis later.

This choice-making deficiency can extend in later years into almost every area of a survivor's life. It becomes very difficult to make any decision—from picking out a shirt to choosing a college or profession. What is always looming in the unconscious is the threat of being killed if she or he makes a mistake.

In attempting to empower survivors in choice-making, Ms. Irwin tries never to tell them what to do. Rather she gives them choices about many things—which outside Twelve Step meetings to attend, which topics to address in discussion groups, which treatment goals to set for themselves.

Another recovery area Ms. Irwin focuses on in treatment is either reclamation or further development of the victim's spirituality. She works with survivors to determine how they tapped into a source of goodness to survive growing up, with all the evil and mayhem going on around them.

"For every minute they spent with the demons, I believe they also spent a minute with the angels," said Ms. Irwin, speaking both figuratively and literally (the latter, according to her own spiritual beliefs). Ms. Irwin said she has never encountered a group of people more capable of "deep spiritual connectedness," because of the strong sense of spirituality satanic abuse survivors had to draw upon consistently in order to survive.

For example: "Some people put themselves into a monastery and lead contemplative lives just to experience what a satanic abuse survivor [because of their past experiences] can sometimes draw on in only seconds while driving down the freeway," Ms. Irwin said.

It is her personal belief that, in working with these survivors, therapists should come to terms about their own ideas of good and evil on a spiritual plane, because good-vs.-evil becomes such a consistent dynamic in dealing with a survivor's recovery. "If you [the therapist] can't believe in evil, or a concept of a loving God, patients are sometimes going to get stuck [in therapy]," she said, adding that, if that were the case, it would then be best to refer the person to another therapist.

She also believes it is imperative that therapists understand that there is meaning to almost all ritual abuse in the ceremonies, that these are not random acts (see chapter 2). "If we don't understand the theology, we often don't know where to take people to get them out of the horror," said Ms. Irwin.

For some survivors, reaccess to belief in the spirituality they drew on as children isn't accomplished until some of the repressed anger and shame are worked through. Some of this happens in therapy group situations at the Meadows. One of the best shame-reduction tools is to talk about the abuse with others, she said.

The groups at the Meadows are mixed, with people from all types of abusive backgrounds. Part of the treatment philosophy at the center is that abuse runs along a continuum of severity, and, while the symptoms abuse produces may also vary in severity, they involve basically the same issues—such as the codependency characteristics. Likewise, no matter what the degree of severity may be, many of the recovery stages are basically the same for most abuse victims.

Since at times in group a ritual abuse survivor's sharing

becomes pretty intense, Ms. Irwin does a number of things to help the other patients deal with this intensity. She spends a lot of time talking to patients about erecting psychological and physical boundaries, so they can experience the sharing without taking it on internally. Also, sometimes group members experience "feeling dirty" when hearing an incest survivor or satanic abuse survivor graphically describe the abuse. If this happens, she recommends that after group people wash their hands and their faces and take showers, as a physical manifestation of reinforcing the psychological boundaries they have set.

Another way that has been devised on a group level to maintain these boundaries after a satanic abuse survivor has shared something particularly heinous is for the group to "go on cosmic record" by shouting NO! repeatedly, said Ms. Irwin—NO! to more abuse to the survivor. This is also a declaration that other group members are not psychically taking on any of the abuse by simply hearing about it.

Ms. Irwin tells other group members to try to stay as open as possible to a satanic abuse survivor's sharing, because there might well be a spiritual reason for their ending up in this particular group. *The sharing may trigger aspects of some type of abuse they, too, may have repressed from childhood.*

Another recovery focus for ritual abuse survivors in treatment at the Meadows is the diminishment of survivor's guilt. Besides allowing a person to talk and process some of the feelings about this, the Meadows has gone a step beyond and started a Survivors' Quilt, with felt graphics and painting done on 12" x 12" squares. The quilt serves two purposes: it honors the memory of those killed during the ceremonies, and it symbolizes that those who did survive now continue to choose life.

Ms. Irwin said that the length of treatment at the Meadows for ritual abuse survivors varies, depending on such factors as how they react to the memories, how quickly they assimilate recovery tools, whether or not they have multiple personalities (see chapter 17).

As part of treatment exit planning, she always recommends ongoing therapy for the survivor. Also, she recommends that a person think about attending a Twelve Step ritual abuse group or an Incest Survivors Anonymous meeting. However, she realizes that some survivors are not ready to talk about this issue in a forum of this kind, and this needs to be a personal choice for each individual.

Ms. Irwin believes that treatment centers like the Meadows will see a substantial increase in ritual abuse survivors as it becomes safer to talk about the abuse in Twelve Step meetings, in therapy, and in treatment. Like other counselors interviewed for this book, she sees parallels between this growing awareness of tramatic ritual abuse, especially satanic abuse, and the recent evolution of incest/sexual abuse awareness.

Working with Children Exposed to Ritual Abuse

Pamela S. Hudson, LCSW, is a child therapist with a county mental health outpatient department in California and author of the book *Ritual Child Abuse: Discovery, Diagnosis and Treatment.* Ms. Hudson has presented training sessions for professionals on child abuse in the United States, England, and Canada.

Ms. Hudson first began to identify the symptoms of satanic ritual abuse in several children who had been referred to her at a county mental health agency in early 1985. What was to follow was a most frightening phenomenon: throughout the remainder of 1985 and into 1986, twenty-four children, all from the same day-care center, all exhibiting many of the same satanic ritual abuse symptoms, were brought to her by concerned parents. What is even more amazing is that the cases came to her individually, without the parents initially talking among themselves.

Common symptoms seen among these children included phobic reactions about water; extreme anxiety about being alone in bedrooms, going to the bathroom, eating certain types of food. In addition, some children exhibited such behaviors as using needles, pens, and other sharp objects to poke the eyes out of people in magazine photographs. And thirteen of the twenty-four children, many of them under the age of ten, consistently attempted to masturbate and have sex with other children or animals.

Most of the children also were experiencing frequent night terrors, night sweats, and extraordinary anxiety on other levels. For example, eighteen out of the twenty-four felt extreme separation anxiety if the mother was out of sight even for a short time.

Early in her work with the children, Ms. Hudson reported the cases to the county's Children's Protective Services. (The names of the day-care center and the mental health center have been omitted at Ms. Hudson's request, to avoid legal or other repercussions.)

About six months after Ms. Hudson began working with one girl, the silence finally was broken about the specific nature of the abuse. The girl named a particular supervisor at the day-care center and described this person inserting sticks in her vagina and other orifices—an abuse frequently reported by satanic ritual abuse victims.

Shortly afterward, other children started to talk as well about specific abuses, and Ms. Hudson began to compile corroborative data. Abuses reported included being locked in a cage the perpetrators called a "jail"; being buried in "boxes" (coffins); being told their parents, siblings, and pets would be killed if the childen talked; being held underwater (the genesis of phobic reactions to water); being injected with needles, threatened with guns, defecated and urinated on; being forced to watch animal and human sacrifices. One child reported helping kill a baby, as an adult female perpetrator put her hand over the child's, gripping the knife and forcing it down into the baby.

The children also described being taken off the grounds to other day-care settings, to private homes, even to a cemetery.

As the stories surfaced, the parents started coming together and talking. It was at this stage in the revelations that Ms. Hudson began to work with the parents rather intensively. In these sessions, she allowed parents to vent their grief, their rage, and revenge fantasies of killing the perpetrators. Ms. Hudson says these feelings are normal. Often the emotional devastation becomes so pervasive that that even basic tasks—cooking, cleaning, getting the children to school, going to work—are disrupted. So part of the therapy emphasizes just maintaining the normal "rhythm" of the family.

Ms. Hudson teaches the parents therapeutic techniques to help with the child's stabilization and recovery. In the case of night terrors, for instance, Ms. Hudson teaches the parents not to discount the dreams, but rather to let the child talk about them and then reassure the child that everything is fine now, and the child is safe.

Parents are taught to help children process anxieties and repressed feelings triggered by everyday occurrences. For example, one of the abused children, with her parents at a fast-food restaurant, looked up to see someone enter the place with a shiny red jacket on. This sight triggered her memory of seeing a perpetrator dressed in a devil's outfit during a ceremony. The anxiety was so overwhelming that she actually crawled under the table to hide. Instead of the parents responding by telling the child, "It's nothing," or to stop misbehaving, they had been trained to talk to her about what scared her and what this incident was evoking for her from the past. Afterward, they offered the child more reassurance that she was safe now.

Ms. Hudson also asks parents to keep a written record of the child's behavior during the week, as well as any memories of the abuse that are disclosed.

Besides the twenty-four from the particular day-care setting, Ms. Hudson has since worked with twelve more children who reported being abused in the same manner, from another day-care center, by members of the extended family, and by neighbors.

Ms. Hudson devised a questionnaire and polled a group of parents involved in litigation cases of purported ritual abuse around the country. She procured names from an organization called Believe the Children. This group was formed by parents involved in the highly publicized McMartin Day Care Center case, and included parents from seven other similar day-care center cases in southern California.

Using her questionnaire, Ms. Hudson did telephone interviews with parents whose children were involved in the McMartin case, and in day-care cases in San Francisco and New Jersey, and in a satanic ritual abuse case in California involving a baby sitter. She talked also with parents in Texas and Oregon. In all, she interviewed one set of parents from each of ten cases across the country. In the findings, she also included data from the cases she had worked with.

No matter where in the country the abuse had taken place, the children demonstrated many of the same post-traumatic stress symptoms—night terrors, fear of the dark or of being alone, uncontrolled vomiting. All the children in the survey had demonstrable medical indicators of sexual assault. Many reported being photographed during the ceremonies. Of eleven victims, ten reported being threatened with guns and knives, and nine reported watching people killed as part of the ceremonies. (A full report on these findings is included in Pamela Hudson's book, *Ritual Child Abuse*.)

She said that the similarities in these cases across the country are not only alarming but an indication that perpetrators actually follow prescribed rituals that are fairly consistent and calculated. What's more, she said that the types of torture and mind control reported to her by the children derive from conditioned response techniques reportedly developed for use with political prisoners or prisoners of war. These include sensory deprivation and physical tortures, such as electric shock or drug-induced states.

In recent years, Ms. Hudson has visited England and reports that therapists there also are seeing similar types of ritual abuse symptoms in some of their patients, both children and adults.

As she works with ritually abused children, Ms. Hudson said the disclosures of abuse generally come incrementally. The reports range along a continuum, from what seems most credible to, much later on, what seems least credible. A child might at first report that a day-care worker or baby sitter touched her or his "private parts." Later, children may talk about someone "pooping" on them, then maybe about being tied up, then having to watch an animal being killed, then maybe even a baby.

Sometimes a child talks about being taken away by "aliens." Ms. Hudson said it became apparent to her that perpetrators actually set up stagings for incidents of abuse. Perpetrators dressed as space aliens or cartoon characters, so that later when a child was questioned by a therapist, lawyer, or police officer, the child might say that the abuser was an alien or Mickey Mouse—and the whole story might be dismissed as fabrication.

"Some of these people are extremely clever," said Ms. Hudson.

In therapy, Ms. Hudson uses a combination of techniques: psychodynamic therapy (helping parents determine underlying psychological dynamics in their children), role play, behavior modification, play therapy, art therapy, family therapy, and group therapy. She said the art therapy is extremely helpful in bringing up data around the abuse.

"Simply, the children were threatened about talking about the abuse, but not necessarily drawing about the abuse," she said.

Often, Ms. Hudson said, a therapist doesn't need to make concerted efforts to have a child regress to the trauma. As the therapeutic rapport is established, the child often regresses spontaneously. During this regression, a child may go back to the behaviors of the developmental stage when the abuse took place. A five-year-old child beginning to deal with repressed trauma that took place at age two may, for a time, go back to two-year-old behaviors, using baby talk, occasionally wetting or soiling.

Working with ritually abused children, therapists also often encounter multiple personality disorder and need to move the alters through the trauma toward integration, just as with adults (see chapter 17).

During the course of therapy, if the child is now in school, Ms. Hudson consults with the teacher(s) on an ongoing basis. Early in therapy, Ms. Hudson coaches the parents in apologizing to the child. Not that the parent is really at fault in any way, but, according to the young child's perception, he or she was taken by parents each day to a place to be hurt.

"The parents need to apologize to the child, and also continually tell the child they have been tricked too," said Ms. Hudson. "And it has been my experience that, eventually, the child will forgive the parents."

Also early in therapy, the child has extreme fear about being alone, sleeping alone. Ms. Hudson advises that the parents spend as much time as possible with the child, and in the beginning let the child sleep with them as often as he or she wants to.

She adds that it is important for the therapist to try to maintain a presence of calm and confidence that the situation is going to get better. While she realizes that this might seem elementary advice at first, it takes on a whole new meaning as the therapist enters into the maelstrom of disruption the abuse has caused for the child and the family, in the school system, even in the judicial system.

She also recommends that a therapist develop as much peer support, individual and group supervision as possible, in order to stay professionally and personally balanced while dealing with this.

Ms. Hudson agrees with Maggie Irwin's belief that a therapist can't gloss over the spiritual aspects of the abuse and recovery. She said it is common to hear ritually abused children say things like: "I can't go in the bedroom—the devil is there," or "I know the god below wants me to . . . " Ms. Hudson said it is ineffective to simply ignore the underlying references to evil and deal only with behavior modification. Since much of the abuse revolved around "dark side" spiritual abuse and programming, children continually need to be reassured that there is another, "good" spiritual power that is stronger and can protect them.

Maggie Irwin and Pamela Hudson agree that, in working with such abuse victims, therapists need to come to terms about their own beliefs around the spiritual dynamics of good and evil. Pamela Hudson also recommends that parents do a lot of education with the child around spirituality.

In the case of the twenty-four children reporting ritual abuse from the particular day-care center, Ms. Hudson said that, although most of the parents professed some type of religious affiliation, few were actively practicing it. On the therapist's recommendation, most parents became involved again with their churches. They began to learn as much as they could to counter with their respective church's beliefs when a child began talking about a "dark side" philosophy or fear. Children need to be assured over and over that they are inherently good, that what was done to them or what they did to others could not be helped, Ms. Hudson said.

She added that some of the parents scheduled time to go over a picture book about Jesus with their children—his life, his professed power over satan. Ms. Hudson said that, even in dealing with biblical subjects, the parents had to be careful. She cited Old Testament stories (Abraham about to "sacrifice" Isaac, for instance) or pictures (King Solomon poised with a sword over a baby) that need to be edited out, so they don't trigger a child's fears, and so the child won't connect these in any way with satanism.

As careful as one might be, a scene as seemingly innocent as the baby Jesus lying in a manger might even bring on hysteria for some ritually abused children early in recovery. She encountered reports of children forced to watch as perpetrators killed a baby around Christmas time. Then they forced the children to chant, "Baby Jesus is dead. Baby Jesus is dead."

A major concern for parents, Ms. Hudson said, is what will happen to their children later in life as a result of being exposed to this kind of abuse. Are they more susceptible to being drawn back into a satanic cult? Are they more likely to become perpetrators of physical or sexual abuse? With effective therapy, and good spiritual and family support, these possibilities are measurably diminished. However, Ms. Hudson suggests a long-term study with children now reporting this abuse, in respect to predilection for emotional, physical, and sexual abuse patterns, drug and alcohol abuse, and suicidal tendencies.

Because of the sophistication of the perpetrators in keeping it hidden, Ms. Hudson said she had no way of knowing the extent of this kind of abuse worldwide. However, "Anyone who's had a brush with it [therapists, friends of victims, or law enforcement representatives] can't seem to drop it." As people learn about its insidiousness, the heinous nature of the abuse, the sophistication of the cover-ups, and the possible organizational ties, they "begin to recognize it as a threat similar to the growth of Naziism—and they need to keep telling other people about it."

As for the day-care center case involving the twenty-four children, the District Attorney's office made a decision not to prosecute. A disappointed Ms. Hudson attributes that decision to the lack of physical evidence, the children being perceived as too young and also considered to be too emotionally traumatized for the stories to appear credible to a jury. Other similar cases around the country have gone to litigation.

Her book (see Bibliography, page 264) deals at length with techniques for working with children exposed to ritual abuse.

As a Ritual Abuse Specialist

Holly Hector, M.A., specializes in working with satanic cult ritual abuse survivors, and she presents professional seminars on the subject around the country.

She didn't start out to be a ritual abuse counselor, or for that matter, a counselor at all, she explained in an interview. She had gone to Colorado State University to major in business. However, while doing volunteer work for Campus Life Ministries at CSU, she came across several teenagers who were involved in satanism.

"A lot of these kids were from dysfunctional homes, and were just trying to fit in anywhere," she said.

As a college student recognizing the danger of satanic influence on these kids, she began reading whatever literature was available on satanism, so she would be in a better position to understand and to help.

This experience turned her toward counseling as a profession, and she eventually went on to get a master's degree in counseling psychology from the University of Colorado at Denver.

As part of the master's program, she did an internship at the Menninger Foundation Psychiatric Hospital in Topeka, Kansas, where she worked in the children's wing. By this time she was quite familiar with satanic cult ritual abuse symptomatology. She said she saw a significant number of children she believed had been abused in just that way.

After graduating, Ms. Hector began specializing in post-traumatic stress disorder (PTSD), which afflicts many abuse victims and cult abuse victims in the extreme. During this time, she continued to study and research every aspect of satanic cult dynamics.

"If I had gotten out of school then and billed myself as a satanic ritual abuse specialist, it would have scared people away," she said.

A short time into her professional career, Ms. Hector began to work with a trauma and dissociative disorders unit at Centennial Peaks Hospital in Louisville, Colorado. Again, a significant number of people being treated at the trauma unit turned out to be ritual abuse victims.

What is excellent about the concept of a trauma unit, she said, is that it is not referred to as a "psych" unit, which often implies—to some people anyway—that a client is somehow "crazy."

"In a trauma unit, we are saying, you [the client] are not crazy," she said. "The world around you was crazy."

Ms. Hector has seen more than she has wanted to of the damage and pain cult victims carry with them. She affirms that she is committed to helping these people, no matter what it takes.

In Mental Health Counseling

There are few therapists at this point who specialize in the treatment of satanic ritual abuse victims. However, many therapists now are coming across this kind of abuse occasionally and sporadically in their counseling practice. Ellen Luepker is one of these.

Ellen T. Luepker, MSW, is a licensed psychologist and licensed independent clinical social worker in Minneapolis. Like many mental health practitioners across the country who are not specialists in ritual abuse, she has nevertheless confronted the needs of certain clients who demonstrated symptoms of this kind of abuse.

Ms. Luepker has been counseling for over twenty years in child and adult mental health services. Besides her general practice, she also specializes in working with psychotherapists and clergy, dealing with inappropriate sexual misconduct in therapeutic settings. She is co-author of the book *Psychotherapist Sexual Involvement with Clients: Intervention and Prevention.*

Ms. Luepker is quick to point out that she is not an "expert" on satanic cult ritual abuse. But, as she worked with two particular clients, one an adult, the other a child, on posttraumatic stress disorder (PTSD) symptoms, the satanic cult abuse issues surfaced.

As she continued to work with these two individuals, she attended seminars on the topic and networked with other therapists who had been working longer with satanic cult ritual abuse victims. She said, basically, that the therapy matched that of work with sexual abuse victims, or victims of other types of physical or emotional abuse where PTSD symptoms had developed.

In general, in the early stages of PTSD work, Ms. Luepker helps the victim begin to make sense of the sensorial memories, and bits and pieces of flashbacks they are having. "That is, I help the client to find words that assist them in organizing the traumatic experience," she says. Later, the therapeutic role progresses to helping the victim go back through the full memories and repressed feelings around incidents of abuse.

Ms. Luepker notes that the process is the same with satanic cult victims, although "it is harder to treat them because the systematic installation of fear regarding talking about the abuse is so insidious and ritualized." She also notes that both clients had come to her initially with extreme and unrelenting anxiety.

Being sensitive to client confidentiality, Ms. Luepker only talks about client memories in a composite fashion. She said the reports included people dressed in dark cloaks often standing in circles, burning candles, being placed in boxes (coffins), drinking urine, or smearing feces, as well as animal killings.

During therapy with cult survivors, another area Ms. Luepker has found integral to address is work with a victim's family, whether a spouse, siblings, or children. They must be educated about the issue, so that they can be as supportive as possible. And they also need emotional support in dealing with the person's mood swings, or perhaps multiplicity. (Multiple personality disorder—MPD—is addressed in chapter 17.)

Ms. Luepker believes cult ritual abuse will continue to come to light more and more in the next few years, accelerated by an increasing awareness in the therapeutic community. And she draws an analogy with sexual abuse issues.

Ms. Luepker is respected nationally for her work in the area of sexual abuse issues, issues that are now talked about quite openly, and which we have found are frighteningly prevalent in society. However, back in the mid-1970s, Ms. Luepker, like most therapists at that time, knew very little about sexual abuse dynamics, "So I didn't know how to ask about it [with a client]," she said. And consequently, much went undetected.

5

IT ISN'T 'ONLY A DREAM'

As ritual abuse survivors who haven't yet had or processed the memories move further into therapy and/or Twelve Step recovery, their dreams often become more intense and more macabre.

The human unconscious seems to use dreams like this to begin to prepare the person for later flashbacks to actual events. These dreams are somewhat analogous to preview film clips.

However, in many of these initial dreams, some of the components of the cult abuse may appear in slightly altered form—often because the victim isn't prepared yet to face the reality of *exactly* what happened and *exactly* who was involved.

A satanic ritual abuse victim had been in therapy and codependency recovery about two years when these dreams started to come up for him.

One dream in particular really scared him. And relating it he was somewhat short of breath. The description came haltingly.

> He described sitting rather high up in an oval football stadium. (For some reason—he didn't seem to know exactly why—"oval" was significant.) It was night. The stadium was empty, except for—strange—a couple of older people from a neighborhood he had grown up in. He hadn't really even known them that well; they were just neighbors. There was a coffin on the fifty-yard line. Eerily it began to open on its own. A very young girl began to levitate up, then turn toward him. Blood was streaming from her eyes and mouth. "It was like a scene from the worst horror movie you can imagine," he shivered. The dream ended.

Mark eventually was to have flashbacks to being exposed to a satanic cult growing up—one that involved his parents, the neighbors who had appeared in the dream, and others. He recalled being forced to watch the murder/sacrifice of young children.

It is also important to note the feelings that accompanied the dreams—in this case specifically fear. What the unconscious seems to do in this early stage of awareness is to use dreams to evoke feelings that have been repressed. Releasing these feelings is imperative to the recovery process.

Dissociation

During cult ceremonies, in order not to incur the wrath of cult members, and to stay intact psychically, victims often have to dissociate from the actual experience. Dissociation is defined as segregation of any group of mental processes from the rest of the psychic apparatus. Simply put, instead of coming toward an experience to join or associate with it, a victim of trauma, for instance, will move away psychologically. In some of the most extreme case, this "moving away" can mean the development of multiple personalities to deal with wave after wave of new abuses. In other words, this process becomes a defense mechanism against psychological and physical overload. Multiple personality disorder is defined as a condition in which two or more distinct personalities or personality states are an essential feature *(DSM-111-R)*. This is further explained in chapter 17.

Again, trauma victims dissociate to numb the feelings registering inside as well. Fear, of course, is one of those feelings. A person who is scared will experience an increase in adrenaline. Fear can be expressed through shortness of breath, "the shakes," talking at an accelerated pace, or just generally appearing to be "freaked out."

Again, however, during a cult ceremony, showing fear is dangerous, so emotions become frozen.

Some ritual abuse survivors experience specific frightening, recurring dreams.

The following is a dream one satanic cult ritual abuse victim reports having had repeatedly since early childhood:

> Mary describes being on an elevator going down. Down
> into a sub-basement. The doors open. There's a room full
> of children, a few adults. They're all laughing, playing. But

there's something wrong. Just . . . something.
As she moves into the room, a trap door suddenly pops
open. Mary tumbles through into another room.
In this room, there's fire. There are adults. But these adults
look sinister. There is laughter here, but it is coming from
demon-like figures near the walls. There are kids here too,
but they're not laughing. They're screaming. Mary always
wakes with a start right here.

Through the recurrence of this dream over a period of
years, Mary's unconscious has attempted to keep a clue to her
ritual abuse close to the surface. Mary had no conscious memories of the abuse. And while the particulars of the dreams are different, these recurring dreams are common for some satanic
abuse survivors.

Upon analysis, the sub-basement in Mary's dream probably is symbolic of the memories being buried in the unconscious. The laughter and gaiety in the first room is a facade—the
facade cult members construct to hide their undercover activities.

The fire is symbolic of hell. The sinister expressions of the
adults attest to their extreme dysfunctionalism, and just plain
"evilness." The presence of demons in her dream indicates that
Mary may have seen some supernatural manifestations of demonic possession during some of the ceremonies and/or demonic stagings. In addition, some of the demon imagery could be
symbolic of the heinous nature of the abuse and Mary's unproc-
essed feelings of shame and anger. (See chapter 20.)

Violence and Symbolism

Satanic ritual abuse survivors' dreams often are violent in nature.
They often include dream experiences such as being pursued,
shot at, or knifed. During a Twelve Step ritual abuse meeting recently, a member talked about a dream he remembered from a
few weeks back.

He recalled being chased by an army in a canyon. He franti-
cally scrambled along paths, up cliffs, through a river. And
still they came, and came, led by—he wasn't sure—but it
seemed like some strong, armed dictator "like [Saddam]
Hussein, or maybe [Manuel] Noriega. Whoever it was, I
sensed he was extremely evil."

>At one point he was actually able to turn the tables and kill
>one of his pursuers. Shortly after that, the dream ended.

This dream was significant on a couple of levels.

For one, this dreamer saw himself "running to freedom." Through his recovery process, he was escaping from the problems the cult had caused in his life, even years later. Also, confronting and killing one of his pursuers could be symbolic of his reaching a stage in his growth process where he has been able to confront other repressed feelings and get closer to actual flashbacks.

Colorado therapist Holly Hector also has heard many cult-related dreams from her clients prior to their having the actual memories. In these dreams, she said, clients talk of being chased, or of having a sense of being watched. They also dream about never being left alone, of their boundaries being constantly invaded by people either physically or emotionally, in school settings, on the street, at home. This perhaps is symbolic of the cult seeming almost omnipresent to the victim.

They also dream about being at family-of-origin gatherings, she said, like picnics or parties, and feeling not at all safe. In fact, they feel extremely scared. This, again, may be the unconscious's way of providing another clue, further preparing the victim for the truth.

"As they get closer to the memories, I've observed that a lot more blood imagery starts to surface in the dreams," the therapist said. "And people will also start dreaming about giant, almost monster-like animals. Dogs, cats, rabbits."

Some of the dreams about giant animals can be symbolic of the huge impact that watching animal (and perhaps human) sacrifice has had on their psyches. Also, Ms. Hector notes, the significance of animals, like dogs, in the dreams, may be related in part to acts of bestiality that a victim may either have had to participate in or watch.

Dreams can be important in any recovery process. They offer insight into the past, clues to how the dreamer was *really* affected by past events. Sometimes they can be a window into the future, or they provide a gauge as to where someone currently is in the recovery process.

For example, if you're an adult child of an alcoholic in recovery, and you're having dreams in which you're confronting an abusive parent or some other authority figure, this probably is an indication that you're doing just fine in your process. While you may not be actually confronting the person in real life yet, this dream confrontation is symbolic of your progress in going back to confront the truth, the real truth, about your past.

Many therapists agree that whatever happens in dreams is usually symbolic. The situations are symbolic. Oftentimes the people, too, are symbolic.

Unraveling the meaning of dreams requires some thought. It is helpful to run them by a professional therapist, or an experienced Twelve Step sponsor, to gain some insight or at least another perspective. Self-analysis of dreams may be too subjective. That is, people might read into dreams what they *want to hear*. Or, if they tend to be overly critical, they might read into dreams what they *don't need to hear*.

Another misconception about dreams: you'll hear people say something like "Aw, I just dreamed about the monster because I saw one of those B horror flicks before I went to bed last night." Usually, your unconscious doesn't dredge up these images for no reason at all—like, "Hey, let's really freak him out with this monster thing tonight!"

What the unconscious seems to do regularly is pick out images a person is familiar with or perhaps has just seen, as in the case of the movie, and transplants them into a dream to represent something else. Maybe, in this case, the monster signified a compulsion that is rampant in the person's life. Or it is symbolic of the overblown stature this person has allowed an authority figure to take on in his or her life. Or perhaps the monster is representative of something out of the person's past, as Ms. Hector explained.

Recording Dreams

For many, it is important to write down the dream right after waking up. Dreams are recorded in the brain's short-term memory bank, and the simple act of writing them down can transfer them to long-term memory—much the same as taking notes in class helps you recall.

Usually it is not essential to write everything down—just note the main scenes. The rest seems to come back when you need to draw on it.

I advise my counseling clients to keep a notebook and pen

somewhere near the bed. And if for some reason they are having problems remembering their dreams, I have them repeat to themselves a number of times just before going to sleep, "I will remember my dreams . . . "

I know that sounds simple, but it usually works.

6

OTHER CLUES

In systematically exploring areas of a counseling client's life, therapists find that a distinct mosaic starts to appear. And while each person is unique, granted, similar character patterns start to emerge among people who are, say, chemically dependent, or codependent, or, for that matter, ritually abused.

Colors and Themes in Art Therapy

While doing art therapy with a specific client, a therapist may begin to notice that the two dominant colors used in many of the drawings are red and black. These colors seem to stand out in almost every drawing. Red trees, red grass, red clothes, black clothes, black birds, black horses, black clouds.

This is a common phenomenon among satanic cult ritual abuse survivors.

These two colors are most dominant in satanic cult ceremonies. The black represents the robes. The red represents blood.

It is as if the unconscious is working hard to keep the reality of the abuse as close to the surface as possible, as in the recurring dreams. On another level, it is almost as if the unconscious is trying to purge some of the residuals of the abuse by calling for these colors over and over.

One satanic cult survivor was an artist. In his work, he

combined the abstract with realism. Many of his works were centered in or were accented by multicolored squiggly lines. They were so prominent they became almost a trademark, a signature of sorts.

Several years into codependency recovery and therapy, this artist started to have satanic cult ritual abuse memories. Among these, he recalled several times as a child being locked in a small cage during the ceremonies—a cage teeming with snakes.

Understandably, this type of torture, also reported by other cult survivors, instills massive amounts of fear and makes the child much more malleable, willing to perform certain acts during the ceremonies without rebelling.

Throughout these years, the artist's unconscious was keeping the memories of the snakes close to the surface through his art, and again, on another level, his painting served as a partial purging process.

(However, I believe—and many other therapists agree—that the only way for survivors like this man to experience recovery fully is to go back to confront the memories and uncover the painful, repressed feelings.)

Other themes that sometimes appear in cult victims' drawings, even before the memories surface, are depictions of extreme violence and evil, supernatural imagery.

For instance, one survivor who was well into codependency recovery believed that the most extreme form of abuse he was exposed to growing up was neglect. Yet, as his anger surfaced during the recovery process, he began to draw graphic depictions of his mother or father standing over him as a young boy, with a hatchet or knife buried in his head or back. Blood was splattered all over. (Typically, the drawings were all done primarily in red and black.)

When his therapist pushed a bit, expressing the belief, based on the violent images in the drawings, that there might be more in his past than neglect, he became extremely defensive. "It's parental neglect that *kills*," he said adamantly. *"It all but destroyed me! What more do you want?"*

Sometime during the following year this survivor began having satanic ritual abuse memories. At the time when he had first been confronted about the possibility of other abuse, the cult programming kicked in, triggering his extreme defensiveness.

One of my clients, who demonstrated many of the satanic ritual abuse symptoms but hadn't yet found the memories, would draw swirling circular masses around the outside edges of all his pictures, with guns and knives jutting out from every angle. All were aimed at a child positioned in the center of the picture, often curled in a fetal position.

The child was always proportionately very small. This "smallness" is common among survivors' drawings, indicative of low self-esteem, as well as the overwhelming feeling of powerlessness while the abuse was going on.

This client early in his recovery saw the swirls as merely symbolic of the maelstrom of abusive authority figures around him as a child—parents, teachers, neighbors. And the knives and guns? Well, they again symbolized the verbal and emotional abuse aimed at him during this time.

On one level, that was probably all true.

However, as he continues his recovery process, it is my professional belief, based on similar stories, that he will also find that the swirls are reminiscent of cult circles. And the guns and knives also may be just what they appear to be: guns and knives.

Several years ago the *Cleveland Plain Dealer* ran a series of articles on people across the country beginning to report satanic cult ritual abuse. The following are a couple of excerpts:

> "A patient will recount stories of satanic rituals in which she saw babies stabbed to death and eaten. Often, the woman will say that she too participated in human sacrifice, and killed her own children."

> "In Los Angeles, 3-year-old children tell a doctor they know how to cut up people, accurately identifying the areas of the body where a knife can and cannot penetrate, and offer descriptions of what internal organs look like when they are exposed."

Addictions/Compulsions

As mentioned earlier, a percentage of cult survivors will use alcohol or other drugs excessively as an escape, to medicate pain, to get over fear.

Likewise, other ritual abuse survivors will use overeating, overworking, excessive sexual activity, or compulsive gambling for the same purposes. As these compulsions may block the recovery process, it is integral to the process that the victims be working some type of recovery program around these issues in tandem with working on the deeper issues of ritual abuse with an experienced therapist.

Within this context, for example, many satanic cult victims seem to be plagued by compulsive indebtedness. There are a number of reasons for this.

For one, growing up in such acute dysfunction, a child's adrenal glands will constantly be pumping—so much so that victims may actually become physically addicted to the adrenaline and emotionally addicted to the frenetic feelings that go with it.

Satanic abuse victims have a difficult time feeling calm and will unconsciously create situations to keep their adrenal glands pumping—whether that's getting involved in a dysfunctional relationship or a high-stress work environment, or continually creating debt situations to worry over.

Another angle is that satanic cult victims sometimes become compulsive paupers, remaining underemployed, doing without, or becoming overly frugal.

Because of the abuse, victims were made to feel worthless, and later in life this can lead them into abusive relationships, or the unconscious belief that they don't deserve financial prosperity.

Debtors Anonymous, Overeaters Anonymous, Workaholics Anonymous, Gamblers Anonymous, Sex Addicts Anonymous, Sex and Love Addicts Anonymous are examples of Twelve Step groups that deal with these other issues.

Slow—Very Slow—Realization of Cult Experiences

Again, many cult victims are in therapy and/or Twelve Step recovery for their own addictions, or for codependency or as adult children of alcoholics, usually for years before the cult memories start to surface.

However, if a therapist starts to suspect ritual abuse, based on some of the symptomatology being displayed, it is advisable, in as nonthreatening a way as possible, to start to move the client toward acceptance—much the same as you would start gradually to move a suspected incest victim, who hasn't had the memories yet, toward the realization of the incest.

It is important to note here that this process must be very

cautious and measured at first because of the extreme secrecy of the messages a cult victim carries. Approaching the idea of ritual abuse too blatantly, or too early, can cause the client to become frightened and back out of therapy.

Ritual abuse recovery is still so new and professionals are still learning, and no matter how cautious a therapist may be, some clients are going to get scared and drop out. That's just the nature of this work. Personally, I just pray they come back or find other help.

An advisable approach for a suspected ritual abuse survivor would be to first explore, over time, some of the ritual abuse characteristics in a generalized fashion.

For instance, if the subject of family violence comes up during a session with such a client, after some processing about the specific issue, the topic could be taken to a more generalized form.

Sensitivity to Violence on the Screen

Another indicator of traumatic abuse is how the person reacts, say, to graphic violence in TV shows or movies? How does he or she react to plots that contain evil supernatural phenomena? Does the reaction go beyond fear and revulsion to actual panic? Can the person watch them at all?

Fears

How does the person react around authority? Is there some fear? A lot of fear? Does the person become nearly paralyzed with fear? Does the person have any phobias? What are they?

The Need to Regain Personal Power

Some survivors identify with the perpetrators. They sometimes remain in the cult and become perpetrators themselves, getting caught up in the same addictive practices as their perpetrators—inflicting sexual abuse and pain. Others, while they don't continue with the cult, later become perpetrators of sexual, physical, and emotional abuse in other areas of their lives.

This is a fairly common psychological reaction to victimization. If someone victimizes you over and over, and you won't, or can't, fight back, this erodes your personal power in all areas of your life. If you don't, at some point, get into a recovery process to work this out, often you will unconsciously turn around and victimize someone else, in order to try to reestablish some sense of personal power and keep your own emotional equilibrium.

Victimization of this kind can set up a domino effect. As an example, while growing up, Dad was beaten and yelled at by *his* alcoholic father. It wasn't safe for him to fight back, so he took the abuse and collected years of repressed feelings. To make matters worse, as an adult Dad also takes a lot of abuse from his boss, and he doesn't fight back here either. Internally, Dad's not feeling good about himself. His self-esteem is extremely low.

However, Dad is *not* afraid of his kids. And so, when Billy screws up or Mary comes home with a low grade, Dad blows up. He rants, yells, beats the kids. What Dad is doing is venting his repressed anger about his own abuse on his kids.

The sad thing here is, this actually works to a degree. While it doesn't in any way fix Dad's internalized lack of self-esteem resulting from his upbringing, it does give him some sense of power, no matter how distorted, and it does give him an outlet for some of his repressed anger.

If some of the anger isn't vented, eventually it can turn into depression, paranoia, destructive compulsions, and any number of other emotional complications.

Since cult victims are often drained of personal power, some, when they are offered a chance later to seize some power back, will take the opportunity, either consciously or unconsciously.

As a youth, another cult survivor from Ohio tortured and killed cats for several years. He had been helpless to do anything about the torture or killing during the cult ceremonies. So he unconsciously turned to victimizing something weaker than himself in order to try and reestablish his own power.

In another case, it was a pattern for a gay, sex-addicted individual just getting into recovery in Los Angeles to act out sexually on a consistent basis with a number of different partners. The specific sexual acts, for the most part, were considered somewhat traditional within the context of gay culture. However, a new partner had expressed that he was into S and M (sadomasochism) and wanted to play the passive role.

"It got really scary for me," he recounted. "At first it was sort of like this bizarre, strained theater. Then something took over inside me, and I really started getting into it—to the point where I started to get scared."

He described hitting really hard, being extremely verbally degrading, not wanting to stop.

"And I can't seem to get it out of my mind, and I keep thinking about when we're going to do it again. It's just not like me," he said, puzzled.

While this man had been in a victim mode most of his life (he demonstrated many satanic abuse symptoms), this incident illustrated the strong, unconscious need to try to seize some power back and somehow gain mastery over the trauma that had all but destroyed him as a child. In much the same way, a person who has been damaged by an abusive parent while growing up may unconsciously seek someone with a similar personality in a relationship, so that he or she can somehow gain power over that abusive personality this time—and finally be psychologically free. It's a phenomenon known in psychiatric circles as "repetition compulsion." And I have never known it to work.

I believe that, as time goes on, we will find that more and more people who are engaging in sadomasochistic practices were ritually abused as children.

Humans have a natural aversion to pain. And most of the time when people start to feel pain, as quickly as possible they try to stop whatever's happening that's causing the pain (unless, for example, an athlete has his eye on breaking a record).

If I have come from a healthy, nurturing family, unless there's been some outside trauma, this is simply how I'm going to react. I'll take my hand off the hot stove, so to speak.

However, if I have been brought up in a setting where I've sometimes been sexually abused or physically tortured by parents, neighbors, or others from whom I am, by the natural order of things, supposed to feel love, my perspective is distorted. I begin to equate pain with love. So I become unconsciously accustomed to, even drawn to, physical pain—just as some codependents are drawn to emotional pain.

Self-abusive Behavior

Another ritual abuse victim characteristic is preoccupation

with—or actual—self-mutilation, without sexual overtones.

As a teenager, Mary, a satanic cult survivor from Massachusetts, would regularly lock herself in the bathroom and cut up her arms with a razor blade—not deeply, and not the wrists.

This self-abusive behavior, quite typical of some cult survivors, can be explained on a number of different levels. Mary often felt neglected, and this act of cutting herself would elicit attention, as did the cuttings for children being tortured during the cult ceremonies. (One of the torture tactics was, as everyone present watched, to trace cult symbols with a knife on the skin of cult members' children to evoke fear as part of the brainwashing. They would trace only lightly on the children's skin to avoid leaving marks that teachers or other authorities could identify.)

For Mary, even though the razor-blade incidents often elicited negative attention, it *was* attention.

On another level, as I've mentioned earlier, cult victims, because of the abuse, have no feeling of specialness or importance, as other children do. Instead, internally they feel unloved and worthless, perhaps even that they are the cause of some of the abuse. (I say "internally" because, in order to survive, people who have been severely abused many times develop a false ego state and sometimes have no idea that their real self-esteem is so weak.)

Because of feeling unloved and worthless inside, when cult survivors act out anger, instead of venting it on others, they often take it out on themselves. Besides cutting themselves, they will sometimes burn themselves, hit themselves repeatedly, attempt suicide. Or they will choose subtle forms of suicide: smoking; not practicing safe sex or abstinence; drug use; driving dangerously.

Also again, victims are often programmed to self-destruct in some way if they should ever get close to the memories.

Perhaps a more obscure reason for Mary's cutting ritual was that, even though the cuts were primarily surface passes, they did draw blood. And many cult victims cut themselves, pick at themselves, or bite themselves, in order to draw blood. From being consistently exposed to dysfunctionalism and evil, many survivors unconsciously believe the "evil" has actually gotten inside their systems. Also unconsciously, they try to "bleed it out," in much the same way as in the once-common practice of bloodletting to cure disease. In the book *People of the Lie*, author Scott Peck, M.D., talks about this phenomenon.

Sexual Problems

Another area to explore, also in as nonthreatening a way as possible, is a suspected cult victim's sexual practices and fantasies.

Because of the traumatic forms of sexual abuse by cult members and exposure to adult orgies, victims exhibit certain psychological effects.

For example, as mentioned earlier, many cult victims are drawn to mild or not-so-mild forms of sadomasochistic practices later in life.

An article published in the *Child Abuse and Neglect Journal*, "Patients Reporting Ritual Abuse in Their Backgrounds," Vol. 15:3, spring 1991, cites a case study of thirty-seven patients, in several clinical settings, reporting ritual abuse in their childhoods. The study indicated that 100 percent of these patients reported experiencing sexual abuse during the ceremonies, and 86 percent reported that they now experience various forms of "sexualization of sadistic impulses."

Some cult survivors will take on the passive (slave) role in sadomasochistic (S and M) encounters, allowing their partner(s) to degrade them, humiliate them, and inflict physical pain on them during sexual acts.

One cult victim now involved in ritual abuse Twelve Step meetings talked about not being able to be aroused sexually at all unless she was cast in the slave role, or was fantasizing about it. She was specifically aroused by being tied up, hit, and screamed at degradingly—all related to the abuse she experienced from cult members while growing up.

This same person had been date-raped several years before getting into recovery. Sadly, it actually required a couple of months and several reality checks with other people in her Twelve Step group for her to realize she actually had been raped.

Some ritual abuse victims have difficulty becoming sexually aroused unless there are pronounced elements of "kink," even devoid of S and M. This is primarily attributable to having witnessed cult orgies, and the bizarre sexual acting out they saw from cult members. Survivors, later in life, may also act out in a variety of ways.

One cult victim from Florida, now in recovery, was an exotic dancer for years. Her choice of profession had very little to do with money, she says. She would, in essence, get a "high" from the attention. And the exhibitionism carried over into all areas of her life: outrageous, see-through outfits, exaggerated makeup, acting zany in public, sexual promiscuity. All of her behavior was highly attention-seeking.

In watching the cult orgies, she had concluded that there was a premium on nudity, which accounted for her exhibitionist tendencies. And she also noticed that the more you acted out sexually, the more attention you were shown. This was the only experience she had to equate love with. Sexual promiscuity never filled the internal void, but it was all she knew before recovery, so she kept seeking sex in an addictive cycle that was taking her nowhere.

Holly Hector relates that a good percentage of her satanic cult survivor clients demonstrate sexual promiscuity/acting out in many different areas. Again, there is an unconscious attraction to this activity because of what they were exposed to growing up. Some survivors are drawn to orgies or hard-core pornography (including child pornography). During the ceremonies, it is reported that children are sometimes photographed in sexual positions, and some of the pictures are sold to pedophiles.

Still other survivors go in an opposite direction. They become shut down sexually. They experience problems with impotency, frigidity, and premature ejaculation (to get the act over with as soon as possible). Because the abuses were so toxic, the acts so reprehensible, some have a hard time consciously or unconsciously equating a sexual act with any sort of pleasure. Even if they don't have a physiological sexual problem, some of these survivors will downplay their sexuality by wearing loose-fitting clothes, no makeup, and no cologne, and avoiding dating as much as possible.

Engaged in some form of sex, these ritual abuse survivors must maintain almost total control over the situation to feel safe.

Body Memories

Body memories may surface in early, as well as in later, phases of recovery for ritual abuse survivors. They are often precursors to flashbacks and are sometimes unconscious cues, set up through the cult's conditioning processes, to try to keep the victim from remembering.

As she got closer to her own satanic cult flashbacks, a

woman from Ohio talked of waking up at 2 or 3 A.M. some nights with what could best be described as a prickling, burning sensation along a stretch of her right shoulder. Again, this is often the time of night the ceremonies are held.

There were no physical marks on her shoulder, she said. But the sensation and the pain were very real, and would last anywhere from twenty minutes to two hours.

Although there were many obstacles, and she had a lot of fear, the woman stayed in recovery, and the cult flashbacks finally started to come. Among them was one memory that put this physical sensation into perspective.

During one of the ceremonies, this woman, who was six years old at the time, was forced to watch a baby being sacrificed with a knife. After the stabbing, one of the cult members took the same knife, pulled her shirt back from her shoulder, and lightly ran the edge of the knife along her shoulder blade to her throat.

The message was clear: If you talk, you will die like the baby. And, as she got closer to the memories in recovery, this old warning started to kick in.

A body memory came in another form for another cult victim. During the ceremonies, he had been sexually abused by cult members who poked stick-like objects in his ears, mouth, anus. (Besides these stick-like objects, survivors have also reported that cult members would push small snakes in the victims' mouths or vaginas.)

Just a few months prior to his first cult flashbacks, this victim was startled out of sleep with the sensation of something being rammed up his rectum, although there was nothing there. "The sensation was so real and startling, I could have sworn someone was standing right there ramming something into me," he said. "And there was enough physical pain that the sensation stayed with me several hours."

Memories also can somatize, taking the form of visible rashes, flaring up at the spot on the body where a victim was at one time cut or burned. Sometimes it is reported that the rashes actually take the form of satanic symbols that were traced on the victim's skin during the ceremonies: 666's, pentagrams, upside-down crosses, and any number of other symbols.

Dr. Marita Jane Keeling has seen a number of these rashes spontaneously appear on her satanic cult ritual abuse clients over the years.

For example, a rash in the form of an upside-down cross

appeared recently on the back of one of her ritual abuse clients.

She said that no one at this point knows the exact process that causes such a physiological phenomenon. But she hypothesizes it's some sort of "conversion reaction," somewhat similar to that which can be induced in a deep trance state.

For instance, someone under deep hypnosis can be given the suggestion that a part of the body is burning, and sometimes a rash will appear in the designated body area. "This is a fairly well documented occurrence," said Dr. Keeling.

Likewise, if a cult victim has been burned or cut as a past warning about not talking, it seems that in some of these cases this early programming can actually be activated in the form of body memories years later.

Counseling ritual abuse clients is not as simple as asking a few questions: "So, do you participate in any bizarre sexual practices? Do you have any strange rashes? Or do you ever cut yourself, or think about cutting yourself?"

These subjects need to be approached delicately, with the client maintaining most of the control and timing on the self-disclosure. Another aspect of this, however, is that many ritual abuse victims have very weak boundaries, because their boundaries had been so thoroughly invaded as they were growing up. And sometimes information about sexual practices and self-abuse is volunteered, often at length, in the first couple of counseling sessions, or even over the first cup of coffee with a person they have just met in a Twelve Step group.

The following lists were developed by Holly Hector, M.A., for use in her practice as a therapist. They provide possible further clues to a client's background of ritual abuse.

SYMPTOMS AND OTHER INDICATORS OF RITUAL ABUSE

Holly Hector, M.A.

- Sleep disorders:
  insomnia, fear of falling asleep, inability to stay asleep, regularly wake at certain times of night, nightmares, night terrors

- High pain tolerance:
  painless childbirth, unaware of injury to self

- Seizures/epilepsy with or without organic evidence

- Liver malfunctions

- Adrenal gland malfunctions

- Digestive tract disorders

- Genito-urinary problems

- Chronic bladder/kidney infections

- Frequent skin irritations, disorders

- Headaches/migraines

- Asthma

- Overweight

- Gynecological maladies and symptoms:
  - ▶ vaginal/penile/rectal scarring
  - ▶ frequent, persistent vaginal discharge
  - ▶ urinary tract infections/diseases
  - ▶ sexually transmitted diseases
  - ▶ uterus is sterilized/scarred/absent

- Unusual scars (shape, location, design) various places on body

- Exaggerated reactions to particular olfactory stimuli:
  the smell of blood, urine/feces, alcohol, formaldehyde, burning hair, smoke from fire, incense

- Significant pain/numbing/psychic paralysis in different parts of body

- Exaggerated startle response: loud noises, surprises

- Easily triggered into "fight or flight" syndrome
- Hypervigilance
- Panic attacks
- Allergies
- Missing digits (fingers, toes)
- Chronic pain

BEHAVIOR INDICATORS OF RITUAL ABUSE SURVIVORS

Holly Hector, M.A.

- Seeks out any form of pain
- Noticeable aversion to drinking water (prefers coffee, pop, juice)
- Extreme fluctuation in behavior and skills
- Self-mutilation/self-destructive behavior:
  - cutting skin
  - burning skin
  - hitting self with fists/objects
  - head banging
  - history of driving vehicle at high speeds or in dangerous manner
  - placing self in physically dangerous locations
  - seeking out physically abusive relationships (conscious or unconscious)
- Artwork/poetry has themes of death, pain, occultism
- Suicidality:
  - long-standing history of suicide attempts
  - obsessive thinking about or planning of suicide
- Speaking in unknown languages
- Chemical dependency:
  - alcohol
  - other drugs, illegal or prescription
- Eating disorders:
  - anorexia
  - bulimia
  - bulimarexia
  - compulsive overeating
- Extreme mood swings
- Speaking in different voices—extreme intonation changes

- Draws or "doodles" occult/satanic symbols
- Often fascinated by or drawn to aspects of:
  - ▶ the supernatural
  - ▶ the paranormal
  - ▶ psychic phenomena
- Multiple psychiatric hospitalizations with minimal alleviation of symptoms
- Amnesiac periods/fugue states [a pathological condition: one is apparently conscious of his/her actions but has no recollection of them after returning to a normal state]:
  - ▶ childhood amnesia
  - ▶ loss of time, identity
- Easily induced into a trance state
- Fear of being photographed/videotaped
- "Fires" or switches therapists frequently
- Avoids or seeks out physical contact
- Sexual dysfunctions:
  - ▶ hypersexuality
  - ▶ sexual perversion
  - ▶ bestiality
  - ▶ sadomasochism
  - ▶ frigidity
- Frequent unexplained crying or laughing
- Frequent regressive behavior
- Strong negative responses to certain holidays
- Fear of one's birthday
- Compulsive washing of body/genitals
- Sense of panic when one becomes the focus of attention
- Bedwetting (as child or adult)
- Strong reaction to circles, even discomfort when sitting in group formed in a circle

PSYCHOLOGICAL INDICATORS OF RITUAL ABUSE
Holly Hector, M.A.

- Fear of talking to therapist, authority figures
- Extreme reaction to animals killed on roadways
- Frequent diagnostic labels:
  - multiple personality disorder
  - dissociative disorder
  - paranoid schizophrenic
  - borderline personality disorder
  - manic/depression, bipolar
  - psychotic disorder
  - addictive disorders
  - depersonalization disorder
  - psychogenic amnesia
  - psychogenic fugue
  - post-traumatic stress disorder
- Frequently labeled "malingerer," "liar," "hypochondriac," "imaginative," as a child
- Occult obsession/revulsion:
  - drawn to or repulsed by occult themes, books, art, concepts
- Imagined taste of blood in mouth
- Extreme claustrophobia
- Pervasive sense of impending doom
- Convinced they are "possessed," "evil"
- Belief that they are controlled by something/someone outside themselves
- Imaginary friends/playmates as a child or adult
- Unexplained loss of time—hours, days, more
- Intense paranoia/dreams of family being hurt/killed
- Auditory/visual hallucinations
- Sense of surrealism, unreality
- Feeling that they could belong to satan

- Black and white thinking
- Sense of being "dead"
- Contempt/rage at God, Jesus Christ, Christianity
- Different styles of handwriting
- Exaggerated trust issues
- Flat or blunted affect
- Claims of being "haunted," seeing spirits
- Acquired items they cannot account for (clothes, books, jewelry, toys, etc.)
- Use of "we" rather than "I" in referring to self
- Unusual fears/phobias
- Denial of behavior witnessed by others
- Sudden shifts into unusual behavior
- Conversion symptoms, hypochondriasis
- Numerous diagnostic labels
- Hearing voices/chanting inside or outside of body:
  - ▶ voices often urge/demand self-mutilation or suicide
- Belief that they are "crazy"
- Belief [that they are] always being watched or followed
- Depression
- General sense of terror
- Repressed tears or repressed screaming
- Perpetual fear of abandonment
- Belief that they will be institutionalized for the rest of their lives

RITUAL ABUSE SURVIVORS' OBSESSIONS/REPULSIONS

Holly Hector, M.A.

Survivors may be either obsessed or repulsed by the following:

- Death
- Dead humans/animals
- Costumes/masks
- Fire
- Violent, bloody films/books
- Mutilation (self/others)
- Telephone
- Certain colors (red, white, black)
- Raw meat
- Blood
- Feces/urine
- Satan/demons
- Knives, blades, sharp objects
- Menstruation
- Bestiality
- Pornography
- The supernatural realm
- Occult themes

POSSIBLE FEARS AND PHOBIAS OF RITUAL ABUSE SURVIVORS

Holly Hector, M.A.

- Christian symbols/artifacts:
  - ▶ crosses
  - ▶ Bibles
  - ▶ altars
  - ▶ robes
  - ▶ chalices
- Churches
- Authority figures:
  - ▶ lawyers
  - ▶ law enforcement personnel
  - ▶ doctors
  - ▶ judges
  - ▶ teachers
  - ▶ therapists
- Incarceration/imprisonment/confinement
- Hospitals
- Medications
- Any type of surgery
- Bones
- Needles
- Blood
- Feces/urine
- Certain symbols/designs (often occult)
- Coffins, trunks, boxes, cages
- Cemeteries
- Ropes, chains, wires
- Water
- Raw meat
- Crying babies

- Pregnancy
- Pits/holes
- Certain letter/number configurations
- Certain animals:
    - goats
    - cows
    - pigs
    - rabbits
    - cats
    - dogs
    - birds
    - rats
    - snakes
    - spiders
- Camera/video equipment
- Being photographed
- Electrical stimuli
- Hypnosis, relaxation techniques
- Mirrors
- Receiving mail, phone calls
- Particular colors (red, black, white)

MIND CONTROL

Many cult members are highly sophisticated in the art of mind control and torture.

As mentioned earlier, it is important to stay measured and cautious while exploring the possibility of cult abuse in someone's background, whether you're a therapist or a friend. If you get to the core of the problem too fast, and the person doesn't have a strong support network, as, for instance, a number of friends in Twelve Step self-help, you risk losing that person because of cult programming.

Even if the person has telling dreams, and other symptoms are coming to the surface as well, this doesn't mean she or he is ready yet to face the possibility, let alone the reality, of satanic cult abuse.

An example of the satanic cult programming came up in a conversation I had recently with a therapist in Ohio. He is working with a client struggling with satanic cult flashbacks from her childhood.

One of the client's memories was that, as a child of four, during one of the ceremonies, a small incision was made in her stomach. Then one of the cult members told the girl they were placing an eye—that's right, an eye—of another cult member in her stomach.

That eye, they told her, would watch her the rest of her life, would know her every move. And if she should ever talk about the cult in any way, she would be found and killed by the cult.

Certainly, the story about implanting the eye may sound ludicrous to an adult, but to a child of four, it's all very real—and threatening. And a message like that, recorded in the unconscious, doesn't reverse on its own.

As a mild analogy: Do you remember as a child your parents telling you something that was out of their parental "universal truth" file? You know, a collection of statements that aren't based in reality, but are imparted to you as truth, with all-too-dead-serious inflections. One day, when I was about six years old, I spilled some salt. My mother solemnly and oh-so-authoritatively said, "You know, whenever someone spills salt, it's an omen they are destined to get into some type of fight or argument during that day." Now how inane is that, right? Yet to this day, every time I spill salt, guess what my first thought is?

So magnify that about a hundred times and you can imagine what was going on in this cult victim's unconscious anytime she came close to having the memories, not to mention *having to talk* about them—even in the confidential setting of a therapist's office.

What's more, when someone is being threatened with death by people they've watched actually kill, the threat hardly seems idle.

To take this a step further, many survivors report that they were forced sometimes to participate in the murders. Knives, for instance, were placed in young children's hands, then a cult member's overlapping hand would help push the knife down into the victim.

This makes the youth feel like an accomplice, and if you're a child, you believe you *are* an accomplice. This tactic further ensures silence, as well as helps to block the memories.

A woman who grew up in Indiana was exposed to a satanic cult. Her mother was the high priestess, and the girl was being trained to take over that role. Initially, when the girl was a young child, her mother would wake her and they would practice carving into frozen and thawed chickens and turkeys at two or three in the morning.

Later, she would be forced to help kill animals as part of the ceremonies. And also in her youth, finally, she reports having had to help kill two humans, again, as part of the ceremonies. This woman was in therapy almost three years before any memories of the cult started to surface.

According to the *Child Abuse and Neglect Journal* article

mentioned earlier, out of the thirty-seven patients reporting cult ritual abuse in that particular study, thirty-one reported witnessing and being forced to participate in human adult and infant sacrifice.

In 1988, the Los Angeles County Commission for Women established a task force to deal specifically with ritual abuse. The task force includes lawyers, therapists, law enforcement people, social service workers, victims, and family and friends of victims.

In one section of a *Ritual Abuse* pamphlet they've published, they list some of the types of threats and brainwashing they've heard reported by victims. The following are a few excerpts:

> Threats of punishment, torture, mutilation, or death of the victim, the victim's family, or pets.

> Victims are told it is futile to disclose because "no one will believe you."

> Children are threatened with the parents perhaps no longer wanting them, and that the cult will become the child's new family.

> Victims are sworn to secrecy, again, under the penalty of death. They are subjected to mind control regarding how to harm themselves, or even commit suicide, rather than to remember or disclose cult activities.

The Danger of Suicide

The latter point about suicide is another reason to approach the subject of ritual abuse carefully, and to make sure the person has some support in place.

Cult victims in a recovery process sometimes do begin to be suicidal as they are approaching the memories.

Just prior to having cult-related dreams and initial flashbacks, a cult victim from Akron, Ohio, made three serious attempts at suicide.

Because the cult programming is so ingrained, it's important for therapists and friends to establish suicide contracts with a person who is in any way threatening to take her or his life, or even just mentioning it in passing. The contract should be a written statement, signed by the person, agreeing to call the other party, or an alternate, before making an attempt at suicide.

Although no such technique can in any way be guaranteed to prevent a suicide, in many cases this has worked. And what is more, when someone takes the time to create the contract, the person often really feels cared about. ("I must matter at least to someone.") Sometimes just feeling cared for is enough to avert the suicide.

Another factor to be considered if the person has multiple personality disorder is that the "lost" person might not be suicidal, but one or several of the alter personalities may be. (This will be explained further in chapter 17.)

If you have a serious concern that someone, anyone, is suicidal, and you cannot intervene directly, or feel incapable of intervening, *contact your community mental health agency immediately. They can connect the person with professionals specifically trained in suicide intervention.*

Bringing up the Topic of Ritual Abuse

The following is a firsthand example of what can happen in broaching the subject of ritual abuse too early with a client.

Jean had been in therapy with me approximately a year, and with another therapist for about nine months prior to that. She also had been going to Twelve Step meetings for adult children of alcoholics and other dysfunctional families for about three years.

As more was revealed about her lifestyle and character patterns during the sessions, I became increasingly convinced that Jean might be a satanic cult ritual abuse survivor.

Even though Jean was in a supervisory capacity at work (she was a counselor) and made fairly good money, she would compulsively spend it on eating out or buying expensive gifts for people. As for providing for herself, she had virtually no furniture in her apartment. She slept on a mattress on the floor, and she had three or four outfits, at most (an example of the compulsive pauper syndrome mentioned earlier).

This again was indicative of how little self-regard she had, which also indicated some type of pronounced trauma in her past.

She was also extremely passive, compulsive about sex and work, and couldn't seem to keep a long-term relationship. In addition, she was starting to have dreams with cult themes, like being chased, or being drugged, but there wasn't, as yet, any overt satanic symbolism.

In putting all this data together, I decided to bring up the subject of satanic ritual abuse as subtly as possible.

Jean had mentioned something about violence in her family while she was growing up, and later in the session I made an allusion to another type of "violence" I had been reading about that had really shocked me. I asked her if she had ever heard anything about satanic cult ritual abuse.

Just as I got the words satanic ritual abuse out, Jean's eyes shot wide open. She started to hyperventilate and was literally frozen in panic in the chair.

It took a couple of minutes to talk her back into a semi-calm state. Then we explored what had happened.

Yes, she said, she had heard of it. In fact, there had been a training session recently on it at the place where she worked. However, even though she had panicked at the mention of satanic ritual abuse, she denied it in her own case; there was no way it could be in *her* background—no way.

Her father and mother went to church. Her father worked hard. They had raised three children. Sure, the parents were somewhat dysfunctional, but "Come on!" she said. "Ritual abuse?"

At that, I almost let it go for the time being. But, just before the session ended, I said, "Jean . . . being a counselor yourself, you know that when something happens, like what happened today, there usually is some significance, even if there is no conscious awareness of it yet. So I'll say nothing more other than to hope you stay open to anything."

If I had just left it there, even that would have probably been all right. But, no. I brought it up a bit in the next session, and in the session after that, each time explaining more about the general dynamics of these cults, and exploring whether any more feelings or awareness had come up between sessions.

Jean started to miss appointments sporadically. Then, she called, saying she needed to take some time off from therapy, even though we had been progressing extremely well with her codependency issues, as she had noted several times during the year.

Then Jean called one day, saying thanks, but it was time for her to move on to another therapist. She had some issue or other—I can't even remember what it was now—that she thought this other therapist would be better at dealing with.

That would have been fine, if that had been the real reason. But I felt sure it wasn't. And I also knew, in this case, I had not used the best judgment in pushing her toward something she was not yet ready to deal with.

All I can do in Jean's case now is pray that when she is ready to face whatever caused the panic in her that day, God will put the right people in her path.

Crossover Ritual Abuse and the "Marionette Syndrome"

Some therapists are beginning to see in their ritual abuse patients an alarming indication that some may have been abused by a combination of techniques inherent in more than one destructive cult or group, and that some of this abuse apparently is intended to turn people psychologically and physiologically into "puppets" for the group.

A certified therapist in the Midwest, who requested anonymity for safety reasons, said that some clients who had memories of being abused during cult religious ceremonies also had memories of being abused in laboratory-like settings. This laboratory abuse is seen as being "experimental."

This therapist, who regularly presents seminars on ritual abuse, said survivors have remembered being hooked to electrodes and administered a series of shocks in, for instance, an apparent attempt to curb their "affect"—to make them emotionally numb or robotic.

The electroshock techniques recalled by survivors also indicate that some are designed to set up muscle reactions as a response to cues. That is, if a person is cued psychologically, or even physically within the limits of an electromagnetic field, certain facial expressions or arm movements, for example, may be activated.

In conjunction with these techniques, some survivors remember being trained relentlessly to be more assertive or aggressive.

The therapist said she believes these techniques to be characteristic of some ethnic/religious "supremacy" groups or other special-focus groups. She also believes that the experimental nature of this abuse may indicate that some groups actually have been attempting to program "special" people, as was the documented intent of human experiments carried out by Nazi doctors during World War II.

The phenomenon of certain survivors having memories both of ceremonial ritual abuse and of experimental, laboratory-based abuse may also indicate that some groups network to relay information about abusive behavior modification and other programming techniques.

This therapist said that she has observed reported "crossover" abuse within her own case load as well as in other cases for which she has served as a consultant. She said it has also been reported by other therapists she's talked with around the country.

Holly Hector, noting that the effects of this kind of behavior modification abuse are sometimes referred to as "the marionette syndrome," agreed that crossover abuse is being seen with increased frequency by therapists working with ritual abuse survivors. As therapy has progressed in the past few years with several of her clients who are satanic ritual abuse survivors, symptoms of "the marionette syndrome" also have surfaced. Besides the electroshock techniques, Holly Hector said survivors report having memories of surgical procedures—of being operated on. She said some therapists surmise that this is related, at least in part, to medical experimentation.

Ms. Hector also reported that, in recovery, more than one of these survivors' alter personalities claim they remember being programmed to assassinate people in powerful political positions if cued.

Ms. Hector said that, in her counseling experience, people exposed to crossover abuse have been the most difficult survivors to work with because of the complexity of the abuse and the layers of intricate programming. She also believes that more and more "marionette syndrome" reports will come to light as more ritual abuse survivors seek recovery. Ms. Hector believes there is grave cause for concern about who actually may be involved with these kinds of abuses.

YOU'RE GETTING WARMER . . .

Beyond the caution espoused so far about moving through the process slowly with a ritual abuse survivor, experts advise even more caution as the survivor moves closer to the realization. As in the case of an incest victim, it is still most advisable to allow the person to choose her or his own pace.

Suggested Therapy

A therapist can keep the process moving by advising continued consistency in therapy, even by increasing the frequency of the sessions. The therapist can suggest that the client either begin journaling, or increase it if the client has already begun this practice. In addition, a counselor needs to support persistently the client's efforts to expand outside support networks, such as Twelve Step groups and other friends.

And as each of these support areas grows stronger for the survivor, the unconscious concurrently will release more clues.

Survivors at this stage are not only having dreams, but some are starting to experience millisecond flashbacks to pieces of scenes—like a bloody knife, a person screaming, or a dead cat. The flashes are generally so brief that a setting is usually not even established. Because of the macabre images and the brevity of the flash, a victim often regards this as merely some type of surreal psychological concoction ("My mind is playing tricks on me").

Yet at this stage the combination of dreams and flashes are causing the person to really start to wonder, to become really concerned.

Holly Hector advises that the professional still should not push for revelations, but a therapeutic atmosphere should have been created in which it is safe for the client finally to initiate serious conversation around the subject.

"I want them to ask me something like 'Why do you think I'm having dreams about animals being killed, babies being killed?' " she said. "Or maybe they'll ask about why they are having these strange, scary flashes."

Ms. Hector often will turn the question around. "Why do *you* think you're having them?"

She is careful at this point not to refer to the fragments of flashbacks as *memories*. Instead, she uses an analogy with her clients, likening the discovery process to a puzzle. Each of these dreams or flashes is like a piece of that puzzle.

She sometimes has her clients write these incidents of dreams or flashes on separate pieces of paper and place them in a box or envelope. After enough have been accumulated, they can be taken out, and she and her client together can look at them for any pattern that may be emerging.

"I really try to honor all of the pieces," she said. "The worst thing a therapist can do at this point is to invalidate any of these occurrences, like dreams or flashbacks, by saying things like 'Oh, it's probably nothing. I wouldn't worry about it.' "

After some more seemingly blatant, cult-related dreams and other mini-flashbacks, the client might say something in therapy like: "Does this—oh, it can't be possible—but does this, do you think, have something to do with a cult?"

"At this point, I will probably say, 'Well, anything is possible. Why don't we just wait and see what else happens, or comes up,' " said Ms. Hector.

During this time, it's Ms. Hector's personal bias that, in the case of those clients who are willing, it is very helpful for them to pray for help and insight with the process. I also suggest this with clients who are willing. In addition, we both pray for them as well.

During this time also, Ms. Hector said she works intently on nurturing and helping to bolster the client's ego because when the memories come, it is inevitable that the person will start to decompensate for a period.

"In a way, I prepare them for battle, even before they know they're going into battle," she said.

Compulsive/Addictive Characteristics

Ms. Hector also has noticed that, as a person gets closer to the memories, any compulsive-addictive characteristics begin to be evident—in acts of avoidance. That is, perhaps clients will become obsessive about sex, or they will become more addictive about certain relationships, or they will work more, gamble more, or compulsively eat more.

Ms. Hector's knowledge about the first phases of clients' getting in touch with ritual abuse memories was gathered in her first few years of counseling. Now that she has developed a reputation as a satanic ritual abuse counselor, about 75 percent of her case load is made up of satanic ritual abuse victims who have been referred to her *after* they have begun having the memories.

"My concern is that codependency counselors, church counselors, and a lot of general therapists are seeing people in different stages of this problem, but not recognizing it—simply because they don't know," she said. "My hope is that this will continue to change."

PRIMERS

Longer Flashbacks

The dreams and flashes persist. And for some, now there may be longer flashbacks of cult scenes: black-robed figures standing in a circle, chanting; or a dead cat, then a pail of blood.

While it's still hard to make out any faces or locations, the flashbacks are now starting to gnaw at the person, who may express more openness to exploring the possibilities of cult abuse. Even if the longer memories haven't yet come to light, enough dreams or mini-flashes will often lead someone who is really intent on recovering to become open to the possibilities.

At this stage, it is often helpful for therapists to tell clients their suspicions about cult abuse, based on the data gathered in earlier sessions. This "leveling" should still be rather brief and general, so clients don't feel any more overwhelmed than they're already feeling.

If a client still seems receptive, the next step is to show the person a list of the characteristics of ritual abuse victims (page 67-75) and go over some of these with them, bringing up any observations related to these characteristics that have been noted during prior counseling sessions.

Introducing "Primers"

When a therapist believes the person is ready (although no one is ever totally ready), the next phase is to introduce some rather generalized articles about satanic ritual abuse (not graphic at first) to begin the desensitizing process, as well as to assure the person that recovery is possible.

One of the best primers for this, I believe, is a short chapter toward the end of the book *The Courage to Heal* by Laura Davis and Ellen Bass. This book is a step-by-step look at incest/ sexual abuse recovery, with a series of personal stories in the back.

The chapter titled "Annette's Story" (Annette is a pseudonym) was written by the woman who founded Incest Survivors Anonymous. At the time of the writing, Annette was sixty years old. In the chapter she reports being a cult ritual abuse survivor from an upper-middle-class town in the Midwest. She had been in recovery for her own alcoholism and incest issues for years before any of the memories of the cult abuse started breaking through. The abuse memories included watching orgies, torture, and murder, although she doesn't go into much graphic detail.

The cult members included Annette's parents and other seemingly respectable community members.

If a person is a cult survivor still without specific memories, one of the biggest stumbling blocks to accepting the possibility of cult victimization, as had been the case with Jean, is simply what the person remembers on the surface about who, for instance, their parents and neighbors were. Maybe they did go to church. Or they drove car-pools of children. Or they did community volunteer work. "Dad cut the grass Sundays, then watched the golf match on television. I mean, *that's* the type of family we had!"

Yet what satanic cult survivors find, time and again, is that respectability, even community involvement, can be part of the ruse, and part of what has kept the secret for so long.

One woman remembered that her family doctor was the high priest of the cult she was exposed to. This man went on to be chief of staff at a highly respected hospital.

Other survivors have had memories of police officers, city council members, and business leaders involved with satanic cults. This information has begun to be corroborated by former cult members, like Mike Warnke, who have broken away from satanic cults and have begun to write about their experiences.(See Mike Warnke's book *The Satan Seller*.)

Survivors who suspect cult victimization can at this point supplement their reading of "Annette's Story" with a book mentioned earlier, *People of the Lie* by Scott Peck, M.D. (Peck also wrote the best-selling *The Road Less Traveled*.) While Peck doesn't talk specifically about satanic cults in *People of the Lie*, he does write about the facades (the lies) that people who are genuinely evil construct in order to cover their tracks.

Everything I've learned so far indicates that the fabric of satanic cults is evil—not merely dysfunctional, but a step beyond: *evil*. I hope *Breaking the Circle of Satanic Ritual Abuse* can be another "primer" to help people move closer not only to the realization of their abuse, but to what actually fueled the abuse. Putting the abuse in context makes the whole horror more believable for victims.

In *People of the Lie*, Peck also describes demons and possession within the context of several exorcisms he witnessed. These are dynamics that reportedly come up during cult ceremonies, and reading about them helps the victims accept more easily the reality of what they may see in their own memories later on.

There is another component to "Annette's Story" that, as I've mentioned, is typical of almost every cult victim I've ever met. Annette had blocked out all memories of the cult abuse, even though it had gone on until she was in her late teens.

This is a documented psychological phenomenon called repression, also mentioned earlier. That is, sometimes when a person is exposed to extreme trauma, the memories of it are buried in the unconscious in order for the person to be able to keep her or his psychic (emotional) balance.

For example, if a child is exposed to torture or murder with a cult, the child usually has nowhere he or she can feel safe to get help. The child has to continue to live with the parents, go to school, do all the things other kids do. It would be too emotionally taxing, at the same time, to be consciously grappling with the guilt, the confusion, the sense of betrayal that this awful reality fosters. So the unconscious flips into a survival mode, and files the memories somewhere outside of the conscious mind.

And, as also mentioned before, it is often not safe for a victim to express outwardly the feelings registering when the trauma is going on, so the unconscious again takes over and actually numbs the feelings. A cult victim may experience waves of fear, rage, sadness, even nausea, during the ceremonies. But since the emotions cannot be expressed at the time, obviously because of possible repercussions from cult members, they are repressed as well.

However, memories and feelings do stay alive inside and start to fester over time. And just as someone who is repeatedly or continually exposed to radiation at some point is most likely to develop cancer, someone who has a build-up of toxic trauma in the form of these buried memories and feelings will start to develop depression, high levels of anxiety, feelings of fear, paranoia, and other emotional disorders.

Most of these conditions are symptoms. And at some point, for those afflicted—whether they're codependent, incest survivors, cult survivors, or survivors of other kinds of abuse—to become really free, long term, they must begin a recovery process based on taking them back into the past to unearth and deal with both the memories and the feelings.

REACTIONS TO VIOLENCE

Beyond the dreams and whatever flashbacks the survivor is experiencing so far, at this stage in recovery the person also will have intensified reactions to seeing or reading about graphic depictions of violence.

For instance, one satanic ritual abuse survivor, while reading about a young child's leg being severed by a falling structure during the San Francisco earthquake, was racked with waves of almost debilitating repressed fear and nausea. Later he remembered watching people being killed and dismembered during the cult ceremonies.

Prior to therapy and Twelve Step recovery in an ACA group, his reading of such accounts provoked nothing even remotely close to that reaction. When he thought back about this, there had been a few isolated occasions over the years when reading something similar did produce stronger than normal reactions. Again, this is the unconscious keeping the reality of the abuse as close to the surface as possible, before the survivor gets into a recovery process.

Also, it's important to note here, if someone is in therapy and/or Twelve Step recovery, many repressed feelings around the cult abuse often surface long before the truth of cult involvement is even suspected.

In the book *Out of Hell Again*, by Joe S., a personal saga of satanic cult abuse and recovery, the author describes an incident in which he accidentally ran over a jackrabbit one night. Almost immediately he was overcome by waves of almost paranoid fear, then extreme fits of rage for ten to fifteen minutes after the incident.

He had been in Twelve Step codependency recovery and therapy some five years at the time of the incident. And it would be almost two more years before he would uncover the real significance of his reaction that night. As a child of four, he was forced to help stab an infant to death as part of a satanic cult ceremony. While this horror was going on, he had to numb all of his feelings.

In another case, a woman was trying to be supportive of a friend struggling through satanic ritual abuse memories. The woman had been in codependency recovery about a year. As she allowed the cult survivor to vent some of the memories with her, she herself would sometimes break down almost convulsively in tears, and later, after the conversations, experience waves of rage.

The woman interpreted this merely as sympathy for the victim and outrage at the abuse. While some of that was true, about a year later the woman would begin having her own satanic cult ritual abuse flashbacks. And she would understand that she was reacting substantially to her own repressed feelings, which were triggered through the conversations with her cult survivor friend.

As is often the case, the woman was not yet able to deal with the whole reality of the abuse, but because of her own recovery work with codependency up to that point, she was ready to cope with at least some of the feelings.

Sequentially, as a person begins to deal specifically with the issue of cult abuse in therapy, and develops a support network for that as well, more of the repressed feelings are apt to come to the surface, and are even more intense.

For some, fragmented flashbacks also persist during this time. And while some of the flashes may now last longer, the faces of the perpetrators are often still undiscernible. It is still hard to identify the setting, and no specific acts of abuse are seen.

One of my clients experienced a somewhat prolonged flashback during this stage.

We were in the midst of a visualization exercise, in an attempt to take him back in time to explore more of his past. Just as he was about to recall a time in his early childhood, the client tensed, and froze in the process. He was also visibly shaking.

I asked what was happening.

The client said he was seeing a black-robed figure standing over him. The figure's arms were folded defiantly and, although the face wasn't visible, the client sensed he was being glared at. His overriding feeling was that it wasn't safe for him to continue further in the regression.

Shortly after that we ended the exercise.

In the following weeks, I suggested that the client become involved with a Twelve Step ritual abuse group to increase his support. As a suspected ritual abuse survivor moves into this phase, some therapists will recommend, for instance, limited viewing of violent movie scenes that may involve knives, guns, or other instruments of abuse. This may help some victims with the densensitization needed to face the graphic violence of the memories. This approach needs to be used with caution, after assessing the psychological state of the survivor. (It is not for every survivor.) Also depending on the psychological state of the survivor, it may be recommended that he or she view the scenes in the presence of a therapist.

From what we are learning about cult activity, many of these movies are actually tame compared to some of the actual cult abuse.

According to the *Child Abuse and Neglect Journal* article referred to on page 63, the following are forms of abuse reportedly experienced by the thirty-seven people in the case study reporting ritual abuse exposure:

A majority of these people from around the United States reported witnessing animal mutilation; witnessing and being forced to participate in human adult and infant sacrifice, cannibalism, and drug use; and being temporarily buried alive in either graves or coffins.

In addition to movies, there are several books available now that describe, in graphic, first-person accounts, satanic cult abuse. These also can be helpful with the desensitization.

Some of these include *Out of Hell Again* by Joe S.; *Michelle Remembers* by Michelle Smith and Lawrence Pazder; and *Suffer the Child* by Judith Spencer.

Adrenaline Addiction

About graphic violence on television and in films and some psychological effects on people in general: people may go to these extremely violent movies for an adrenaline high, or "fix." These people often grew up in homes where there were varying degrees of chaos and confusion, as well as pronounced mood swings. Physiologically, this type of atmosphere keeps the adrenaline levels high, as mentioned earlier, and eventually a child will become addicted to this feeling. Later in life, the person will seek out experiences that will continue to keep the adrenaline pumping fairly consistently.

Now, there's nothing wrong with some healthy excitement or fun that gets your adrenaline going at times. That's all part of life. What I'm talking about is way beyond that.

Adrenaline-addicted people will be drawn toward crisis-oriented jobs, for example, air traffic control, fast-paced journalism, or emergency room work. Or a person will continually create crisis situations, like becoming heavily in debt, or becoming involved in chaotic relationships or thrill-seeking sports. Or, again, she or he may be drawn to the slasher film genre.

I believe that this adrenaline addiction is a basic psychological reality. Otherwise, how psychologically healthy, or for that matter, even natural, is voluntarily watching people get sliced up and shot?

Another dynamic to this, and an insidiously scary dynamic at that, is that exposure to this type of movie does, over time, desensitize people to this type of violence. Just the same way as, say, continued exposure to classical music, over time, often cultivates a preference for classical music; or exposure to romantic novels often increases one's sense of romanticism. Or, if you eat spinach often enough—even if you don't like it—you're probably going to start to like it.

If you're exposed to an experience consistently, you often acquire a taste for it, or an immunity to it.

This dynamic becomes particularly significant in the scenario of someone being drawn into a satanic cult.

First of all, you don't just walk down the street one day, and someone comes up and says, "Hey, if you're not doing anything, would you like to join a satanic cult? Torture a few cats? Kill some people?"

No. As explained earlier, people are first lured into the cult, without their even knowing it is a cult, through promises of sex or drugs or power. And if they're drawn in further and areexposed to actual graphic violence, they have less natural aversion to it if they have been desensitized earlier by violence in movies or other media.

Family Dysfunctions and Vulnerability to Cults

It's an extremely good bet that people drawn to cults that engage in ritual abuse didn't come from the best of homes. And I'm not talking the "other side of the tracks" here. I'm talking about coming from a home, rich or poor, where parental dysfunction eroded the child's personal self-esteem, leaving the child with a lot of fear, a poor sense of self, and little sense of belonging.

Counselor Marty Smith, who has been working in the Los Angeles area and on research around the addictive nature of perpetrators of ritual abuse, concurs. The degree of childhood trauma often dictates the degree of "ontological [sense of being] insecurity," said Smith. People raised in dysfunctional homes often live under a created superstitious belief system that he compares to "Newspeak," the mythical language described in George Orwell's novel *1984*. That is, children's development does not follow natural emotional growth, but is instead oriented more toward overt, or covert, forms of self-destruction. Later in life these people look for things that offer power and a sense of belonging, good or bad.

Along comes someone perhaps with demonstrable clairvoyant capabilities. The person apparently can move an object with his or her mind (telekinesis), or he can tell you something accurate about your past. Or you can turn over a card in another room, and the person can tell you what it is.

Paranormal phenomena such as these do exist, and have been documented over the years, through studies at Duke University and elsewhere.

Now this particular person with the clairvoyant powers just happens to be a witch. But a good, or "white," witch. Or, maybe the person claims to be a mystic. But, again, a "good" mystic.

Some people gravitate toward this power, this kind of person. They, too, begin to try to communicate with the "spirit world." Perhaps they personally experience some paranormal— some would even say supernatural—phenomena. "Good" phenomena. Seemingly harmless phenomena.

However, as is sometimes the case, as things progress and these seekers' trust grows, they are moved closer and closer toward the "inner circle," so to speak. They are now invited to some alcohol and other drug parties. Then they're connected sexually with others. A while later, they're invited to stay after the party for a small orgy.

And a while after that, at least some may be lured into a full satanic ceremony, where they watch, for example, a cat being killed. Later they may see people being killed, or witness what appear to be demonic possession and other "dark side" phenomena.

Now, the natural reaction to watching a person being tortured, then stabbed to death, is extreme aversion and disgust. However—and this is key—if someone has grown up watching violent films, that person usually has become somewhat desensitized to violence and so may react with less than normal revulsion, may not be as shocked. The person may actually get a vicarious thrill from watching or participating in such horrible deeds.

In spite of some studies which seem to show otherwise, I believe that these movies have an effect on personality and behavior—not to mention broader aspects of societal violence they may directly or indirectly influence as well.

Negative Excitement

Marty Smith also said that the more insecure perpetrators are, the greater the payoff in masking their own internal fear and pain by acting out on their victims during the ceremonies. This also feeds the addiction to negative excitement, he said, and dominos into cult members continuing to support each other in their "craziness" once the cycle is under way.

The addiction to negative excitement and patterns, like that generated in a satanic cult, Smith attributes not only to a chaotic/dysfunctional family of origin but also to what he calls "neophobic" learning. This is a learning that comes from the most primitive of senses and is often overlooked, but nevertheless is important, said Smith. "At one level, man somehow still internally believes if we sacrifice someone in a volcano, the crops will be plentiful the next year," he said, trying to explain how perpetrators unconsciously rationalize some of their behaviors on this base level.

THREATS AND INFILTRATION

As mentioned before, ritual abuse survivors have often been programmed to believe they will be hurt, even killed, if they ever talk about the abuse. And, so far, some survivors who are now talking about the abuse in the media, or to law enforcement officials, or at Twelve Step meetings, are experiencing some forms of harassment and threats. Others have had none. But this threat can definitely become an issue in a survivor's recovery process.

Shortly after a man in Cleveland started talking about his ritual abuse issues in Twelve Step ACA meetings, he received a threatening early-morning call from a person talking in what sounded like backward jibberish. However, a couple of key words like "satan" and "death" were discernable.

The satanic alphabet reputedly is comprised of a backward pattern of letters. The significance of the backward alphabet is just another part of the overall cult theme, standing for the reversal of all societal norms, including the alphabet.

Monitoring by Cult Members

In their May-June 1990 issue, *Changes* magazine for adult children did a comprehensive piece on satanism, including how it is being talked about with more frequency in Twelve Step meetings across the country. The article also included talk about the fear that some cult perpetrators were attending some of the meetings, in essence, to monitor what survivors were saying.

According to Myra Riddell, chairperson for the Los Angeles County Task Force on Ritual Abuse, this type of monitoring is often a given, in her opinion. She is convinced some cult members do attend Twelve Step meetings, and, for that matter, also seminars on satanic ritual abuse, and public meetings conducted by the task force.

Holly Hector also said she believes many of her seminars are attended by a percentage of cult members as well.

"They want to learn everything they can," Ms. Hector said. "It's important for them to know the latest in counseling techniques with this, for instance, so they can devise strategies to reverse and undermine the effectiveness."

Ms. Riddell adds that she believes some cult members are actually designated to infiltrate organizations, like task forces, the court systems, and the police forces, to gather information.

In the *Changes* magazine article, Washington, D.C., investigator Larry Ziliox, former director of the New York/New Jersey Cult Awareness Network, seemed to agree with other experts that many satanic cults have lawyers, judges, and police officials among their members. Besides influencing public policy, Ziliox said, these kinds of people would also be quite adept at disposing of incriminating evidence.

In *The Satan Seller*, Mike Warnke, who reports having been a satanic cult high priest before leaving the cult, not only talks about infiltration on these levels, but also says there are actually select cult members targeted to influence those in top governmental positions all over the world.

And as hard as it is to believe how heinous and far-reaching these crimes may be, it is even more unbelievable that they have been kept so secret for so long. Yet the revelation process isn't without precedent. It seems to me that it's somewhat analogous to the Mafia exposé in the 1950s.

Up until the fifties, the public heard about the Mafia occasionally, but it was only rumors. And the public heard about the killings too, but they were just isolated homicides, right? I mean, a whole organized group of people planning "hits"? Extortion? Selling drugs? Running numbers? Influencing government officials? How likely was all that?

But then came Joe Valachi, a former member of La Cosa Nostra who finally broke the code of silence. Yes, there was a highly organized network. Yes, they did operate "front" businesses. They did extort money, sell drugs, torture, kill, influence government officials.

Now, all these revelations were amazing enough then. But what was even more amazing was how long this had gone relatively undetected.

It seems these transgenerational satanic cults are somewhat like the Mafia, only even more secret.

"Code of Silence" Programming

Another tactic cult members reportedly use sometimes is to follow victims who are starting to get in touch with the memories in recovery and harass them by trying to trigger the "code of silence" programming.

Ms. Riddell said she knows of victims in recovery who have been conspicuously followed and have received threatening late-night calls. She talks of cases in which the victim's therapist is harassed as well; there may be, for instance, plants in the therapist's case load to level trumped-up malpractice lawsuits.

Shortly after a man in Ohio started talking publicly about his satanic ritual abuse, his therapist received a threatening letter from the victim's family. About the same time, in what appeared to be a totally unrelated issue, one of the therapist's clients threatened to bring a malpractice suit against the therapist for sexual inappropriateness.

Because of her intensive work with cult survivors, Ms. Hector said she also worries about being the target of faked malpractice charges. And she, too, has had to deal with the threats.

She has received harassing calls from cult members and death-threat letters, some even written in blood.

Another woman from Ohio had been having satanic cult memories for more than a year when she decided to share the memories with a brother, and, in addition, did a four-hour police deposition about the crimes.

Shortly afterward, she started getting cult-related harassing phone calls and letters. Her husband was roughed up one night, and the brakes went out twice on her car. They sold their home and moved to another state because of the harassment.

However, if she had to do it over again, she said she would. Getting in touch with the memories, going to the police, and taking a stand is the only way she could really be free inside.

A counselor who works in an adolescent chemical dependency unit in Toledo, Ohio, has had a lot of experience with teens involved in satanic cults. She also presents ritual abuse seminars.

During one of her seminars at a college in Ohio, this woman reported that other cult members start to get scared when one of the members comes into the unit for a chemical dependency problem. They are afraid cult activities will be revealed during treatment.

One of the tactics cult members on the outside will use to try to ensure silence from the member in treatment is to send what appears to be a wholly innocent message, such as a "get well" card. However, the intent of the card will be anything but innocent.

If the person, for instance, has watched cats being killed as sacrifices during some of the ceremonies, the patient may receive a card with a cat on it. Or the card will be primarily red and black. Or the person might receive a card with specific words underlined, such as "power," "sacrifice," "father" (satan), "silence."

Shortly after going public about his cult abuse on a radio talk show, a man in Los Angeles received a Christmas card from his mother. The cover displayed a pristine forest snow scene that also included a small deer and a young girl. Inside, all she wrote was "Love, Mom."

That night the man woke in a panic around 2 A.M., and began having flashbacks to a little girl being stabbed to death during a cult ceremony—stabbed to death by his mother, who was the cult high priestess.

Not everyone who has begun to talk about satanic ritual abuse has experienced harassment.

For instance, several survivors who have been regularly attending a particular Twelve Step ritual abuse meeting have had no forms of threats.

Also, at the end of "Annette's Story" in *Courage to Heal*, an addendum was added by Sandi Gallant, a special investigator in San Francisco P.D.'s Intelligence Division. "Many adult survivors believe they are at risk talking about these things," she said. "And in some cases this may be true. But in many cases I believe they are feeding off the threats and intimidation they experienced as children [in the cults].

"I've never been threatened, and I've been the most outspoken person in law enforcement in the country on this issue."

Colorado's Dr. Marita Keeling said she too has never been

threatened and she has been very visible in her work with survivors, as well as in conducting seminars and writing on the subject.

In early 1991, Dr. Keeling wrote an article that dealt with threats. While she stated that, conceivably, there is a real possibility of threat to some survivors, many of the reports may simply be paranoid reactions.

Because of the extreme abuse and systematic programming by cult members, said Dr. Keeling, many victims are naturally fearful, and may perceive attacks from many sources (friends, acquaintances, strangers) that are in no way based on reality.

In the cases of survivors she's seen with multiple personality disorder, this issue may be further complicated. That is, a survivor may, for example, find threatening notes or some type of object, for example, a knife, lying around.

Initially these are seen as real threats from the cult, but later in therapy the survivor may find that these were left by one of the alter personalities, with the "host" personality having no memory of writing the letter or leaving the knife. (See chapter 17 for more about the phenomenon of multiple personalities.)

A Personal Story

One of the most courageous sagas (although these are all phenomenal stories) is that of a woman who chose to break away from a satanic cult in Oklahoma several years ago. And breaking away wasn't without risk—a lot of risk.

While her story is about the trauma she faced getting out of the cult, it is also about the help she found from some extremely caring people. (For this woman's entire story, see page 218).

In late July of 1989, the Mothers Against Drunk Driving (MADD) crisis hotline in Texas received a call from a woman—let's call her Gina—in Oklahoma, claiming her daughter had recently been run over and killed by a drunk driver.

The details were sketchy, but the phone counselor realized that the woman was extremely troubled and decided to keep the lines of communication open by talking with her every couple of days and offering emotional support. The woman sounded very distraught and had made some allusions to suicide.

Janice Lord, MADD's National Director for Victims' Services, was brought in to consult on the case, and began talking to the woman as well.

Over time, Gina shared the information that her daughter had been run over by a cult member in retaliation for Gina's starting to rebel against the cult. And now the woman was trying to leave the cult altogether. She had been what is known as a "breeder" for the cult, forced to turn her babies over for sacrifice.

Mrs. Lord, although she had had no similar experiences either over the MADD hotline or in any other way, still found the story credible. She was disturbed because the woman seemed to have nowhere to turn for protection.

After she talked it over with her husband, a minister in a Disciples of Christ church in Texas, the couple decided to help. "We, at that point, took the situation out from under the umbrella of MADD and took it under our own personal umbrella," Mrs. Lord said.

Mrs. Lord and her husband, Dick, helped get Gina situated temporarily in a women's shelter close to their home in Texas. The couple then arranged to move her into some subsidized housing, also nearby.

"We were frankly afraid to take her in because of the possible repercussions from the cult at that point," said Mrs. Lord, who is also a licensed professional counselor and a certified licensed social worker.

The cult eventually did track her to Texas, and one night she was physically assaulted and raped. After she was released from the hospital, the Lords decided to take her into their home for protection, in spite of the possible risk to themselves.

Several nights later, when they took Gina to her apartment to pick up the rest of her things, they found a plastic bag that had been left on the front steps by cult members. The bag contained animal entrails and dismembered animal body parts, with a note. The note said this was a reminder of what had happened to Gina's babies and would happen to her if she didn't return to the cult. This was the beginning of a series of notes and threats both to the Lords and to Gina. All of this evidence has been turned over to the police.

Shortly after Gina moved in with the Lords, the story took on another dimension.

Gina was having a particularly restless night. Janice Lord attempted to lead her in some deep-breathing relaxation techniques she had developed in her professional counseling. In the midst of this, Mrs. Lord said that Gina's eyes, and her overall countenance, took on what she reports was a "demonic-looking appearance." Then, in a foreign voice totally unlike her own, Gina began speaking in a backward-sounding language, which Mrs. Lord today identifies as satanic.

Janice Lord said she had the presence of mind to invoke the name of Christ, and began speaking back to what she believed to be the demonic spirit.

"She doesn't belong to you anymore, but to us," Mrs. Lord spoke emphatically. *"This is a child of God."*

A big scene ensued, culminating in Gina's running to the bathroom and attempting to slit her wrists with a razor blade. Mrs. Lord reported struggling with her, finally getting her to release the blade before any major injury happened.

The next day, the Lords contacted an Episcopal priest who specialized in exorcisms. The priest quickly gathered an exorcism team, and the Lords took Gina to the Episcopal church that evening.

Initially, some of the symbols in the church were "triggers" for Gina—candles, a gold bowl, crucifixes. These were all things Gina had seen used during cult ceremonies. She lost control, and ran wildly out of the church. Eventually, however, she came back.

First she asked the exorcism team to pray for the souls of the babies she had turned over for sacrifice. After a while the team began to pray for her deliverance from any demons.

The experience culminated for Gina in violent episodes of coughing, vomiting, and retching.

The next day, Janice Lord said she noticed a marked difference in Gina. She seemed much more calm, and also more willing to talk about spirituality.

"You know, if you would have talked to me a couple of years ago about cults, much less demons, I would have thought you were crazy," said Mrs. Lord. "But now that I've had these experiences, I'm convinced all that exists."

Another thing Mrs. Lord is now convinced of is the existence of angels. She said she has been providentially assured their home is protected by a circle of angels.

At the time of this writing, the Lords have had Gina in their home a year and a half, and no harm has come to their family.

However, there have been other complications.

Shortly after the exorcism, it also became clear that Gina

had multiple personalities, not unusual for someone who has been subjected to such extreme abuse. Using her counseling skills, Mrs. Lord has spent countless hours helping counsel and nurture these alter personalities toward integration.

Then, while working toward recovery, Gina was again abducted and raped one night—it happened on a Good Friday. A satanic symbol, a circle with an upside-down cross, was branded on her stomach. She was able, however, to make her way back to the Lords and continued to work on her recovery.

Eventually, Mrs. Lord came across several other cult survivors in her area, and she decided to start a closed support group for these people. The group has been meeting for around a year, and has proved to be of significant help in each survivor's process of recovery.

THE INNER CHILD

Probably you've heard about the "inner child."

You could have heard about it in relationship to an ego state within the study of Transactional Analysis. Or you could have heard about it more recently as it relates to codependency recovery.

What some therapists are starting to believe as they delve further into codependency study is that there actually is a "child" who exists within each adult. If you've come from a dysfunctional family, it is a child who needs to be nurtured through the developmental phases that weren't negotiated all that effectively the first time around. (The similarities and differences between the inner child and child alter personalities will be explained in chapter 17.)

One of the main keys to lasting recovery, whether from codependency, incest, or ritual abuse, is to find this child and begin the nurturing process in some tangible ways.

Usually, this inner child doesn't just suddenly reveal himself/herself. The revelation generally happens in phases, and many times only after the person has been in Twelve Step recovery and/or therapy for a time.

When first approaching the issue of the inner child with clients, for instance, I will ask them to tell me how old they think their inner child is. At the most I give them five seconds to answer.

Now, while consciously they usually don't have a clue,

somehow their unconscious always seems to come up with an answer. And what I've found in my work is this: Always trust the first number that's given.

After the age is determined, the next step is to begin to establish some trust. For example, Tim, who's a thirty-seven-year-old computer programmer, guesses his inner child is six. We then discuss things that six-year-olds like to do. (And you can be sure it won't include reading Tim's *Wall Street Journal*.)

Six-year-olds, as a rule, like to color, watch cartoons, have stories read to them, build sand castles . . . well, they like a lot of things.

Tim's next task was to do some activities appropriate for a six-year-old.

Now, at first, Tim, who is super-responsible and productivity-oriented, not to mention a product of very neglectful parents, saw all this as extraneous, a waste of time.

However, after ignoring the suggestion for a while, and staying stuck in his process (and probably getting very tired of hearing me mention it every week), he grudgingly gave in.

He had also begun using the Sixth and Seventh Steps (see page 256) to help with his lack of motivation in this area:

Step Six: Were entirely ready to have God remove all these defects of character.

Step Seven: Humbly asked Him to remove our shortcomings.

Tim first went to the children's section of the local library and picked up some books for six-year-olds. Then, at night before bed, he would read to his inner child, out loud and with expression, as you would to any child. He later got some coloring books for his inner child, then started a baseball card collection.

During this time, he was also doing daily affirmations with his inner child, holding a teddy bear and talking into a mirror.

As he did each of these things, he kept getting the impression that his inner child was moving closer and closer to the surface, which is generally what happens.

(Early on, the inner child often holds back, does not reveal himself/herself, primarily because to be revealed and then ignored would amount to the ultimate rejection, would hurt too much. So the child holds back to see if the efforts are going to be somewhat tangible, somewhat consistent.)

After a time of these real efforts, the inner child will sometimes simply show up in such a way that the person finally knows the child is, in fact, there.

Tim, for instance, had an overwhelming feeling of childish excitement while picking out a particular children's book in the library one day. "There's no way that could have been me," he said, still astonished. "No way."

Or take Bianca, a forty-year-old loan manager, who, also reluctantly and skeptically, was doing some experimental inner child work. She was skeptical, that is, until she found herself late for a conference meeting one day because she had somehow found herself engrossed with a doll house she was playing with. Or, rather, that her inner child was playing with.

A Guided Meditation

Another way the inner child will sometimes show up is through a guided meditation.

During a therapy session, I'll ask the client to relax. Just relax, sit back, breathe deeply, rest. (Also before we move into the next part, I will suggest, if the person is okay with it, that she or he take a few moments to pray, as I do, for help.)

After this, I have the client breathe deeply some more . . . close the eyes . . . and begin to drift . . . then, that's right, drift some more . . . farther, then farther away . . . leaving the stress of the day, the week . . . behind. Drifting farther . . . and farther . . . .

When the client is ready I ask him/her to picture a place from the past. A safe place. A place to go as a child to get away. I then allow time for that image to come into view.

It's usually a place, well, for instance, by a lake. Or off in the woods. Or maybe it's a favorite room in an old house. Perhaps this client is a man. I tell him I want him to be in this place, not as a child, but as an adult. Then I have him describe what he is seeing and experiencing in detail.

What does the sky look like? What's the temperature? What kind of trees are around? Is the pond calm? Or, what's in the room? Where is he standing in the room? What kinds of books are on the shelves?

Then I have him go to a place in the scene to get comfortable, to sit in a chair, on a log, whatever.

"Now I want you to breathe deeply some more. That's

right, relax . . . just let the relaxation happen."

Also, at this point, I'll often have him say another prayer to himself for help with the next phase.

"Without any preconceived notions, I'd like you now to ask if there's anyone else there that would like to come join you. You can ask either out loud, or to yourself. But ask. Then wait."

Sometimes it happens right away. Other times it takes awhile. And sometimes, it just doesn't happen.

Say another client is a woman. Often she will see the child, a hesitant child who will walk into the scene.

The client reaction will vary at this point, but I can usually tell the moment the child shows up as well. The woman will start to cry. Or she will smile, or look perplexed. Sometimes, for some inexplicable reason, *my* inner child can tell when the *other's* inner child has shown up, and there's this feeling—I guess the best way I can describe it is, this feeling of inner excitement.

After she acknowledges that the child is there, I direct a bit more at this point. "Tell her you love her. And that you're there to protect her. Ask her also if she'd like to join you."

Sometimes the child immediately comes over. Other times it takes some patient coaxing. And other times, well, the child doesn't trust enough yet, and keeps some distance.

Other times, the client will sense the child is there, but just outside the picture, because, again, the trust level isn't there . . . yet.

I then either ask the client to hug the child, or hold the child's hand, or, if the child is still at arm's length, I have the client just talk to the inner child reassuringly.

As the conversations are going on, I ask the clients periodically to share with me some of what's being said. Then, a bit later, I have the persons ask the inner child if there's any place the child wants to go. On a path through the woods? To the other side of the lake? Or does the child just want to stay here? (It's important at this juncture that the child feel in control of the situation.)

Then, generally, if the client has taken his/her inner child on some sort of junket or journey, periodically I ask the person to describe where they are going, what they're seeing.

Then I again direct the person to ask the child what the child likes to do.

Some like to play jacks or hopscotch. Others like comic books, playing ball, playing with dolls. The list goes on.

Sometimes, as with their initial appearance, some inner

children will remain hesitant about letting the adults know what they like to do—merely because if a person knows, and then doesn't attempt to follow through on any of this, an inner child will feel extremely rejected.

I then allow the client the last couple of minutes to say some closing things to the child, and vice versa. And then I suggest some more hugging.

At the end, I have the person ask the child if he/she wants to come back. If so, fine. If not, I suggest the person tell the child he/she will be back again, and again.

"Now, take a couple of deep breaths and slowly, slowly . . . start to see yourself back, and back . . . And when I count to three, you'll be back in the room.

"One . . . another deep breath . . . two . . . three."

Generally, what's left of the session is spent processing what's happened—often after a kind of stunned silence about what really seemed to have taken place.

Again, it's one thing to hear, or even believe, there's this inner child existing in some psychological dimension of the unconscious. It's another to not only meet the child, but to realize that the adult and inner child are somehow separate beings, with separate likes, dislikes, moods, feelings . . .

Reviewing the Meditation

How was the experience? What were the feelings? How did the child seem? Pensive? Fun-loving? Sad? What?

What did the child look like? What was she wearing? What did he say he liked to do?

For instance, one inner child says she likes to swing. "Can you, maybe, three times this week after work, stop by a playground and swing?" Then I add I would like for the client to report back to me the following week on how that went. This adds a little incentive, and shows I'm interested.

If some inner children don't show up for the first meditation, or even for several meditations, this is often merely an indication that they are still hesitant, for any number of reasons. In this case, I simply praise the clients for the progress they have made, and continue to focus on getting them to do more affirmations and generalized play reparenting in preparation.

I also ask them to make a conscious effort to keep focusing on the Sixth Step.

When it is time, it inevitably happens—the child shows up.

Reparenting

There are at least three good reasons why getting in touch with the inner child and reparenting are keys to many recovery processes, including recovery from ritual abuse. Note: Many of the same therapy techniques and rationale about dealing with the inner child apply to child alters in the case of multiple personalities. (See chapter 17.)

One reason for reparenting: there seems to be a direct correlation between the amount of tangible reparenting and the rate at which the buried feelings and memories come back. Since the inner child, along with any child alters, has to re-experience both as well, the unconscious seems to gauge where a person is in the reparenting process—how much actual time and emotional support the person is able to give to these inner entities—before releasing each wave of feelings and memories.

The second reason: the inner child and child alters are saturated with the old dysfunctional programming, whether it's the highly sophisticated cult messages that came from Cousin Charles about being quiet during an incestuous act, or just the free-floating, funky messages you got while growing up in a just generally dysfunctional home. The more time you spend with the inner child, the more the child accepts you as the new "parent" and the more the child will start to accept, really accept, new messages from you.

During the middle phases of the ritual abuse recovery process, one of the most important new messages is: It is now okay to remember.

The third reason to connect with the inner child is that, through this connection, some of the fun-loving, trusting innocence still left in this child rubs off on the battered, understandably jaded adult.

What I've seen as a consistent pattern is that, once the person really connects with the inner child, the adult and child go at the tangible reparenting with a newfound zeal. They increase the play time. They become more consistent.

However, there's a psychological catch after a while. As I mentioned, as the reparenting increases, so does the catharsis. And, as more of the buried memories and feelings move to the surface in direct correlation, this starts to become uncomfortable for the person. The natural reaction is to do something to cut back on this process, or to even stop the reparenting altogether.

Another dynamic here is that, generally, the things the child likes to do aren't necessarily what the adult likes to do. (I mean if you're, say, twenty-nine years old, hopscotch and jacks don't really capture your attention.) So reparenting also entails sacrificing adult time. This does not come naturally when you've come out of a home with chronic abuse and neglect and no parenting models you could depend upon.

So, when the reparenting process starts to sour a bit, I suggest a couple of supplemental things.

For one, I have the person at this juncture start to focus on the Eighth and Ninth Steps of the Twelve Step Program:

Step Eight: Made a list of all persons we had harmed, and became willing to make amends to them all.

Step Nine: Made direct amends to such people whenever possible, except when to do so would injure them or others.

The inner child becomes one of the top people on the list, once a person realizes he/she is treating the child in somewhat the same way dysfunctional parents had treated him or her.

And in consistently relying on God for help with this, the client realizes that a lot of things just evolve serendipitously.

Say your inner child lets you know he'd like to start a baseball card collection. Yet you keep just, well, putting it off. Oh, sure, you're going to get started on it; it's just that it's been busy at work, repairing the house, and the car keeps breaking down.

When a person realizes, to his consternation, that he's been sounding a lot like his parent(s)—he starts turning to the Eighth Step on a daily basis, to the best of his ability.

And wouldn't you know . . . the next day at work, a co-worker is talking proudly about his kid's baseball card collection. And, in the newspaper a couple of days later, you see an advertisement for a baseball card show the next weekend, or you notice there's a sale as you're passing by a card shop, or . . .

Then, seizing the moment, or the day, or Darryl Strawberry for that matter, you use the Ninth Step and buy your inner child some cards, then some more, then even a folder to organize them. And before long, you're back on the reparenting track—which moves you ultimately into deeper levels of recovery.

And if you're a satanic cult survivor, this may mean more painful memories and feelings may shortly be in store for you.

13

UNCOVERING ADVANCED CLUES

There are more flashbacks now, still of the fragmented variety. More milliseconds of what appear to be black-robed figures standing in what appears to be a circle. No faces yet. Or there's a flashback to a bloody knife, or flickering candles, or to someone screaming in terror. Yet, the survivor still can't see who it is.

Concurrently, cult dream themes are becoming more prevalent. Dreams of being drugged or chased. Dreams of seeing a person or animal being tortured, or killed, but in settings outside of a cult ceremony. Then, in some of these dreams, neighbors may start to appear as perpetrators of the violence.

It seems weird to the survivor " . . . because, I mean, Mrs. Smith up the street would never, I mean NEVER be involved with anything like a cult. She sang in the choir at church. She volunteered at the Red Cross. She . . . "

Dream Symbols

Other survivors, during this phase, will dream of their current friends or acquaintances, who, in the dreams, are also perpetrators of violence. But upon analysis, it becomes apparent their unconscious is using these people as symbols of other destructive persons in their backgrounds.

For instance, Jane dreams of Bill, an acquaintance who, in the dream, stabs a young child.

Now Jane has known Bill for a long time, and knows pretty

115

assuredly Bill's not like that—at all. However, upon analysis, it's learned that Bill's personality is sometimes moody, authoritarian, narrow-minded—much the same as Jane's father's was.

And while in therapy at this time Jane is not ready to accept consciously that Bill in the dream is the symbolic representation of her father, this idea does get filed somewhere and becomes another clue—another step in the desensitization phase.

Again, the unconscious uses these dreams as a way of continuing to prepare the victim for the eventual shock of what happened, and who was really involved. To get there too fast would overload the psyche. Again, it's important to respect the client's pace.

Revisiting Familiar Places

If the client is ready, besides the violent movies, there are other ways to jog memories. One is to go back to the neighborhood(s) one grew up in. Drive around, even walk around, if possible, remembering, or trying to remember—remembering the adults in the neighborhood, remembering the children. What were their personalities like? Did anything ever seem odd? Odd, especially in the light of what the survivor might be learning now?

What was quirkish about a certain adult? Do you remember any adults who seemed especially sadistic, or overtly sexual, so that you always felt uncomfortable around them? Also, what's happened to some of the children who lived in the neighborhood? Did some develop psychiatric disorders? What kind? Is there a possibility the disorder is related to extreme trauma?

If at all possible, arrange to go back through the old family home. While the cult memories still might not surface consciously, there's a good bet that familiar settings can trigger memories for the inner child, and for alter personalities if the person has MPD. Of course the safety of the survivor must come first. The possible dangers of such a visit must be weighed carefully.

This moves survivors into an even more active role in their own recovery process. They, in effect, become investigative reporters, viewing their past almost from a safer, third-person perspective, at least for the time being.

Meditative Techniques

Another helpful therapeutic adjunct is for clients to learn some type of meditative technique, like self-hypnosis or other relaxation techniques, and schedule times each day to work on slowing their systems down, to allow time and a clear passage for the memories to come. (In this phase, there's again an unconscious tendency to turn to compulsive behavior of any sort—sex, work, gambling, shopping—to block both the memories and the feelings.) Also, it is important for a person to stay as regular as possible with Twelve Step meetings, therapy, and the meditation, if that's been incorporated into the process.

SUPPORT FOR SURVIVORS

Part of the recovery equation is that the more support victims have, the more quickly and effectively they move through the process.

As victims move into the phase in which they start to accept internally the reality of the cult abuse, it is important to hook them up with other people going through the same process.

This can be facilitated on several different levels.

Inpatient Treatment

At first it is sometimes advisable to send victims to inpatient treatment. There are a number of hospital settings across the country now set up for people reporting satanic cult ritual abuse. (For a list of some of these, see Resources.)

Twelve Step and Other Groups

Another avenue that is extremely helpful is referral to a Twelve Step group focusing specifically on ritual abuse issues. As more people working other Twelve Step programs, especially as recovering chemical dependents and codependents, have started to have cult memories during the past few years, these Twelve Step ritual abuse groups have begun to evolve and now can be found in some major metropolitan areas. They have either formed as autonomous Ritual Abuse Anonymous or Cult Survivors Anonymous groups, or they have been incorporated into ACA or ACoA as special-focus groups. (See pages 256-259 for the Twelve Steps, Twelve Traditions, and Promises of AA, as well as the Twelve Steps for ritual abuse survivors.)

Cleveland's first Twelve Step ritual abuse group was incorporated as a special-focus AcoA group in the fall of 1989.

The format for this particular meeting varies. Once a month someone volunteers to share his or her story of abuse and recovery for anywhere from fifteen to forty-five minutes. The group comments on the sharing afterward. At another meeting, someone will give a mini-talk on one of the ritual abuse characteristics, its genesis in and how it has affected that person's life, and what the person is doing to get over it.

At another meeting there will be a general open discussion. And the remaining week of the month is spent discussing one of the Twelve Steps.

The atmosphere in the group is very supportive, or at least as supportive as it can be, given the circumstances. Everyone is given a chance to share, but no one is forced to.

The meeting is often quite dynamic and cathartic. As people share some aspect of their abuse, it will often trigger others' recollections of experiences, evoking repressed tears, anger, fear. And, as these feelings come, group members often show an empathy that can only come from other survivors. During all of this, the group bonding strengthens.

For newcomers, the group helps them move further into recovery.

However, getting newcomers to attend one of the meetings can be hard. For one thing, the individuals are extremely self-conscious. ("Well, I'm not as sure now whether it really is ritual abuse. I mean the dreams, and those flashes, could have meant anything.") Also, they worry that the group might be infiltrated with cult members. ("Besides, even if it is ritual abuse, can't I just deal with it in therapy?") And then, unconsciously, they're worried that they are going to relate with the group, which will really force them to look deeper.

After the meeting, people often go for "fellowship," over coffee or whatever, and friendships begin to develop.

It's important to note that these meetings are far from perfect. People attending them are hurting emotionally. Many have major fears and trust issues. Some people are more empathetic than others. And because the groups are still new, there will be organizational problems. (Well, after all, that's how AA started.)

So the first experiences at meetings are not always entirely positive for some who are new. However, it's important to encourage those who didn't particularly take to the first meeting to go back, and back again. And if they still don't like the meeting, and if they have the luxury in a particular city to find a different one—it's recommended they try another meeting. Sometimes the group chemistry happens right away. Other times the assimilation simply takes time.

(See chapter 15 on the evolution of these groups, and also how to get one started.)

If there isn't a Ritual Abuse Anonymous meeting in the area, another possibility for survivors is an Incest Survivors Anonymous group. Since incest/sexual abuse is part of the cult experience, this can also be a forum for starting to talk about the trauma.

It is often the case that once people have worked through some of their codependency issues, then have started to deal with incest issues in these more specialized groups, the cult issues, if they are there, finally start to break through. So it isn't unusual now to hear talk of satanic ritual abuse in the incest groups as well.

Also, as Holly Hector pointed out, the closer a person gets to the memories, the more that person's primary addictions or compulsions start to kick in. And it may also be necessary for victims to be in other Twelve Step groups concurrently, actively working on these issues as well—Overeaters Anonymous, AA, Narcotics Anonymous, Workaholics Anonymous, Gamblers Anonymous.

Besides Twelve Step meetings, groups led by professionals, such as incest therapy groups, ritual abuse therapy groups, and groups for people with multiple personalities, also provide supportive/intensive settings for cult survivors.

TWELVE STEP RITUAL ABUSE GROUPS

One Group's Beginnings

The meeting started tentatively, a couple of minutes late. It was late July in 1991. A muggy evening in Cleveland. An old fan clacked in the corner of a basement meeting room.

The format was a free-floating group discussion this night, and the first person to talk, a man about fifty, spoke about this being the first Twelve Step ritual abuse meeting he'd been back to in a couple of months. He had also temporarily dropped out of codependency Twelve Step meetings and therapy as well. And, as a result, he said he really noticed himself starting to slip back into depression and some old dysfunctional emotional patterns.

He went on to say that he knew, in order to continue to recover, he needed to keep coming back to the meetings.

Later, however, he said some of the memories were still continuing to come despite his lax attitude toward recovery.

"I was driving on a rural back road recently and had just pulled up at a stop sign. At that second—and I don't even know what triggered it—a crystal-clear memory of a [satanic] ceremony abuse scene came into focus. So clear, it was as if I was standing right there again.

"And, as for how horrendous that was, I thank God He's allowing the clarity so I know, really know, exactly what happened."

At first the man wasn't able to describe the actual scene. However, as the evening went on, his description became more graphic.

Another man talked about remembering having the inside of his eyelid cut as a seven-year-old, as part of a torture/brainwashing ritual. He trembled as he recounted the memory, unable to look up at anyone as he talked.

A twenty-five-year-old woman talked about lying down for a nap earlier in the week, when, all of a sudden she flashed to a bathtub covered with blood and dismembered animal parts. "I HAVE TO WASH THE BLOOD OFF. I HAVE TO WASH IT OFF!" She screamed, wide-eyed, looking around the room imploringly. Then she broke down sobbing.

Respectful of her process, her tears, the group members remained silent.

After a while, one of the other members asked if she needed a hug. She did.

And as they hugged in the center of the circle, some members were now crying, too. Others, somewhat dissociative perhaps, were staring off into space. Others reached out to hug her too, with an empathy only one survivor could have for another.

Others there that night weren't having the actual memories yet, but were having cult-related dreams and intense feelings. Also, they could relate to any number of the satanic cult ritual abuse characteristics. They, too, were just as welcome.

The meeting lasted an hour and a half. There were more tears. There was anger, and even occasional laughter to break some of the sustained tension. There was also hope, hope that this could get better.

This night, there were ten people at the meeting. Sometimes there are more, sometimes less. At the time of this writing, this is the first Twelve Step ritual abuse group in the northern Ohio area. It had been in existence about a year and a half.

At this stage of the group's development, a small core is attending regularly, with another group coming sporadically, and a couple of newcomers generally are added every week or two.

Soon, a few of the core group people will probably spin off to create other Twelve Step RA groups, typical of new Twelve Step group evolutions.

This group's founder, Pam, said that since the group started, about thirty-five people have come through the doors.

She has observed the new group ebb and flow as it has

struggled for identity. Initially there was a lot of enthusiasm among the people coming together to form the group, and attendance and group participation were fairly consistent during the first couple of months. It wasn't hard to solicit participation in group tasks, such as setting up the meeting room or volunteering to be the monthly chairperson or treasurer.

However, said Pam, as the months went on, getting volunteers got harder and harder, and attendance started to drop off. For about five meetings, only one person showed up.

Yet Pam and a couple of the other core group members kept pursuing it, and eventually attendance started to increase again. The nucleus began to grow larger, get stronger.

In order to get the word out about the group, a couple of members have collaborated on putting together a flyer to be distributed to treatment centers and therapists throughout the area.

Besides fluctuating attendance and a fluctuating level of volunteering, Pam also cited some other struggles the group has had, in order to give those thinking about starting one of these groups an idea of what to expect.

A Place to Meet

First of all, she said, finding a place to meet was somewhat of a struggle, because of preconceived notions about any group having to do with "satanism," even if it was purely recovery-oriented. Though she had thought about describing the group just as a "ritual abuse" group to those who rented the meeting halls, she felt it was important to be totally straight with them up front, so there would be no problems later. Plus, if the group was meant to happen, said Pam, "God would work out the details."

A church was finally found, a Catholic church with an open meeting room in the basement.

The location proved a mixed blessing. For some who had been exposed to the cult's mock religious stagings and had just started working through this issue, coming to a religious center, with its traditional Christian symbols, was a trigger for them at times. Cult members may have dressed up as Christ, priests, or ministers and raped children with crosses, or made them drink blood from chalices. However, this triggering did cue some of their repressed memories and feelings, which, although painful, are necessary for their recovery.

The positive side was that some who had relied heavily on God as a protecting force over the years found the setting felt extremely comforting and safe.

Another issue had to do with meeting in the basement, said Pam, because some survivors had been exposed to cult ceremonies in basements. Although one survivor said that, by forcing herself to go into the basement week after week, she has gotten over some of her claustrophobic fear about being in confined spaces.

Fear of Infiltration

Another concern that comes up consistently for cult survivors is fear of the group being infiltrated by cult perpetrators.

This particular group has adopted a mini-screening process. Since Pam's phone number is given to people interested in coming to the group, she usually conducts brief conversations with prospective newcomers about their backgrounds. Reciprocally, Pam describes what the group is about and its format. Although this process admittedly is in no way guaranteed to keep out infiltrators, it may give some preliminary clues about newcomers' backgrounds.

Format

The format of the group, as mentioned earlier, varies.

Some nights it will be an open discussion. Other nights a specific Step or RA characteristic will be discussed. However, even on these nights, no one has to stick specifically to the topic if other issues are pressing. And some nights there is a lead—someone shares some of what happened in the past, how recovery began, and what he or she is doing now in recovery.

At the beginning of the meeting, the RA Steps, the characteristics, the Twelve Traditions of AA, and the following description, drafted by Pam, are read:

> Ritual abuse is that physical, emotional, mental, sexual,
> and/or spiritual abuse that is perpetrated in a ceremonial
> (or ritual) manner most often by a group of perpetrators.
> However, the same damage can be caused by a single per-
> petrator when performed in the same ritualistic manner,

such as a parent who perpetrates the abuse in the same
order and place, and often at the same time of day.
Group perpetration includes such cults as satan worship-
pers, witches' covens, pseudo-religious groups . . .as well
as fringe and mainline churches. (Because the intent of the
group is basically good doesn't mean that an individual
within the group can't twist beliefs and standards to meet
his or her own sick needs.)

Pam notes that watching the group evolve has been an extremely
positive experience, especially seeing some of the people in the
group get significantly better over time. A combination of the support group and concentrated work on the Steps seems to move
people through the process more quickly, taking them to deeper
levels of recovery.

There is not much to starting a group, she said. A group
starter packet basically consists of what is read at the beginning
of the Cleveland meeting, and any specific policies about the trea-
sury, group literature, and so on. These policies can be worked
out during monthly "group-conscience" meetings.

Note: It was a group-conscience decision of this particular group to allow me to use vignettes, somewhat altered, from
this meeting.

On a Twelve Step recovery level, it is often advisable for
ritual abuse survivors to attend either Codependents Anonymous
(CODA) or Adult Children of Alcoholics (ACoA) Twelve Step
meetings, where there is a concerted focus on reversing the
codependency characteristics that usually affect the survivors to
the extreme.

TWELVE STEP APPLICATIONS FOR ABUSE SURVIVORS

The First Step: Admitted we were powerless ...

The First Step for cult ritual abuse survivors in Twelve Step self-help is: "We admitted we were powerless over the effects of ritual abuse—that our lives had become unmanageable."

This, like all the Steps, is multilayered. Deeper and deeper awareness of the effects of ritual abuse comes to a survivor over an extended period of time.

First, the part about being "powerless."

The nature of children for the first nine or ten years of life is often narcissistic—not in an adult-vanity, addicted-to-mirrors way, but in the sense that children believe what happens around them is usually directly *because* of them.

If exposed to a satanic cult, child victims often believe that something they've done creates this prevailing climate of evil mayhem. Much the same as kids in families with other kinds of dysfunctions believe that if their conduct were just a little better, or their grades were higher, Dad wouldn't drink so much or Mom wouldn't yell so much.

Ritual abuse survivors unconsciously carry an enormous guilt; if they had somehow just been different, none of this horror would have happened. This guilt fuels extreme shame, shame that erodes self-esteem in the survivor.

Without a sense of their own worth, many survivors find it virtually impossible to meet their potential in relationships, careers, hobbies, or other pursuits. Some even drift aimlessly, not really living, just surviving.

Added to this shame is the survivors' belief that somehow they could have stopped the sexual abuse, the torture, the killings. And, of course, they didn't—couldn't—which adds to their survivor's guilt.

Cult survivors, like many people in other forms of Twelve Step recovery, are afflicted with massive amounts of shame. Shame, more often than not, is one of the core problems in recovery.

An excellent book on this subject—though not specific to ritual abuse problems—is *Healing the Shame That Binds Us* by best-selling author John Bradshaw.

When survivors first enter ritual abuse recovery, much work must be done to help them come to terms internally with the indisputable fact that they *really* were "powerless." While an adult can often accept this cognitively, it's quite another thing to accept it internally and actually begin to let go of the shame.

Generally, this acceptance will take time, talking with other survivors, reading other survivors' stories, and a lot of dialoguing with their own inner child. If they have developed multiple personalities, this also may require dealing with alter personalities as they work toward integration. (See chapter 17.)

Survivors need to reach another level of awareness about powerlessness. Gradually they come to find that they were not only powerless over the situation in their youth, but that they are powerless over something now—the long-term effects the ritual abuse has had on them, especially the survivors' typical characteristics.

What's often the case is that they begin therapy or become involved with ritual abuse recovery groups and learn some of the reasons behind the "unmanageability" in their lives. At this point some will drop out of formal recovery and, armed with this new information, go out to try to change things on their own. (Doing things "on their own" is not unusual for ritual abuse survivors; in fact, they've relied on this kind of independence for most of their lives.)

Realizing now that the boss isn't *really* life-threatening, they set off to confront him or her—only to balk at the last minute, or to end up shaking through the whole attempt at confrontation, just as they've done so often before.

Or, now realizing why they are attracted to dysfunctional

relationships with a certain kind of person, they set out to choose someone different—only to find that, after a time, much to their chagrin, they've chosen the same type of person all over again.

The painful realization—which is, in fact, all a part of working the First Step—is that it will take time, support, and the working of the rest of the Steps to really effect lasting change.

To work the First Step—actively work it—simply means to keep showing up for recovery—for the meetings, for therapy, and for seminars—and to make use of whatever supplemental reading is available.

The Second and Third Steps
(or, Turn My Will Over to Whom?)

Step Two: "Came to believe that a power greater than ourselves could restore us to sanity."

Step Three: "Made a decision to turn our will and our lives over to the care of God as we understood Him."

Recently, during a satanic cult ritual abuse seminar, a counselor asked how distorted one's sense of spirituality can become from being exposed to this type of cult while growing up.

The answer: *very*. On many different levels. And it will be important to address these within the recovery process.

First of all, a child's internalized sense of who "God" is comes primarily from how the parents act toward the child. It's the psychological phenomenon of transference. In this case, a child usually can't see "Our Father who art in heaven." But as kids, we can clearly see our father (or mother) who art on earth.

And if the parents, or first caregivers, are controlling, perfectionistic, and punishing, that becomes the child's—later the adult's—internalized sense of who "God" is. (No matter how many times he or she has heard about a loving and caring God.)

To take this a step beyond, or actually a lot of steps beyond, a transgenerational cult victim's parents and other neighborhood role models were people bent on total control, blatant abuse, even killing. On top of all that, they worshiped an entity that epitomizes dark power, evil.

In addition, because of all the contrived abuse to discredit Christ, explained in the chapter on satanism, many victims have developed a strong unconscious aversion to Christ.

Some victims consciously do believe in "God." However, their internal perception is often that God is extremely controlling, judgmental, and punishing.

Burdened with this belief system, many cult victims before recovery are plagued with extreme scrupulosity, or guilt obsessions.

The situation becomes even more complicated when a victim gets into Twelve Step recovery.

The Third Step reads: "Made a decision to turn our will and our lives over to the care of God as we understood him."

The message that comes from a cynical cult victim's unconscious may go something like this: "Yeah, right. Sure . . . I'm really ready to turn my life over to some maniacal god or other!"

So this Step really can be a stumbling block for many survivors.

However, the Second Step reads: "Came to believe that a power greater than ourselves could restore us to sanity."

That "power" for many cult victims, no matter what they believe, can be the new kind of love they begin to feel from others in the Twelve Step fellowship or from a caring therapist. (Or for that matter, the kind of love cult survivor Gina felt from the Lord family; see chapter 11 and the appendix.)

Survivors in Twelve Step groups are accepted basically for who they are, cared about, empathized with. And yes, while people in the fellowship have their problems (cliques, gossip, some closed-mindedness at times), who's perfect? I believe that God nevertheless seems to use these Twelve Step people as channels for healing. Through these groups, victims gradually start to feel some unconditional love. Slowly, sometimes very slowly, they also learn to trust for the first time in their lives.

Through this love and acceptance, a victim becomes open enough not only to begin to trust others in the group, but also to develop the trust necessary to begin to turn his or her will and life over to the care of this God talked about in the Third Step.

The Third Step lays the groundwork for the Eleventh Step: "Sought through prayer and meditation to improve our conscious contact with God as we understood Him, praying only for the knowledge of His will for us, and the power to carry that out." These Steps become a continuing process of praying for God's will, then actively taking the time to listen, so to speak—whether it's intuitively sensing that you're hearing God talk through someone else one day, or taking note of a part of a book that seems to speak to a situation you find yourself in, or in countless other ways.

I've also observed that a percentage of cult survivors seem to have had an extremely strong spiritual belief in Christ, even before they got into recovery. In the ritual abuse Twelve Step meeting, some would talk about going to church regularly, always wearing a cross, keeping pictures of Christ all over the house, praying to Him a lot.

Frequently they talk about this not so much in a free- flowing, "God is love" sense, but rather as a reliance on God in almost a hypersensitive need for protection. What sometimes emerges is a memory of some sort of seemingly tangible supernatural experience in which Christ did actually come to protect them during a ceremony—and they have held strongly to the experience.

The Fourth and Fifth Steps

Step Four: "Made a searching and fearless moral inventory of ourselves."

Step Five: "Admitted to God, to ourselves, and to another human being the exact nature of our wrongs."

As recovery progresses in any Twelve Step Program, the individual will work the Fourth and Fifth Steps. There are several formalized guides for these Steps, whether a person is in AA, Al-Anon, Codependency Anonymous, or whatever. Generally a person who has been in another Twelve Step Program prior to getting to the satanic ritual abuse memories has often done a Fourth and Fifth Step.

While the Fourth Step format varies a bit from program to program, there are some basic common denominators.

In this process, people basically go back over their lives in an analytical fashion. They look at times they've been dishonest with others or themselves, times they've been verbally, emotionally, or even physically abusive to family members or friends. They also look at things like problems around sex. Many of these Fourth Step guides also call for making a list of fears. If victims are codependent, they'll also look at things like their own controlling behavior, their own victim behavior, choices of people they've gotten into relationships with, choices of people they've got into relationships with (no . . . this is not a typo, it's just that this is often repeated behavior and a big area for many codependents), being overly responsible, or really irresponsible.

Now some will attempt the Fourth Step in one fell swoop, while a lot of others will approach this Step as a journaling process over time. That is, as they move along the recovery continuum, they remember more of their past, and also become more and more aware of their present dysfunctional behaviors, as is the case in any good therapeutic process.

While cult survivors become clearer about their behavior as they move through therapy and Twelve Step recovery, they generally don't achieve deep, lasting levels of recovery until they've finally gotten to the "exact nature of our wrongs" talked about in the Fifth Step.

And the exact nature of much of the core dysfunctional behavior seems always to be rooted in the cult abuse. Again, it is integral in this process not only to get to the memories, but to the repressed feelings as well.

Also, the patterns often can't be significantly reversed until the genesis of the "exact nature of our wrongs" is actually seen, then actively worked on through different therapeutic techniques, including a reparenting process (see chapter 12).

In many Twelve Step recovery processes, people go through notebook after notebook of emerging memories and realizations as part of working the Fourth Step.

The Fifth Step is a process of sharing with God—yes, actually reading the Fourth Step analysis to God, coming to terms with it oneself, and then admitting it all to someone else. For a cult survivor, as intimidating as this last part seems, this sharing becomes an essential part of the process and an excellent shame-reduction tool.

As mentioned earlier, cult victims have tremendous internalized shame around whatever type of involvement they had with the cult. Some of that dissipates as they progressively accept their "powerlessness" in the First Step.

However, the next step in this acceptance process, and an even more tangible way to reduce the shame, is to share the details, as they become available, with a therapist, sympathetic friend, sponsor in the Twelve Step group, priest, rabbi, or minister.

The Sixth and Seventh Steps

Step Six: "Were entirely ready to have God remove all these defects of character."

Step Seven: "Humbly asked Him to remove our shortcomings."

Okay, so a person is moving closer to the memories.

Another way to help accelerate the process at this point is consistent work with the Twelve Step Program's Sixth and Seventh Steps.

It is recommended in this phase that the person pray daily, or at least as frequently as possible, to become "willing" to have the "defects" removed.

This becomes the free will part of the Step for the person. And from what I've observed, once God has the green light, so to speak, He'll begin to take over.

Some of the main "defects of character" for ritual abuse victims are fear, and more fear, and yet even more fear (this is quite understandable, given their background).

This can be fear of the intensity of repressed feelings that may surface, fear of authority, fear of being sent to a psychiatric unit, fear of being harassed or even killed by the cult if they re-member or talk—and, paradoxically, fear of getting better.

Now, it seems to be the experience of many in recovery when working the Sixth Step that God doesn't come down with this magic wand or something and do a pseudo "poof" routine. Hardly.

What instead seems to happen is that circumstances "*co-incidentally*" seem to come about that start to help push the cult survivor through fear.

As an example, Ralph knows he has more repressed anger, sadness, and nausea that need to come out, but he's been balking of late—cutting down on the Twelve Step meetings, therapy sessions, and prayer time.

However, another self-help group member notices this, and confronts Ralph on it. The confrontation brings Ralph out of some of his denial. In order to get back on track, because he doesn't seem to have enough motivation on his own, Ralph begins working the Sixth Step daily.

As he does—wouldn't you know it?—he meets a couple

of other people with satanic ritual abuse in their backgrounds. And someone at another meeting, seemingly out of the blue, recommends a book that has triggered a lot of repressed feelings. Or, perhaps, a potential confrontation situation evolves at work with Ralph's boss. This situation offers an opportunity for Ralph, through confronting this authority figure, to take back some of the power that he lost to the abusive cult authority figures in his past.

Now the cause and effect here seem to be that through praying for the "willingness" in the Sixth Step, these situations have seemed to materialize, as they do for many working the Sixth Step. But again, there is no guarantee that Ralph is going to take action to increase his support network of friends, read the book, or confront the boss.

That's where the Seventh Step comes in.

When faced with one of these situations, then Ralph, ideally, will go off and pray specifically for any fear (a "shortcoming") to be removed—so that he can start to respond and change.

There is no guarantee that the fear will be totally removed, allowing Ralph to go in and do an ultra-assertive routine with his boss, or smoothly establish a rapport with these new people. For that matter, Evelyn Wood's speed-reading skills will probably not mysteriously infuse into Ralph's brain.

However, generally through this process, Ralph will be given just the motivation or strength to get through. And each time that happens, he will grow a little bit stronger emotionally. And his faith will grow a bit stronger with each of these experiences as well.

I also need to say here that people who are intently working these two Steps consistently will know they're really working them if, at times, they really hate the process, hate the situations they need to react to, hate all the effort. But it is through this very process that people—I hate to sound like a Pollyanna—reach deeper and deeper levels of recovery.

This brings up another point. A lot of people, whether satanic cult survivors, alcoholics, codependents, whoever, are unconsciously, and sometimes even consciously, afraid to recover. Oh, some will do enough recovery work to pull themselves out of a deep depression, or to get over some debilitating fear.

However, when it comes to pushing through the barriers and working toward long-term consistent emotional health, they are afraid. Afraid of success, of the added responsibility that comes with success, of the unknown. All that.

The way to get beyond this fear is to rework the other Steps that relate to this. Other defects, such as fear, are in the list generated during the Fourth Step.

The Eighth and Ninth Steps

Step Eight: "Made a list of all persons we had harmed and became willing to make amends to them all."

Step Nine: "Made direct amends to such people wherever possible, except when to do so would injure them or others."

People working the Steps can usually derive most of the Eighth Step list from their Fourth Step inventory. This list basically includes people in our lives we've somehow abused, whether physically, verbally, or emotionally.

Some satanic abuse victims, upon first getting to these Steps, as with the Fourth Step, have a hard time looking at those they may have abused because they are so focused on how they themselves had been abused and how damaged their lives had become as a result. (This is entirely understandable.)

But after a time, as they begin to work through issues, it becomes more and more apparent to the survivors that there are people they have harmed. Maybe by being too controlling with a child, a spouse, a friend. Maybe by transferring some repressed anger onto someone who didn't deserve it, through physical or verbal abuse. Or maybe in a more passive-aggressive manner— consistently showing up late for appointments, not returning someone's calls, being neglectful to a child.

As recovery progresses, it becomes more clear who those people we've harmed are.

And as one prays for the "willingness" to make amends, the timing and how to go about that begin to become clear as well.

The actual amends in Step Nine can take several forms— going to someone personally, explaining about one's recovery process, and directly apologizing to the person for past wrongs, or writing a letter to the same effect.

Also, there may be gestures, "living amends." Besides the apology, the person in recovery makes a consistent effort to be more caring, more concerned for the person they've harmed.

As in AA, there are times when making these amends

could prove "harmful," as, for example, walking back into an old lover's life to apologize for some past indiscretion when the person is involved with someone else. Or, it might be dangerous for a cult survivor to go back and attempt an apology with people who may be still cult-involved.

While doing this Step, it's important to consult continually with a Twelve Step sponsor, your therapist, and friends, on the timing and appropriateness of the amends.

The Tenth, Eleventh, and Twelfth Steps

Step Ten: "Continued to take personal inventory and when we were wrong, promptly admitted it."

Step Eleven: "Sought through prayer and meditation to improve our conscious contact with God as we understood Him, praying only for the knowledge of His will for us, and the power to carry that out."

Step Twelve: "Having had a spiritual awakening as a result of these steps, we tried to carry this message to other ritual abuse survivors, and to practice these principles in all our affairs."

These Steps are referred to as the "maintenance" Steps in most Twelve Step fellowships, and that holds true for Twelve Step ritual abuse groups.

As ritual abuse victims get more and more insight into some of their distorted character patterns and how they affect others and themselves, especially from working the Fourth Step on an ongoing basis, they have a frame of reference to gauge their daily behavior. Their patterns may include being overcontrolling, overcritical or overly fearful, lying, or being compulsive.

The Tenth Step is all about taking spot-check inventories, in as timely a way as possible, and continuing to make amends for wrongs affecting others (or oneself).

Say a victim has been in recovery awhile and has just gone back to college. On his first Economics test he gets a 78 (a high C). Fine. Passing. However, being afflicted with perfectionism, the victim goes into a funk and spends the better part of a day beating himself up emotionally, constantly going over the questions he missed.

Then that night, reviewing the day in the light of the Tenth

Step, he catches what he's doing here.

The next day, he spends some time affirming himself and his inner child for having the courage to go back to school and, for that matter, having the courage to hang with the recovery process.

Perfectionism is often extremely strong and deep-rooted in satanic cult survivors, simply because if they didn't do everything *just so* during the ceremonies, it would mean terrible abuse for them, even death.

With the Tenth Step, as with the Fourth Step, it is just as important to highlight and note the positive as well as the negative. This helps reverse a tendency to self-criticism and at the same time helps rebuild a highly damaged ego structure.

For example, it's important to acknowledge facing a certain fear, even thinking about facing that fear. Or, to applaud oneself for a project at work, for taking time to relax, for going to a self-help meeting. (Some days just acknowledging having gotten up is a big thing!)

Step Eleven: "Sought through prayer and meditation to improve our conscious contact with God as we understood Him, praying only for the knowledge of His will for us, and the power to carry that out."

Again, for some satanic cult survivors working Step Eleven, prayer and meditation, because of the programming, is not always easy. However, as people progress in Twelve Step recovery, they begin to even out emotionally, and it is in this calmer psychological state that they can open the door to work on deeper spiritual levels.

In this more balanced condition, more time is allotted for both prayer and meditation. And in this state, the quality of both generally improve as well. Typically, before recovery, many satanic ritual abuse survivors often exist in an almost frenetic state of racing thoughts and compulsive behaviors, all functioning to keep the memories and feelings repressed. Or a survivor may exist in an almost catatonic state of numbness.

Like almost anything else, meditation takes practice and is also multidimensional.

Some people in the Twelve Step Program incorporate relaxation techniques they've learned through any number of the "deep breathing" methods, to slow themselves down to listen to God. Others will take reflective walks or runs. Or they will just quietly watch an occasional sunset, listening. (Well, *sometimes* listening.) Or they will read daily a passage from any one of the many Twelve Step or spiritual reflection books, in order to increase their understanding of the God they have found and the knowledge of His will.

While knowledge about His will becomes more apparent as time goes on in recovery, there seems to be at least one constant in this emerging realization. Each person seems to have been sent to this planet with talents—a talent for athletics, for painting, for writing, for mathematics or science. Or the ability to work with people, to parent, to do public speaking, to . . . the list is endless. Anyway, it would seem that part of the plan or God's will would be to use the talent(s) to the best of one's ability, giving the credit to God.

Because of the abuse cult survivors have been exposed to, they are often saturated with fear that blocks talents. However, since the recovery process can help alleviate fears, survivors can get on with their lives the way God intended them to, carrying out His will, His plan.

Step Twelve: "Having had a spiritual awakening as a result of these steps, we tried to carry this message to other ritual abuse survivors, and to practice these principles in all our affairs."

As survivors work the Steps, they experience spiritual awakenings, often again on different levels. Many people experience serendipity as they go on—coincidences that they have a hard time writing off as just coincidences.

The Twelve Step fellowship is filled with countless "You're not going to believe this, but . . . " stories. Someone has a specific problem, then miraculously hears an unsolicited answer at a meeting. Maybe you need a job in a specific field and—wouldn't you know it?—you meet Harry, who knows George, who just happens to have a job opening in that very area.

However, while these things go on quite frequently, another level of spiritual awakening happens in quite a different way. As the Alcoholics Anonymous "Big Book" describes this, the person in recovery "finally realizes he has undergone a profound alteration in his reaction to life; that such a change could hardly have been brought about by himself alone." What this means is that, through working the Steps, the recovering person has learned to tap into another Source for insight and guidance.

Most of us think this awareness of a Power greater than

ourselves is the essence of spiritual experience. Our more religious members call it "God-consciousness," the "Big Book" goes on to say.

For cult ritual abuse survivors, this relying on a supernatural source is often doubly hard because of traumatic and detrimental supernatural experiences.

"Carrying the message" (the Twelfth Step) means that those who are established in Twelve Step ritual abuse groups become involved in outreach work with others who are ready to begin recovery.

This may include meeting with a prospective newcomer—making what's known as a Twelve Step call, and sharing their own stories, or offering to take these new people to meetings.

Another aspect of "carrying the message" is sharing with other members what the Steps mean to them and how they work them.

Other Twelve Step work entails helping schedule the meetings, or setting up intergroups and, just as important, taking on some of the weekly meeting responsibilities—like set-up and clean-up, and treasurer, secretary, and chairperson duties.

Some people also give Twelve Step work a broader application—going public with their stories in the media or at seminars, most often anonymously, other times not. If you're a satanic cult ritual abuse survivor, of course this public openness can be a risk. But for some, because their stories may help someone else break free of the cult programming, and because they take personal power back by speaking out against the cult, it becomes worth the risk. (There is also belief that the more public survivors are, the safer they are because of the cult's worry about drawing attention in any way.)

MULTIPLE PERSONALITY DISORDER

A desperate call came through on a national youth runaway hotline. A sixteen-year-old girl was calling, reporting that she had been raped violently.

The call was referred to a social service agency in New York. The girl was extremely distraught and presenting strong suicidal tendencies. She was brought in for shelter and observation, and concurrently assigned to a counselor with a rape crisis center. The social service program director, Robin Jones (not her real name), described observing a pronounced "injured child persona" (an alter that was extremely vulnerable and damaged) in the girl. Another of the personalities was adult and very cold and impassive. ("I'm tough. I can handle this. Leave me alone.") A third personality demonstrated a strong degree of aggressiveness.

Another disturbing dynamic was some of the poetry the girl had written. Ms. Jones described it as "dark poetry," dealing with pain, despair, suicide, and demons.

Often, experts are coming to find, a child exposed to extreme and consistent forms of ritual abuse will develop multiple personality disorder (MPD), or multiple personality syndrome (MPS), as others prefer to call it. While usually referred to as a disorder, because of the multiple problems of living it can cause for a person, it's important to note that the initial development of MPD in an abuse victim is actually a coping mechanism that helped the victim survive the trauma. According to the Los Angeles Task Force's *Ritual Abuse* booklet, MPD is:

> The existence within the person of two or more distinct
> personalities or personality states (each with its own rela-
> tively enduring pattern of perceiving, relating to, and think-
> ing about the environment and self).
> "At least two of these personalities, or personality states,
> recurrently take full control of the person's behavior."
> (DSM III-R, 1987.)
> Richard Kluft, in describing the kinds of events that trigger
> the creation of new personalities in children, delineates the
> following criteria: 1) the child fears for his or her own life;
> 2) the child fears that an important attachment figure will
> die; 3) the child's physical intactness and/or clarity of con-
> sciousness is breached or impaired; 4) the child is isolated
> with these fears; and 5) the child is systematically misin-
> formed or brainwashed about his or her situation. These
> criteria are certainly met in the events encountered by the
> ritually abused child.
> It is important to remember that multiple personality dis-
> order is not a thought disorder, and that although different
> personalities may be in touch with different pieces of mem-
> ory and reality, they are not delusional. The memories that
> they express, however painful and frightening, should not
> be dismissed as hallucinatory fantasies.

As one example of how MPD can develop: During a cult ceremony,
seven-year-old Shawn is locked in a cage with snakes, then physically tortured, and finally sexually abused. Shawn's psyche can
only take so much (as can any of our psyches). So when Shawn is
ready to snap, a new personality, a tougher personality in this
case, is developed to handle the next wave of abuse. Or to handle
the next scene—maybe of one of his parents sacrificing an infant
or having sex with a neighbor.

Each time a new personality is developed, it becomes an
inherent part of the host person's system. Later in life, this can
really cause some problems.

Note: In codependency recovery, as mentioned earlier, we
are working with the phenomenon of the "inner child." If a person
has come from a dysfunctional home, some of the stages of the
maturation process get stunted. And, as also mentioned earlier,
there are now ways to contact this child and take him/her back
through the growing phases in an emotionally healthy manner.

People who have developed MPD often have many inner
children (teen and adult) personalities that have developed because of the trauma. As will be explained, some of these person-

144

alities have been developed by the victim as a response to dealing with the waves of abuse. And if the MPD is cult-related, some of the personalities actually have often been systematically formed by the cult as well.

With the inner child and with alter personalities, the task in recovery is basically the same—that is, nurturing them in a healthy fashion and supporting them through reliving that trauma.

Recognizing MPD

There are a number of classic signs for early detection of multiplicity.

According to Dr. Marita Keeling, one indication is when a person loses blocks of time he or she can't account for.

"A man, for instance, will lose some time during the day," said Dr. Keeling. "Several hours may have passed and he suddenly finds himself in a different place without knowing how he got there." (This can also happen in shorter or longer spans.)

As another example, a woman will come across an item in the house she can only assume she bought, but doesn't remember buying. The variations on this are endless.

During these times, what is happening is that one or several of the alter personalities have taken over and bought something, or driven somewhere.

"Or, and this can be quite embarrassing," said Dr. Keeling, "an acquaintance will come up and say hi, and the person has no recollection of that acquaintance, because it was originally through one of the alters that they met."

Over time, this gets more and more troubling and complex for the persons experiencing it. They often start to doubt their sanity.

"This starts to add to the problem," said Dr. Keeling; "because of the fears about sanity, a client sometimes doesn't readily offer the information that these lapses are going on."

In these cases, if Dr. Keeling has started to suspect multiplicity from other signs, she will sometimes confer with outside observers, such as spouses, about incidents they are seeing.

"Maybe a husband will tell me his wife is getting up at night and doing things, not remembering any of it in the morning," Dr. Keeling said.

Or an outside observer will note the person is prone to extreme mood swings, and sometimes, for example, takes on the distinct persona of a little child or a recalcitrant teenager. Or maybe, if the person is generally quiet and shy, a personality will occasionally emerge that is bold and dynamic.

Besides worrying about their sanity, multiples are often merely too embarrassed to disclose this type of thing, or they simply don't consciously realize it's going on.

Another indicator of multiplicity is variable handwriting, distinctly different scripts at times.

"A person with MPD might get a check back with a monthly statement, and the signature on one of the checks is so different, the person thinks it may have been forged," said Dr. Keeling.

Also, many multiples will actually, at times, hear voices talking to them, sometimes voices that are very critical, even vile, depending on which alter is speaking. At other times the person will hear the alters talking back and forth to each other.

Because of this, Dr. Keeling said, it's been her experience that a lot of patients are misdiagnosed as having a psychotic disorder.

According to Holly Hector, misdiagnosed psychotic disorders in these types of cases include paranoid schizophrenia, bipolar disorders such as manic depression, and depersonalization (that is, actually being chronically out of touch with their physical/psychological functioning).

Because of all this, Ms. Hector said, multiplicity is currently referred to as the "hidden disorder."

"Family, friends, even therapists sometimes have a hard time believing it," she said.

As Ms. Hector also noted, research indicates that it takes an average of 6.8 years of therapy before multiplicity is diagnosed. (However, how fast this happens is also contingent on the type and consistency of therapy, and how much Twelve Step recovery or other support is being used.)

Tanya, a woman Ms. Hector had been treating in the trauma unit in Colorado, is a typical example. She had been in therapy, on and off, for seven years for schizophrenia and manic depression. A suicide attempt preceded her coming to the center.

During the evaluation process, Ms. Hector diagnosed multiplicity, and as her therapeutic rapport with Tanya grew, the rest of the "system" (alter personalities) began to surface.

Ms. Hector knew that this particular woman had a sports car and would often drive fast—90 miles per hour fast—on the freeways. When questioned about this during a session, the woman simply explained it away as one of the few "escapes" she indulged in.

Something in that explanation didn't jibe for the therapist. For the most part, Tanya demonstrated what therapists call flat affect—extremely flat affect. Which is another way of saying she wasn't animated in any way, her nature was quite depressive, and she showed little emotion or motivation. For a woman like this who isn't multiple, a radical "escape" might be to stay up an extra hour to watch a TV program she'd construed as risqué, like the "Arsenio Hall Show"—*not* to turn a Denver expressway into an autobahn.

Over time, through therapeutic empathy and acknowledging the alters, Ms. Hector, in effect, was giving the whole system permission to start to appear.

During one session, as Ms. Hector questioned the woman more about the driving, all of a sudden her eyes fluttered a bit, her facial countenance and expression changed.

"And up comes this bubbly, funny, actually hilarious person," said the therapist.

"I love to drive fast, fast, fast," said Gwen, a teenage-sounding alter, in this fast-forward sort of falsetto. "I love it, just love it! And don't you try to get her to stop. Don't!"

Ms. Hector learned Gwen had been created so that the core personality could have fun, essential to keeping the human equilibrium.

Since Gwen was the first alter to surface distinctly, Ms. Hector asked her why she hadn't let Tanya know she was there, or that any of the other alters were there.

"Oh, we couldn't let her know," said Gwen, speaking for the rest of the alters as well. "She would have thought she was crazy."

Ms. Hector said this is a common answer from alters early in therapy.

When alters come up, as described earlier by Dr. Keeling, many times they take over completely and the host loses blocks of time.

Co-consciousness

Other times, there's a dynamic called co-consciousness, in which the alter will come up while the host, in effect, merely slips into the background, watching as a sort of third-party observer. And if the host person isn't aware of being multiple yet, she construes this as merely another part of her personality coming out, albeit, an uncharacteristic part or even what she sees as a "weird" part.

One reason for the co-consciousness is that the psyche sometimes allows this so the "birth person" doesn't lose some of those blocks of time, while continuing to believe the switches between alters are merely shifts in personality. The birth person simply is not ready to deal with multiplicity yet.

However, during the "discovery phase" in therapy, when the personalities are becoming more overt and pronounced, it is this same co-consciousness that helps the birth person then accept the multiplicity more easily, because she or he is able to watch, with new information, some of what's going on during the switch.

Another dynamic in all this is, the alters are often co-conscious with each other as well as with the birth person.

"The alters are hypervigilant in order to be able to 'come up' instantaneously if there is any trauma," said Ms. Hector.

Also, an alter is able to come close to the surface, but sometimes not all the way out, just to transfer specific feelings to the birth person, such as anger or sadness.

Physiological Cues

Just before Gwen came up, Ms. Hector noted Tanya's eyes fluttered, which in some is a physiological cue that an alter is taking over. Other indicators include eyes darting back and forth rapidly, or eyes that will open extremely wide for a moment, then go back to normal. Other times the eyes will twitch or roll up into the head briefly.

Sometimes the change is subtle, almost imperceptible, while at other times it's very discernible.

Another obvious physical change is that the person's voice will change, sometimes slightly, sometimes radically. The mouth itself will actually sometimes change too, from what Ms. Hector described as a soft mouth to a hard one. That is, the lips will be drawn tighter.

"All this [physical change] isn't something someone could easily manufacture," said Ms. Hector, who has observed the changes in many clients.

As Ms. Hector built more trust with Tanya's system over time, memories of satanic cult ritual abuse started to surface as well, but not without a struggle.

Antagonistic Alters

As fragments of the abuse started to come to Tanya, and then through some of the alters, another alter broke through abruptly during one session.

"YOU ARE A _____ JERK!" this alter screamed at Ms. Hector. "YOU'RE GETTING INFORMATION THAT WILL GET US KILLED! KILLED!"

This type of abrupt volatility is common, said Ms. Hector. And at these times she tries, to the best of her ability, to stay even and calm to avoid escalation.

In responding to this antagonistic alter, Ms. Hector will at first try to be as sympathetic as possible to the concern. She'll say something like: "You've been through a lot. It must be really hard for you. If it was me, I'd be scared too."

Bruce Leonard, M.D., Clinical Director at Columbine Psychiatric Center, Littleton, Colorado, takes a tack similar to Ms. Hector's when dealing with an antagonistic alter. Columbine has a program specifically for the treatment of people with dissociative disorders, including many people reporting satanic cult ritual abuse clients. (Dissociative disorders, such as MPD, are marked by amnesia and disconnected experiences of which a person is unaware.)

Dr. Leonard gave an example of an alter he had to deal with recently who had an extremely hardened personality. (This alter had been developed to deal specifically with any cannibalism the host had to participate in during the satanic ceremonies.)

The alter would burst out, challenging, shouting obscenities, glaring at him.

Dr. Leonard said he will first sit back and not respond to the hot anger, or the barbs either. He said he's come to know that the bravado and hostility of these alters is usually a cover for fear. And once that's played itself out, he tries to get the alter to talk about the trauma.

"I wonder what that must have been like for you [in this case, the cannibalism]?" Then Dr. Leonard will listen actively. (Listening actively is more than the stereotypical therapist's "unh-huh" at the appropriate places. It is regularly repeating back verbatim what the therapist has heard the client saying, and asking probing questions to get the client to elaborate more along his or her own train of thought, not necessarily where the therapist wants to direct the train of thought.)

After listening, Dr. Leonard tries to empathize as much as possible, and reassures the alter that he is not a perpetrator, and is not there to hurt him in any way.

"These [alter] personalities fully expect to be mistreated once they risk coming out," said Dr. Leonard, because in the past their trust was constantly being betrayed.

Based on his experience, Dr. Leonard advises bypassing dealing with the antagonistic personalities as much as possible in the early phases of working with the system, until there is an alliance built with the whole system.

Building Trust with Alters

Ms. Hector also makes every effort to assure the alters she's not a perpetrator. "I'd never do anything to hurt you purposely," she often says.

She said the child alters especially want to believe this. However, again, because their trust has been betrayed so often, systematically building an emotional bridge is hard.

In starting to build this bridge or alliance, Ms. Hector will often say something empathetic, like, "It's good you don't trust just anybody. And it's probably because you have been hurt by so many people. I'd be guarded too."

This often begins a new orientation because the latter statement isn't what a typical cult member would say at all.

Instead of just hearing the words, Ms. Hector tells the victim to watch her behavior toward them over time. And she, in turn, tries to remain as consistent and caring as possible.

However, inevitably there will be a time when she isn't able to call back right away, or is late for a session. And because a cult survivor is typically hypersensitive to even a hint of what they imagine to be betrayal, they will sometimes lapse into a temporary nontrusting stance.

"You said you'd call back right away, and you didn't," Ms. Hector said she will hear in suspicious, frustrated tones sometimes. "You said you weren't going to hurt us, but you did!"

This is when Ms. Hector reiterates what she had said earlier about never "purposely" trying to hurt them, which is often enough to begin to appease the system.

Cult Mock Therapy Sessions

To give another indication of how cunning and thorough satanic cult members are, some of Ms. Hector's clients have had memories of mock therapy sessions in which a cult member posed as a therapist. Then, while the victim relaxed into a regressive state, or carried out a visualization technique, the cult members abused the victim in some way, sexually perhaps, or through electric shock.

This staging was designed to set up an internalized distrust of any therapist who later might help the person remember.

"These people are extremely smart, extremely advanced," said Ms. Hector.

Dr. Leonard corroborated the stories of mock therapy stagings by cult members. He said he has to be very careful, for instance, in doing imaging with a client during a session, because victims recount being hypnotized or drugged by cult members, then taken through guided imagery, then being tortured or sexually abused.

Within the context of the cult mock therapy session, some words become trigger words for the victim. Ms. Hector said she is very careful to note responses to words like "relax," or "have faith," or "you'll heal." Sometimes because the abuse was going on while the cult member was repeating these words, if some victims hear them in session, they begin to dissociate.

In such instances, a therapist can actually be talking to the birth person, or an alter, for a while before realizing that "they have gone away," said Ms. Hector.

"It's like talking to an empty shell," said Ms. Hector, who then will begin to talk to the alter who has taken over. She will emphasize that it is important that the birth person, or the alter who is "up," complete the specific therapeutic work being dealt with. And she reminds the alter who has taken over of the contract she has made with the system: that when she's working with another part of the system another alter can't spontaneously take over like that. At this point the alter is generally fairly cooperative.

Early in the process, Ms. Hector said she establishes ground rules against persecuting alters damaging the office or physically accosting her. She also said it's important to give the system a right to rules, such as contracting with them that, if they are frightened, they have the right to end the session at any time.

A Memory Breakthrough

Ms. Hector had been working with Tanya's system awhile when the ritual abuse memories started to break through.

The first memory was about a snake.

Tanya had a fragmented flashback to a snake. That was all. But it stayed on her mind, and she would try to journal about it. And it kept bothering her to the point that Ms. Hector began to look to another part of the system to bring back the rest of the memory. This was done by simply telling the system it was okay to remember now.

Tanya was around five years old. She was being held down during one of the ceremonies. A snake was placed near the inside of her leg, and it gradually slithered up her body, eventually wrapping part of itself around the young child's head, as cult members stood amidst candles all about, chanting.

Later, a cult member placed an axe in Tanya's hands, and she was ordered to first chop the snake's head off and then chop up other parts of it. Finally, he forced her to eat part of it.

One of the child alters related the story while Tanya, in this case, maintained co-consciousness.

"I heard me talking and I wanted to stop, but I couldn't make myself stop talking," Tanya would say later. If an alter has been with the birth person practically a lifetime, the alter feels very much a natural part of the person.

Other times, Ms. Hector said, the alter will come up to tell the rest, or all, of a particular memory, and the therapist will have to recount the whole thing to the host later.

Because not all of these memories come directly to the birth person, Ms. Hector suggests that they all be recorded in a journal as well, so that a consistent pattern starts to appear for the client. This also makes the reality of the abuse that much more tangible for the victim.

According to Ms. Hector, some therapists working with multiplicity don't see it as a "disorder" because, in reality, it functions to keep someone safe—from a hostile environment, or from a psychotic breakdown. Again, these therapists see it instead as a "syndrome" and refer to it as simply MP, to clarify misconceptions about the condition.

Satanic Alters

As in the case of other antagonistic alters, satanic alters can play havoc with the system and the recovery process.

A satanic alter is also commonly referred to as an enforcer, evil introject, or satanic introject.

According to Ms. Hector, there are several ways these alters are formed.

The first way is sometimes referred to as a "cult split." That is, the cult intentionally creates the alter (a "structured alter") in the victim in what can best be described as a highly sophisticated psychological technique.

First, the cult will evoke a dissociative state in the victim through scare tactics, torture, or some type of sensory deprivation (such as locking a victim in a dark space for an extended period of time, and/or starving the victim).

When the victim has reached the dissociative state, a cult member will actually call forth a new alter, name it, and tell him/her which demon they belong to.

"It's a calculated, methodical split," said Ms. Hector, "designed to bring about total control of this alter."

These alters are given specific tasks. One alter, for example, may be assigned to bring a person back to the cult later in life. Another may be designated to commit suicide if the system starts to get close to the memories.

Cult-created alters often won't give their names early in therapy—sometimes never—because they were led to believe there is power in the names, Ms. Hector noted.

However, as therapeutic trust builds, some do reveal the names. In the interim, Ms. Hector merely assigns new names to them. "And, interestingly, they almost always come up to that new name when they are called," she said.

The other way a satanic alter is formed is by the victim, for a number of reasons. For one, the victim will create a personality to carry out terrible tasks of killing or of skinning the sacrifice, or, if forced to, of having to choose who will be sacrificed.

Also, as the victim is being brutalized himself, he will unconsciously create a (satanic) personality to match the aggressiveness of the perpetrators. "Although difficult to deal with early in therapy, these types of personalities are understandable to me," said Ms. Hector. "You aren't going to create Mickey Mouse to protect you from evil people."

One thing these victim-created alters (or "reactive alters") will do early in therapy to wrench the process is to shout rebellious obscenities at the therapist, or they may try other intimidating stunts.

"I can't tell you how many of them have come up, glared at me with this really sinister look, and bellowed something like 'I AM LUCIFER,'" said Ms. Hector. "Later, as they move along in therapy, they will say something like 'Oh, I was just trying to scare you.'"

Ms. Hector said these victim-created alters are a lot easier to get used to than the cult-created alters, because you can quickly see this personality is merely hiding, say, a frightened six-year-old. These alters, too, said Ms. Hector, are a lot easier to sway about going from the "dark side" to the "good side."

Both the survivor and the therapist need to honor these parts (satanic alters), because without these parts, said Ms. Hector, the survivor probably wouldn't have made it either physically or psychologically.

These parts, in effect, had to learn to like the rituals, almost as an acquired taste. Ms. Hector said a satanic alter will come up, bold, sinister, and blurt out something like, "I LIKE TO KILL!"

And, in turn, Ms. Hector will respond with something to the effect of, "Good for you," with sincerity. "If I was forced to have to do it [kill] I guess I'd learn to like it too."

She always tries to thank satanic alters for what they did, because their actions probably saved the system. Used to feeling chastised, a satanic alter will be thrown off and will often, eventually, respond positively. All this goes a long way toward building a necessary rapport with the alters.

There are other things to be aware of with satanic alters. Some are programmed, for instance, said Ms. Hector, to commit suicide if the memories start coming up. And the suicide can come any number of ways. The alter can take over the system and drive off a cliff, slash the wrists, take a drug overdose, whatever.

As these destructive alters surface, it's important to try to negotiate suicide prevention contracts with them, similar to the contracts mentioned earlier. With some alters, said Ms. Hector, this won't be possible, but intensive work with the birth person around this issue and the rest of the system often works to defuse this.

Another function of a satanic alter is to simply cause the person to bleed if she or he gets close to the memories and to talking about them. This can be the genesis of cult survivors' self-mutilation. Seeing the blood will often trigger the victim back into silence.

Sometimes, said Ms. Hector, the host person will actually "come to," so to speak, find the laceration, and be unaware that the alter has actually drunk the blood. (Again, the cult actually believes there's power in the blood.)

Some of the satanic alters, Ms. Hector said, are specifically designated to keep the person as far away from Christ as possible (see chapter 2).

A survivor might be heading for a church or a Christian bookstore, for example, and all of a sudden turn up across town from either place.

Another simply amazing thing, said Ms. Hector, is that the survivor may be back in a cult without actually knowing it. That is, one of the satanic alters takes over and continues to attend the ceremonies, either on a "dabbler" level, or even back in the mainstream of a hard-core transgenerational cult, perhaps even back in the original cult.

A person who is totally amnesic to the alter will know nothing about the involvement.

The cult involvement, however, said Ms. Hector, often becomes apparent in therapy. And while a therapist can tell the alter not to go back anymore, "it's pretty difficult to get them to stop until the internal parts of the system tangibly see the power of God."

Ms. Hector notes that, from reports she's heard, the cults are especially careful with the victims they detect as not fragmenting into alters. If child victims do not dissociate consistently, they often become afflicted with any number of major psychotic disorders.

Those children, said Ms. Hector, are at risk because they may reveal the secrets. And these are the ones, often, who are killed. They will be reported as missing children. Or there will be staged accidental deaths, such as drownings or car accidents. Or a ritual will be carried out, including torture and ultimately the child's death.

MPD Integration

For survivors who are multiple, one of the keys to recovery is often to achieve some measure of integration. This, too, can happen on a number of different levels.

Dr. Keeling said one level is to achieve a functional group relationship among the personalities. That is, the host and the alters learn to communicate and negotiate as a team.

As an example, the child personalities are often just interested in playing all day, while the adults often like to work all the time, or follow "adult" pursuits.

When a person is in a continual work mode, for example, in rebellion, one of the child alters might take over one day at work, said Dr. Keeling, and begin talking the equivalent of baby talk to the boss.

The negotiated compromise here, as a person moves along in recovery, would be to work, say, eight hours, then reserve at least a couple of hours a day for some sort of play with the child alters.

As multiples keep working on these kinds of compromises, the alter personalities' distinctive traits begin to blur, until one day the therapist can't differentiate anymore, said Dr. Keeling. And after a while longer, the blurring gets to the point where the person can't tell either.

Dr. Keeling said this blurring typically happens in increments over time. That is, a block of five personalities may blur into one. And then another five. And then those that are left start to blur with the host.

Ms. Hector said she consistently sees basically the same process toward integration. She explains that moving the alters toward integration essentially means supporting them through all their past work. That is, the release of the memories, the repressed feelings, and resolution work around anger, fear, paranoia, and the cognitive distortion that is still going on in the present.

An example of distortion could be, for instance, the perception that God is going to rape them if they start praying, since they had been raped during ritual stagings.

"Why do you think that?" Ms. Hector will ask.

Often at this point, the rape memories will surface. And again, it will be explained to the alter that it wasn't God, but rather a cult member disguised as God. This can be reinforced by reviewing instances when the cult had lied about other things as well.

"This work entails a lot of unraveling of distortion, and then the rebuilding of truth," said Ms. Hector. Because this isn't an overnight process, some stopgap measures need to be employed to begin to combat any sabotaging. For instance, said Ms. Hector, just before a person is to go to church or, say a Twelve Step meeting, there will be mystifying local paralyzation of an arm or the legs—or again, all of a sudden a person will end up far from the original destination, unable to remember how she or he got there.

Using the analogy of a mansion, Ms. Hector will tell the sabotaging alters that they have a right to still be afraid and rebellious. However, at the same time, the system has a right to go to church or to a self-help meeting and it is advised that during this time alters simply have the right to go to their rooms and not participate. This usually works because offering them an option, instead of trying to force them, empowers them.

Ms. Hector said it isn't unusual to discover anywhere from several to a whole crowd of "parts" in someone with a multiple personality disorder. However, a therapist will usually have to do intensive therapeutic work with a relatively small percentage of these.

"For instance, if you ask an alter what his/her job was and the reply is 'one of the keepers of the secrets,' you know this is the alter you're going to be dealing with," she said.

Often alters' jobs might have been just to hide emotionally, with eyes closed, during some of the ceremonies. In these cases, there's not much trauma attached to these fragments and no significant resolution work needs to be done.

Ms. Hector said that over time it becomes quite apparent which alters need to be worked with intensively. When there's a question, if you simply ask the system directly, she said, it is usually fairly cooperative about offering the information about which one needs work.

During this phase, it is also important that the birth person do a substantial amount of reparenting with the system. Ms. Hector said she has her clients consistently affirm the system with healthy, loving messages. This can be done tangibly— holding stuffed animals, or doing mirror work with affirmations.

In addition, she has the birth person specifically reassure the system that she/he will do everything in his/her power to keep the system safe. One of the ways to facilitate this type of communication is to have an imaginary room in the imaginary house—a board room, if you will—that has been supplied with a bulletin board or chalk board, where messages are posted.

Another dynamic that's important to be aware of is that there may be varying degrees of resistance throughout—sometimes really strong—to integrating. The alters actually see it as death.

"I don't want to die. I won't get to play anymore, read my books," Ms. Hector said she may hear.

She explains to the alters that integration is not like death, but rather the merger of "two good things." She also reassures them that the alters who have done it are now, in effect, all co-present and have reached a wholeness they could never achieve separately.

She stresses there will be no more power struggles, no more arguing about who's "up."

One phenomenon Ms. Hector has observed is spontaneous integration. That is, she tries to call up an alter, and another alter explains he/she has merged with that alter, and they're now experiencing and feeling the same things.

While sometimes this type of integration is inevitable, Ms. Hector said she will often try to discourage spontaneous integration so that final grief work can be done: grief work around the system losing the distinct personalities, and grief work also for the therapist.

"It's just like terminating with any other type of client," said Ms. Hector.

Sometimes the integration will happen prematurely. Either there will be spontaneous integration or the longer termination process, and another memory might come up involving the alter, and the alter will fragment back out.

Another dynamic to be aware of is that some victims actually don't want to integrate, said Dr. Keeling. She explained that these host personality types are usually quite isolationist and enjoy the company of the alters.

Ms. Hector also has seen this and said she tries not to get into a power struggle about forcing integration in these cases. She said the main focus of MPD therapy is increasing the level of functionality and decreasing the level of crisis. And as this happens in the course of a natural progression, integration takes place on its own.

Ms. Hector said that victims who are multiples also worry about losing the parts of their personalities that function at work, take care of the children, or perform other roles. To diminish these fears, Ms. Hector continues to repeat the refrain about everyone being co-present, that no one gets lost in integration.

One dilemma for some therapists working with MPD, Ms. Hector said, is actually finding the birth person. That is, the system may be set up to protect the person constantly from the therapist as well.

While this may be somewhat unsettling for the therapist at first, said Ms. Hector, this basically needs to become a "non-issue."

In other words, in this case it's important to just keep working with the system and finally the birth person will emerge. Eventually, the system always releases the secret.

Assuming the Persona of Another

According to Ms. Hector, some therapists are seeing another phenomenon: during some of the trauma in a ceremony, a survivor may sometimes actually assume the personality traits of another person involved in the ceremony. And this personality will also stay with the system.

(A simple analogy to this psychological "borrowing" from another personality would be going to a movie and taking on the personality of an actor or actress—viewing *Casablanca* and assuming Bogart's speech or mannerisms, for instance, or *Pretty Woman* and "becoming" Julia Roberts.)

In contrast to cases of multiple personalities, even though this "borrowed" personality is often displayed in the system and can interact with alters, it is not an inherent part of the system.

Ms. Hector said many would just look at this as another

159

alter personality. However, the personality itself will often admit to not being an inherent part of the system, and therapists have been consistently successful in releasing this "part" when it comes up, as opposed to trying to integrate it.

Ms. Hector said these personas usually identify themselves as, for instance, a cult member who has been sacrificed, or a child who has been sacrificed.

The therapist said that once these parts are found and identified, with not much prompting they will describe and do feeling work around some of the specific trauma they were exposed to. For instance, a sacrificed child persona will describe the act of sacrifice in detail, reliving the pain and horror step by step.

There are a number of possible explanations for this phenomenon. Within the cult ceremonies, Ms. Hector said some of their clients have described "transference" rituals. That is, just as a child or adult is being sacrificed, the cult will tell the victim that he/she can choose to have his/her "spirit" enter another person in the room, as a way of "staying alive." (By having the additional preprogrammed spirit in one of the other victims who is to live, the cult actually believes they will be able to exercise even more control over this person—as they believe they can over cult-created satanic alters.)

If that choice is made by the victim to be sacrificed, Ms. Hector said some of her clients report that the cult then goes into a chanting ritual, calling on satan or other demons to effect the supposed transfer. Ms. Hector said the presence of these other "parts" in the system is so real to some survivors that they actually believe the spirit has been transferred, and they also report an overriding sense that the "spirits" of these people seem to somehow be trapped in this dimension, continuing to search for what they perceive would be some outlet for salvation of some sort.

In a related phenomenon, besides cult victims, occasionally these "parts" will actually identify themselves as, say, distant relatives from another century or even historical figures the person may have heard or read about.

Ms. Hector said one psychological theory for this phenomenon of borrowed personality is that a survivor, as a youth, watched a sacrifice. And, because of extreme survivor's guilt, the survivor unconsciously took on the personality of the sacrificed victim in order to somehow keep the victim protected inside—

and also alive, as the survivor perceives—so satan, for instance, can't get to the victim. Or in another case, the transfer ritual may have seemed so real to the survivor and the consequences of not being able to demonstrate that he or she had taken on the "spirit" so dire, that the person actually, in effect, unconsciously forced himself/herself to take on the personality.

Again, it is counterproductive to try to integrate these borrowed personalities in any way. Instead, Ms. Hector said the therapeutic tactic is to release them. Once these parts have done their trauma work, Ms. Hector has developed a releasing ceremony to appease and bring resolution for the system. That is, good-byes are said between this personality (persona) and the alters, host, and therapist. Then this personality is presented with the opportunity of choosing Christ, or the "good side"—as the final part of the ceremony. Ms. Hector notes that if what seemed like a "borrowed" persona is actually an alter personality inherent to the system, it simply won't release.

MPD Integration: A Personal Story

Faith Donaldson had been in therapy on and off since 1979 for a variety of issues. In 1987 she had gotten to a point in recovery where fragments in the form of mini-flashes and repressed feelings around what would turn out to be satanic cult ritual abuse started to break through.

Her therapist, who had some experience working with satanic ritual abuse victims, recognized the symptoms and diagnosed the satanic ritual abuse. Shortly after that, he diagnosed Faith as having MPD as well.

Faith said over the years she was always aware that her mood swings and what she believed were just different parts of her personality were pretty pronounced. For example, she is an entrepreneur, and at almost any time she could "turn on" her extremely professional business acumen. Then, only a short time later, she could flip into consuming rage, or consuming fits of jealousy.

She didn't know what caused the extreme shifts, but continued to try to work on it in therapy. "One of my motivations was that I had children and I didn't want to hurt them with these swings," she said.

As therapy around the cult abuse progressed, the alter

personalities became more and more distinct. All told, thirty-three alters emerged in Faith.

Gradually, each brought back pieces of the memories. However, Faith said this was an extremely hard process, because each time more memories were about to surface, the more the cult programming about not remembering, not talking, would invade the process.

"I had a very good therapist," said Faith. "He persistently and patiently just kept telling me, 'they lied to you, Faith, it's all right now to remember.'

"And the more I faced the memories, and the more I talked about them, the more I realized the cult wasn't coming after me to kill me, or coming to take me to hell."

Faith was exposed to a satanic cult growing up in a small town north of the Twin Cities in Minnesota. She is now living in Colorado. As a safety precaution, she chooses not to mention the name of her home town.

After a time, Faith decided to go public with her story, talking at ritual abuse seminars or on radio shows, and writing articles for several Colorado newspapers.

A short time after she began talking publicly—actually, after her first speaking engagement, she said—the final stage of the integration took place.

She was to give a talk at a seminar on ritual abuse at a local church. Just a few minutes before going on, she said the cult programming kicked in as if it were blaring over a loudspeaker in her head.

"YOU WILL NOT SPEAK! YOU WILL NOT DEFY US!"

Faith said she locked the door to a nearby restroom and shouted back: "YOU HAVE NO CONTROL OVER ME! NONE!"

She then went out and did the talk.

The final integration took place only two weeks later.

"The reason they [the alters] were split was simply to protect me from the abuse and the memories," she said. "Once the memories were out in the open and there was no more threat, they realized they didn't have to do either anymore, and they integrated."

Faith said she hasn't had any threats or other forms of harassment as yet since going public.

Ms. Hector notes that Faith's integration process went fairly smoothly. Sometimes the integration takes much longer.

And, again, not everyone reaches full integration.

Besides talking publicly, Faith and two other cult survivors have formed a nonprofit national organization, based in Colorado, to generate referral information, public training, treatment, and scholarship funds for survivors. The organization, JUSTUS Unlimited, is described in chapter 22.

DRUGS

Both child and adult victims of satanic cult ritual abuse report sometimes being abused with mind-altering drugs.

Drugs as Part of Ritual Abuse

The drugs are administered to the victims by cult members in a number of ways. According to Holly Hector, one of the most prevalent ways she consistently hears about from clients is with hypodermic needles. During the recovery process, victims will have body memories of needle pricks in such places as the arm or between the toes. Ms. Hector also said patients report remembering starting to feel dizzy and/or numb after being forced to drink urine or blood. Other times, the victim merely remembers being forced to take a drug orally under duress.

Re-experiencing a Drugged State

Sometimes, when clients are having such memories, they actually re-experience part of the drugged state. That is, besides re-experiencing the physical sensations, they will also experience cognitive distortion, where objects appear smaller, larger, or wavy, as if looking through convex or concave glass.

"The drugs are mainly used to make a victim more malleable about performing tasks during the ceremonies," said Ms.

Hector. "And they also are used to make a person more passive and accepting of the reprogramming."

Dr. Bruce Leonard said, based on drug states described by ritual abuse patients he's worked with, the drugs used range from the likes of Benadryl, Valium, and other minor tranquilizers to strong opiates.

One ritual abuse patient at one point in her recovery was administered Thorazine, said Dr. Leonard, which triggered her remembering the exact feeling state during some of the ceremonies.

Ms. Hector said these drug-affected memories provide another complication in the recovery process. Because these memories seem somewhat surreal, victims sometimes stay in denial longer about the abuse, trying to pass off the memories as hallucinations.

NEW MESSAGES

Because of the years of cult indoctrination, a survivor's perceptions have usually become distorted, skewed. A major part of the recovery process is to gradually reverse all this.

Messages for Survivors

Therapist Holly Hector has developed the following list of messages ritual abuse survivors need to hear as they progress during their recovery.

> 1. YOU DESERVE COMPLETE FREEDOM AND HEALING.
> You were brainwashed to believe you are worthless, incapable, and useless to anyone but the cult. These lies were to shatter any sense of self or break down any independence you might have and ensure your loyalty and eventual return. You are special, gifted, and worthy of health, of love, and of life as *you choose it*. Believe in yourself. Choose freedom. Choose healing.

> 2. YOU ARE *NOT* CRAZY.
> You were programmed to believe that if you told you would be called "crazy" and would be institutionalized forever. You are not crazy—*the world in which you lived was crazy!* You are having a normal reaction to an abnormal situation. Trust your truth.

3. YOU WILL NOT DIE FOR REMEMBERING OR TELLING.
You were forced throughout extensive abuse, programming, and ritual work, to believe you would die if you remembered or told. This was to ensure your silence. The
present threat may only be perceived—although it would
be important to take as many precautions as necessary to
safeguard against any harm. You must break the silence to
aid in your healing.

4. EXPECT STRONG SUICIDAL THOUGHTS OR DESIRES TO
SELF-MUTILATE WHEN YOU REMEMBER.

5. NOTHING THAT HAPPENED TO YOU OR TO ANYONE
ELSE WAS *YOUR* FAULT.
The torture, the pain, the sex, the killing—*NONE* of it was
your fault, or your responsibility. You were told that you
wanted it, chose it, and deserved it. This is a lie. You were
an innocent victim who was not given any choices.

6. YOU ARE *NOT* A MURDERER.
All children of cults are forced to perpetrate (mentally,
physically, sexually), even to murder. This is to ensure
your silence and the belief that you are one of them, or
"just like them." This is called "coercion to commit a
crime" by law enforcement. You are NOT responsible—the
real murderers are the cult members.

7. EVERY PERSON YOU MEET IS NOT A PERPETRATOR.
You were systematically and calculatedly abused by a variety of people from a variety of professions and authority
positions. This was to teach you not to trust anyone, ever.
But not everyone is a perpetrator. It will be helpful to start
slowly attempting to address the reasons and realities behind these trust issues.

8. DENIAL CAN BE EITHER HEALTHY OR UNHEALTHY.
A sense of healthy denial can be beneficial to put some distance between you and the horror. But denial can also be a
powerful part of the programming to keep you from the
truth. Work on not denying your truth—believe yourself.
Remember: "You can't heal from what you can't feel."

9. BE PREPARED FOR BODY SENSATIONS (BODY MEMO-
RIES) AND FLASHBACKS.
The body will give you pieces of the abuse (body memories) and the mind will also give you pieces of the abuse
(flashbacks). You will feel out of control and feel like you
are going crazy. You are not. Have a plan (written is best)
for this part of the healing process. And try to travel

through it, not *around* it, so that you can get to the other
side of it and not be stuck running from your healing.

10. THE SHAME YOU MAY FEEL IS *NOT* YOURS.
The shame instilled in you by the humiliation and degrada-
tion is real, but—it is *not* yours. It belongs *only* to the perpetrators. It should not be your shame—*give it back to
them.*

11. YOU SURVIVED WHAT FEW HUMANS COULD HAVE.
HONOR THAT.
You employed resources from within that few people could
develop or call on. Honor your survival. Honor your cre-
ativity. Honor your intelligence to cope and adapt. Take
these gifts and redirect them into your healing process.
You are more capable than most—believe it.

12. IF YOU SURVIVED THE ACTUAL EVENT, YOU CAN SUR-
VIVE THE MEMORIES.
Often you will feel as though the reality of this will actually
consume and destroy you. But remember you survived the
event—employ your strengths to survive the memories
and the healing.

13. IF (WHEN) YOUR BODY RESPONDED TO SEXUAL STIM-
ULATION—HONOR THAT.
As children we have *natural, normal* physiological
responses to sexual stimulation. This does not mean you
chose or enjoyed the abuse. Release yourself from that
guilt.

14. GIVE YOURSELF PERMISSION TO FEEL *BAD* [to hurt
emotionally]. As a child you had to lead a double life. You
were expected to behave perfectly in school, in public,
while you were being hideously abused in the cult. Allow
yourself—NOW—to be okay with hurting emotionally. You
deserve to feel bad.

SUPPORTING THE SURVIVOR OF RITUAL ABUSE

For therapists and others concerned with these victims, Holly Hector has these suggestions:

DOs . . .

- DO validate their pain

- DO reinforce that they are not crazy

- DO believe in them. They don't need skepticism; discrediting them plays right into the cult's programming.

- DO remind yourself and them that they need to honor and respect their own survival, even if it included dissociation or fragmentation.

- DO remember healing is a *process,* not an *event.* It will take a lifetime of support and love.

- DO remember it will take courage, support, and commitment from everyone involved to heal from this level of trauma.

- DO learn to *listen*—not advise, criticize, or ignore, but *listen.*

- DO remember survivors learned to lie and manipulate to *stay alive.*

- DO remember it's not the falling down that counts, but the getting back up.

- DO remember survivors were taught "opposite truths." (Bad is good, good is bad; right is wrong, wrong is right; etc.)

- DO find your own support group, therapy, etc. You may need a place to vent your fears, anger, pain, frustrations.

- DO remember Jesus Christ has won the victory over satan. His death and resurrection have sealed the victory. His shed blood has given eternal life. What the cult teaches about satan's dominion over Christ is a lie.

(Ms. Hector is Christian and uses this with counseling clients who profess to being open to the same spiritual belief. However, as explained under the DON'Ts [below], she in no way pushes her beliefs on clients, but instead allows for those who don't believe in Christianity to draw on whatever "good side" spiritual strengths they feel protected by and comfortable with.)

DON'Ts . . .

- DON'T offer pat answers (like pray more, read the Bible more, forgiveness—these may come in time).

- DON'T try to "fix" survivors—instead, support, honor, nurture, and love.

- DON'T shove God [on them]. They have been tortured and brutalized with the concepts of God. They need to be slowly loved into the truth—not battered, or you will reproduce the cult experience.

DEMONS: REAL OR IMAGINED

Another subject that needs to be brought up here, because it often proves to be a block to survivors getting in touch with cult memories, is demons. This chapter presents a range of views on the subject of demons, by victims, witnesses, and clinicians.

A significant number of satanic cult victims report having memories of seeing supernatural manifestations of demons, satan, and the phenomenon of possession with their perpetrators.

During the cult ceremonies, part of the prayer ritual is to call up demons and satan, as Christians call for Christ during a prayer meeting. And as some supernatural phenomena are said to happen in Christian prayer meetings, so they are reported in satanic cult ceremonies as well.

This is a significant enough dimension for the Los Angeles County Ritual Abuse Task Force to have included in their booklet *Ritual Abuse* a section on "Demons and Evil Spirits." Part of it reads:

> . . . spiritual beings who are evil and ruled by Satan. According to Christian tradition, they are angels who shared in Satan's rebellion and were expelled with him.
>
> Ritually abused children and adults are victimized at rituals which invoke such beings. Victims report believing that perpetrators of ritual abuse possess control over these spiritual entities. Some victims are made to believe that these spirits have power to control the victim's life. For some, the fear of being controlled by them is more oppressive and debilitating than the fear of the perpetrators themselves.

Because they are so prevalent, the stories from those who report seeing such demons and appearances of satan are hard to overlook. Whatever a reader of this book may believe about such supernatural phenomena, victims' reports must be respected and dealt with on a clinical—as well as a human—level.

A cult victim in the Cleveland ritual abuse Twelve Step group reported having a memory of being in a room crawling with snakes as a young child. She talked of a cult member forcing a small snake partially down her throat (reportedly a common form of satanic ritual abuse). Then, later, all the snakes in the room seemed to meld into one huge snake hovering over her, and emitting what seemed to her like "so much hate . . . I just knew it was satan," she said. "I don't know how else to explain it."

Some therapists would believe the huge snake was merely a "metaphor" the woman was using unconsciously to explain the horrible trauma she was experiencing. Actually, some therapists believe the whole satanic cult memory phenomenon is a metaphor for other kinds of more ordinary abuse, like systematic beatings, or incest, or emotional torture of some sort. (When I say "ordinary abuse," I in no way want to diminish the significance of the effect of *any* abuse.)

Another reaction by others to the "huge snake" memory is that it is an image caused by hallucinogenic drugs cult victims are sometimes given before the ceremonies, not only to enhance the experience, but also to make the victims more malleable. In *People of the Lie*, Scott Peck, M.D., writes of being involved in two carefully planned exorcisms that included priests, psychologists, and medical workers. During one exorcism, Peck noted seeing the reportedly possessed woman's head actually change into the head of a huge snake, with hooded reptilian eyes. The head would dart forward trying to menace the team, and would hiss and talk threateningly to them, apparently in an attempt to get them to back down. Peck also wrote that he believed that, in this case, it was satanic possession, as opposed to possession by more minor demons.

What's interesting to note is that Peck talks about sensing the "years of hate" in this creature—the same level of overwhelming hate, perhaps, that the child from Ohio felt.

Another widely read author, Malachi Martin, wrote the book *Hostage to the Devil* documenting five specific cases of possession. In this book he, too, describes at length supernatural phenomena connected with possession. There are substantial numbers of other books written about possession, not only in the United States, but in cultures around the world.

Michelle Smith in the book *Michelle Remembers* (1981), written in conjunction with her therapist, reports having seen satan. As a child, Michelle recounts being exposed to a black mass—not just your "usual" black mass either. (As if any black mass is "usual" in the first place!) This black mass was particularly special to satanists.

According to the book, satan comes to the planet in a physical form to preside over this special black mass at regular intervals. This particular ceremony involves high priests and priestesses from around the world.

The one Michelle was exposed to was reported to have been conducted in Victoria, British Columbia, Canada. She reported satan overseeing this world assembly in the form of a half man/half beast. The ceremonies included sexual abuse, torture, and murder.

Michelle Remembers also made it to the *New York Times* best-seller list, and the book and tapes of her therapy sessions reportedly have been sent to the Vatican for study.

Besides apparently seeing satan, Michelle describes being visited both by Christ and by Mary, His mother, during the most terrifying parts of the ceremony, to give her strength to endure and to watch.

In *Out of Hell Again*, the author reports similar supernatural phenomena—of seeing Christ and satan, instances of demonic possession, even a vision of hell.

Interestingly, there's been a heightened societal awareness and curiosity of late about the supernatural plane. *Time* magazine and *U.S. News and World Report* published cover articles in 1991 on spirituality, the afterlife, and evil.

A book about angels and demons, *This Present Darkness* by Frank E. Peretti, published by Good News, a religious press, sold over two million copies.

A major television event in 1991 was the first airing of a live exorcism on the program "20/20." The show first reported on the painstaking preliminary review process by priests and psychologists. The second part of the segment showed the actual exorcism of a teenage girl reported to be possessed by several demons.

During the exorcism, when the spirits seemed to be in control, the exorcism team reported that the girl had bulging eyes and distinctly different voices. Also strong feelings of what seemed to be hatred emanated from her. All these observations are consistent with other accounts of possession.

What I found extremely intriguing was that a priest who had been working all through the process, said that, at one point, one demon, through the girl, was able to talk about places the priest had been during the prior week, places the girl would have no way of knowing about.

Some say that, if this type of demonic power exists, it may be easier to understand how satanic cult atrocities have been kept so secret for so long, given the seemingly heightened ability to know the whereabouts of authorities at any given time—or, for that matter, the power to influence authorities.

Another dynamic of this demon phenomenon is the seemingly possessed person's inability to remember what happens once the demon actively takes over, for example, during parts of the cult ceremony. Is it like an alcoholic blackout? That is, the person continues to function, but doesn't remember? Or is it similar to what happens with some incest perpetrators, who, like some victims, sometimes suppress the memories of the incestuous acts? It is interesting to note that the woman in the "20/20" piece said she had no recollection of the exorcism once the demons seemed to take over and began battling with the exorcism team.

Demonic Imagery

A ritual abuse victim in Ohio reports having a memory of coming face to face with a demon as a child. This woman had been in therapy a couple of years, working through some extreme sexual abuse issues, and had recently begun having flashbacks to satanic cult abuse that included her family, neighbors, and the family doctor, who was also the high priest of the cult.

One day during this time, while seated in the first row of church, the woman glanced down at the carpet in front of her pew. In the carpet, she saw a vision of a baby crying, then what appeared to be hideous looking gargoyles biting and clawing at the baby. She watched transfixed, but didn't understand the significance.

Later that week, she had a flashback to watching a baby being tortured and killed by cult members during one of the ceremonies. She felt that the image of gargoyles in the church may have been God showing her that these particular cult members were possessed by demons as well.

Then later in the month, the woman had another flashback. She was a child of, maybe, six. She was in a dark cave—she believes it was in the Medina, Ohio, salt mines, just south of Cleveland.

In the memory, she was pushed up against the cave wall, terrified. There was a surreal eye pressed up against one of her eyes. As the memory progressed, and her eyes adjusted to the darkness, she could make out a "hideous looking creature" that somewhat resembled the gargoyles in the carpet. After a time, she said, the creature backed away, and was walking about the cave chewing on what appeared to be human flesh.

"This thing definitely wasn't human. I was so afraid, so afraid," she said. "And the stench coming from it was almost unbearable."

She said the cult she was exposed to would sometimes use isolated outdoor areas like salt mines or woods as settings for the ceremonies—a practice reportedly consistent with many cults.

This woman, who now lives in Massachusetts, has started one of the first Ritual Abuse Anonymous meetings in that state. She has also begun to write about her experiences, and is an accomplished artist. She has periodically drawn, or painted, depictions of different aspects of her recovery process, including some of the cult memories.

The Demon Phenomenon: Some Explanations

According to therapist Holly Hector, the demon phenomenon actually may be explained along a continuum.

First, some of the demonic imagery could be caused by hallucinogens.

Second, she said she has heard a number of survivor stories indicating that some of the demon imagery is staged. That is, cult members will ceremoniously call up demons in mock prayer rituals, then one cult member or several members will appear dressed as hideous demons and attempt to scare the victims.

At the end of these staged productions, the disguises often come off in front of the children, with a disclaimer like "just fooling you."

"For a while, this made no sense to me," said Ms. Hector, who in the course of her extensive experience has come to believe that demons exist and actually do manifest themselves during some of the ceremonies. Yet, she related, when she first started working in the field, she adamantly believed demons didn't exist, and that demon images were the result of hallucinogenic drugs, or simply imaginative metaphorical contrivances. "I used to talk about this in all the seminars at first," she said.

However, as she further contemplated the reports of stagings it occurred to her that the stagings were possibly being used as part of the brainwashing, a way to keep the demon phenomenon secret. By watching the stagings, then seeing them as a ruse, if victims did see actual demons, they would become confused as to their authenticity.

And later in life, if they ever got close to these memories, they again would be confused as to what they saw. "Gee, maybe it was all just staging. People are going to think I'm psychotic if I actually talk about seeing real demons. Maybe I did just see the staging."

Another brainwashing technique is to tell victims that if they ever talk about any of the abuse, they will be seen as psychotic and get locked away.

Diagnosis through Drawings

As mentioned earlier, one of the ways to diagnose early whether a victim has been exposed to demonic stagings or, for that matter, the possibility of actual demons, is to pay attention to drawings they do about more general family abuse— drawings done in a therapeutic setting.

For example, when asked to draw something representative of Dad's alcoholism and/or physical abuse, a client may picture a scene with Dad standing over a child. The father may be raging, with a club or other weapon raised in his hand. However, in the swirl of other imagery in the background, there may be, for example, either a small or a looming drawing of demonic shapes or heads with sneering expressions.

The victim often consciously writes off this type of background imagery as merely his or her own way to accentuate the horror of the abuse. But it's becoming apparent with some people who have dissociated to a degree during the drawing that the unconscious has taken over and depicted what the victims apparently saw as children: demons.

If Ms. Hector suspects satanic abuse or, for that matter, other types of abuse, but the person has yet to get to any memories, she will have the client do some drawing with the non-dominant hand. This is a method used by many therapists.

"The technique has a tendency to get a person into the unconscious quickly," said Ms. Hector.

Ms. Hector said she has seen the gamut of cult imagery in these drawings over the years—blood, knives, sabres, coffins, candles, circles, hooded figures . . . .

In the initial stages of therapy for cult abuse, the cult imagery is often vague and only a small part of the picture. However, as therapy progresses, the cult imagery in the drawings becomes progressively larger and more pronounced.

There is one exception to this process that Ms. Hector has noticed with a number of her clients. Sometimes early on in therapy, the cult imagery is not only vivid and looming, but also quite detached and graphic. In clients with multiple personality disorder, Ms. Hector attributes this to alter personalities who, at times, can take over when the person is drawing. She surmises that alter personalities, as a rule, do want to be acknowledged. And clues like these become a way for them to move closer to the surface.

Reactions to Supernatural Films and Literature

Another way to help gauge whether individuals were exposed to demons or demonic stagings early in therapy is to explore their reactions to movies or literature that include forms of evil supernatural phenomena. How did they react to *The Omen* or *The Exorcist?* (Incidentally, William Peter Blatty's novel *The Exorcist* is supposedly based on the true story of a young girl.) Is the person thrown into a state of panic when reading about or watching these? Can the person watch them at all? If not, why not?

Movies like *The Omen* and *The Exorcist* have some overt violence, but the scare component lies more in the supernatural phenomena. So if some clients are reacting with panic attacks instead of "normal" levels of fear, there just may be a connection to their seeing evil supernatural phenomena or supernatural stagings somewhere in the past. In other words, on an unconscious level, it may be more than a movie to these people.

These clues become more and more helpful in formulating therapeutic strategies.

Another dynamic that Ms. Hector has observed somewhat frequently is that, as a satanic cult victim moves further into the therapeutic process, the fearful or even phobic reactions to these types of movies or literature increase proportionately. Most psychotherapy processes are designed to gradually dismantle defenses that have been hiding feelings and memories. And as the defensive walls come down, the intensity of reactions and feelings increases.

Ms. Hector said clients may express bemusement in this phase, that is, before the memories have surfaced. "I didn't used to have such *strong* reactions to these types of movies . . . or to the color red . . . or to being around knives . . . or . . . "

It's also important to note here that some cult victims are actually drawn to, if not obsessed by, movies depicting demons and other supernatural phenomena. They also may be drawn to slasher films and what the porn industry refers to as "snuff" films, said Ms. Hector. (Snuff films purport to show actual acts of torture and murder.)

Ms. Hector attributes the fascination to alter personalities that actually had to learn to *like* the torture and murder they were forced to participate in.

"They had to learn to like blood, the killing, if they were to survive," said Ms. Hector.

Because cult imagery, whatever the source, is so prevalent, it's a good bet that victims will at times be triggered by it, and in many cases construe that they are under some form of supernatural attack. No matter what a therapist's spiritual belief is, it is often therapeutically integral not to discount the fear, but to acknowledge it and allow the victim to talk about it.

Beyond this, it is advisable in a therapeutic sense to suggest that victims begin to make more concentrated efforts to turn to a "Power" that can prove stronger than any evil power. For some, that power becomes the collective strength of the Twelve Step ritual abuse group, along with therapists and other parts of a support network.

Likewise, at this stage, many victims also make a more concerted and consistent effort at what the Twelve Steps term "conscious contact" with a Higher Power. That is, victims will spend more time in prayer and other spiritual pursuits. If the victim has a formal religious affiliation, increased involvement with church activities is also encouraged.

Efforts in these areas often help to begin to counteract the fear, giving victims—as well as their inner child and any alter personalities—a sense of protectedness that will allow them to move closer to the specific memories.

Demons Exorcised (so to speak)

Demons, either real or perceived, need to be dealt with during the memory period, when victims begin to recall their past traumas.

Dr. Bruce Leonard at the Columbine Center said it is an issue that has come up consistently when dealing with satanic cult ritual abuse survivors. He tries to maintain as neutral a stance as possible with his patients as to whether demons actually exist on a supernatural plane or not.

"If that's what they [the victims] believe, it's important to acknowledge it," he said, explaining that discounting the patient's reality in this case erodes trust and is counterproductive.

One theory Dr. Leonard has developed is that some of the demons may be imagery, metaphors for abusive acts the victims were, at times, forced to perpetrate. And since the victims can't deal with the actual, physical act, they unconsciously create a hideous demon of some sort to represent the act—because it can't be blocked out altogether.

If, for example, a victim at age eight was forced to help stab a baby to death, since the memory is too horrible to live with, a horrible demon is created in the unconscious to represent the act. Later, in therapy, the existence of the demon will surface, and the victim will often then offhandedly want to simply reject it as a figment of imagination.

And if the act is uncovered, talked about, and processed—that is, the memory and repressed feelings around it are worked out—then there is reassurance that it was in no way volitional. And this type of demon is often "exorcised."

Interestingly, the older the person is when the act happened, the more ominous or hideous the demon appears to be. Dr. Leonard surmises that the older victims were when forced to carry out these deeds, the more guilty they will feel remembering them, since they believe that they should have had more power in not participating in the abuse—as well as more power in getting out of the cult altogether.

Although Dr. Leonard does not attempt in any way to modify a person's spiritual beliefs, he said he does, at times, try to help illuminate for victims the genesis of some of these beliefs.

He said survivors sometimes find themselves in "this eternal loop of hopelessness," feeling overwhelmed by what they perceive as an "undefeatable" supernatural dark side.

Besides helping them into their memories, then seeing some metaphor links, Dr. Leonard also helps them discern what demonic occurrences were staged by cult members. The demonic stagings are done to further intimidate the victims and are incorporated into the ongoing mind-control scheme. That is, victims are told they will be watched by the demons throughout the rest of their lives for any form of betrayal.

An example of one of these apparent demonic stagings happened with a survivor Dr. Leonard was working with. The survivor had been plagued by what she perceived as a quite haunting demon. And during treatment she had a memory of being married to a "beast," followed by satan supposedly rising through the floor to consummate the marriage.

As the fragments of the memory were fitted together and analyzed, it became apparent that the "beast" was actually the girl's uncle wearing some sort of demonic costume, including a phallic device that was used to rape the girl. (She was eight years old at the time.) But because the girl couldn't deal with the reality of her uncle being a satanic perpetrator, her unconscious reinforced the belief that the perpetrator had been a demon.

As for satan rising through the floor, another costumed cult member created this illusion. What heightened the experience, Dr. Leonard surmises, were two other factors: she may have been given some type of hallucinogenic drug prior to the staging, and also, while she was being raped, she may have had a dissociative, out-of-body experience, common to incest victims, POWs, and others who are severely traumatized. That is, she may have unconsciously "gone" to a place near the ceiling, watching from above, making the whole event that much more surreal—or supernatural—for her.

This is a protection mechanism, because the psyche of a little girl of eight usually can't handle the reality of the abuse without some sort of physical or psychiatric breakdown. And such a breakdown could lead to screaming, crying jags, catatonic with-drawal, or fainting—all reactions that could put a victim's life in danger during a ceremony.

"The mind is amazing, better than any computer," said Dr. Leonard. "It actually can project the unconscious all over like this [for instance, to the ceiling]."

Dr. Leonard also concludes that there is a range of possi-bilities to explain the demon phenomenon. He added that he is convinced it's not the therapist's place to try to convince a victim that demons don't exist, especially because many cult ceremo-nies are focused on calling up demons, in addition to directing these demons into some of the victims.

Because of this, he recommends that this subject be ap-proached with as much objectivity as possible.

Ms. Hector agrees that demons exist for her clients on both of these levels—both as metaphors and as cult stagings.

However, Ms. Hector also believes in the existence of the supernatural realm. She believes it was not only a factor during actual abuse, but that it remains a factor in therapy/recovery.

She believes in the phenomenon of possession both by satan and by demons. Her theory is that demons attach them-selves (or enter a person) at the time of some trauma, attaching to the host personality, or the alter, or even to the actual trauma memory. However, in the case of victims, Ms. Hector believes the person isn't completely possessed, but rather that satan or the demon only has a "toehold," because the victim never specifi-cally or volitionally invited the entity in.

Ms. Hector also said she believes that the supernatural phenomenon of demonic influence has accounted for much of the ultra sophistication of the brainwashing techniques, and the ma-jor reason it has been kept so covert for so long.

After working with satanic survivors and seeing things in therapy for which she had no other explanation, Ms. Hector has changed her original stance of believing demon appearances were always metaphors or stagings. For instance, while dealing with a child alter in therapy, she will often hear the child say something like: "It's really dark in here. I'm scared, really scared . . . " (Ms. Hector explained that at this moment the child is still in the trauma, as if it were crystallized in time.)

If there is a demonic trauma, she will then hear something to the effect of "THE MONSTERS ARE GOING TO GET ME!!!" (Ms. Hector says the child alters often will call the demons monsters.)

Ms. Hector went through a similar scenario with one of Tanya's alters. Because she knew Tanya was a Christian, she got permission beforehand to call on Christ during the session.

Tanya's alter, Misty, was panicked and called out about a "monster."

"You need to feel safe, right?" Ms. Hector said as calmly as possible.

"NOTHING IS BIGGER THAN THE MONSTERS!" Misty repeated, still in a state of panic.

"Yes, there is, Misty. Jesus Christ is bigger, Misty," Ms. Hector said.

"DON'T YOU SAY THAT WORD [Jesus] AGAIN!" Misty screamed. "He hurt me!" (She was referring to stagings of Christ abuse— Tanya had been raped as a young child by a cult member dressed as Christ.)

Knowing some of the history, Ms. Hector repeatedly reassured Misty that the cult had lied. It wasn't Jesus who had hurt her— it was the cult.

"But why?" asked Misty, perplexed. "Why did they lie to me?"

Staying on a somewhat elementary level for Misty, Ms. Hector used an analogy.

"Pretend you were sick, Misty. And there was, like, a green pill you could take to get better. But instead they wanted you to stay sick. What would they do?"

"They'd hide it from me so I couldn't get well, or strong," she replied.

"Yes, and besides that, they might even tell you it's poisonous, to make sure you would never get to choose the good medicine, right?"

Ms. Hector then went on to tell Misty the cult members had done the same thing to her with Christ (the "good medicine"), and that Christ is really a power bigger than the monsters.

Misty then asked if she could somehow have Christ. Ms. Hector said that often the alters really want to believe, and want something they can really trust.

Her response to Misty was, all she had to do was ask Christ to come into her heart. Shortly afterward, Misty, apparently feeling safe, said, "There's light now. It's warm in here now."

Ms. Hector said that in every case (not most cases, but *every* case), when an alter personality has been asked to do this, the light and warm feeling is described.

What also may happen is that a child alter will describe the appearance of these "big white people" (angels). Because this has happened so frequently, if a child alter doesn't describe angels, Ms. Hector will say, "Ask Jesus to give you one." And, again, shortly thereafter, one usually shows up for the child alter. "Whether all this is a product of their imagination, or a supernatural phenomenon, I can't conclusively prove," said Ms. Hector. "But it sure always seems to work."

She said that a number of child alters have reported seeing angels—big angels extending up through the ceiling, with wings and swords, just as they are sometimes described in the Bible. Although she hasn't actually seen them, Ms. Hector said she believes they are there also. She also believes they have been protection for her while she's been carrying out this work.

Ms. Hector explained that, in spite of her own convictions, she does not force her spiritual beliefs on her clients. If a client does not come to her as a Christian, she accepts that, and instead will offer choices between the "good side" and the "bad side" at pivotal therapeutic points, as during the "monster" incident with Misty.

However, Ms. Hector argues that it is therapeutically sound and even essential for complete healing that, at some point, the survivor become emotionally free enough in recovery to choose or reject Christianity (as the opposite of satanism), because that choice has often been taken totally away from these survivors as children.

TO FAMILY AND FRIENDS

To say the least, initial revelations about someone's ritual abuse past and/or multiple personality disorder usually come as a huge shock to spouses and friends. And I'm sure the word "huge" is often an understatement.

It is a particular shock to significant others who have seen some survivors as fairly high-functioning and competent. Oh, maybe there were some marked mood swings, or intermittent periods of depression, or higher than normal anxiety.

"But Charlotte having something as drastic as a multiple personality disorder like Sybil or something? C'mon!"

Multiplicity is hard enough to believe, but ritual abuse too? Orgies? Torture? Murder? And all this going on secretly?

Needless to say, a victim's coming out, so to speak, is often met with varying degrees of skepticism—skepticism that can be psychologically damaging to victims, who are usually struggling to accept the reality of it all themselves.

Education

The most important thing, initially, is to educate these significant others, said Holly Hector.

Ms. Hector stresses that she will work with a victim's spouse, children, or friends. However, she often won't work in any way with a victim's parents, grandparents, or brothers and sisters. "There's a possibility any of these people may still be cult-involved, and you may be walking into a lot of chaos with this," said the therapist. "My first interest is always my client and his or her safety." (Peripheral referrals to other therapists can always be made if other family members sincerely want help.)

Ms. Hector will hold an education session with the significant others to "demystify" the multiplicity in as clinical a way as possible. At this time, she will also explain some of the dynamics of satanic abuse as well.

She will then recommend articles on both subjects, as well as biographies of, or autobiographies by, other cult survivors.

Mood Swings and Uncharacteristic Behavior

During the phase when a survivor starts to deal with the abuse issues, other issues begin to surface for family and friends. For instance, moving into this part of the therapy process, the victim will generally start to decompensate for a while. The alters will start to surface more frequently, and their personalities will be more defined. This will also mean that family and friends will have to cope with the victim's more pronounced mood swings for a time, as well as more uncharacteristic, bizarre behavior (as more of the alters surface).

Also, because an individual's ego boundaries have been temporarily penetrated and partially dismantled through therapy and/or Twelve Step recovery (necessary to release repressed feelings and memories), the person becomes a lot more vulnerable and sensitive than usual for a time.

Let's say, for example, that Charlotte's ritual abuse memories and repressed feelings around the cult abuse have just started to surface. And one day her husband, Matt, comes home to find Charlotte has forgotten to take the car in for a tune-up— and he's planning to take it on a trip the next morning.

Now, this type of forgetfulness is sometimes a pattern with Charlotte, and Matt in this case is understandably frustrated. Not yelling, but in a voice slightly louder than normal, he tells Charlotte he's upset with her pattern of forgetting. He doesn't harp, doesn't dwell on it, just lets it go after that.

However, Matt's frustration isn't all that Charlotte hears. Her father, who had some of the same outward personality traits as Matt, was the high priest in the cult. During the ceremonies, he was constantly after Charlotte to do everything perfectly and he would scream at her or beat her if she got something wrong.

As Matt expresses his feelings, Charlotte unconsciously is hearing and seeing all that past abuse now. And instead of Charlotte just validating Matt's feelings and maybe offering an apology—or even reciprocating with mild anger because Matt has forgotten to bring home some groceries this same night— Charlotte, instead, loses it. She's thrown into a hysterical crying jag, then explodes at Matt (unconsciously screaming at her father). The scene culminates with Charlotte locking herself in her room.

What should have been a mild exchange of feelings to clear the air about something relatively minor has turned into an emotional upheaval beyond their control.

Escalation or Detachment

Now there are a couple of directions this can take. Matt can start screaming back at Charlotte and escalate the whole situation into a veritable world war. Or he can try to reason with Charlotte "as an adult," which in this case probably won't make a bit of difference, especially if one of Charlotte's obstinate child alters has taken over. Of course, this too, will only lead to further frustration for Matt.

Or, Matt can detach. That is, take the dog for a walk, call a friend, go read the newspaper, whatever.

One of the places the detachment philosophy has evolved with a degree of success is in Al-Anon Twelve Step groups for spouses and families of alcoholics. After a while, a spouse in Al-Anon comes to understand that there is no way to deal rationally with the crazy behavior and mood swings of an active alcoholic or drug addict. Through the help of others in Al-Anon, the spouse would learn techniques for detachment—just as children in Alateen and Alatot learn to deal with an alcoholic parent. In recent years, other Twelve Step "significant other" support groups have evolved as other addictions and compulsions have been identified. For instance, there's Gam-Anon for those involved with compulsive gamblers, Nar-Anon for those involved with drug addicts, and so on.

At the time of this writing, I am not aware of a similar group for family and friends of satanic cult ritual abuse victims. However, the founder of the Twelve Step Ritual Abuse group in Cleveland said there has been talk lately of starting a Twelve Step group for significant others. Family members have begun to express interest. She sees this as a trend that will start to happen across the country, along with the increasing number of ritual abuse groups.

Besides learning detachment skills in these groups for significant others, many recovery groups and therapists place a heavy emphasis on family members incorporating the Twelve Steps into their lives as well. This process usually illuminates interpersonal problem areas that need to be worked on—outside of the relationship with the victim. This can involve certain types of fears or compulsions, difficulty with expressing feelings, or, for that matter, having a propensity for being drawn into stressful relationships.

"In this phase, family members have a tendency to tap into their own fear-of-abandonment issues, and their own [family of origin] abuse issues," said Ms. Hector.

With these issues coming up in tandem with the years of accumulated stress from living with a cult victim, Ms. Hector will often recommend that family members get into some form of professional therapy themselves.

If the cult victim is a parent, Ms. Hector also insists on doing assessments of the children. She said that in these cases there is the high probability that the children have been abused by people in the cult, an uncle, grandfather, or perhaps grandmother. And these children will need emotional help as well. Sometimes in such cases the parents will resist having the assessments done, because they realize that they may not have been able to protect the child at times from the perpetrators.

FIGHTING BACK

Awareness of ritual abuse is starting to grow outside the Twelve Step and therapeutic communities as well. Highlighted here are model organizations that have developed to address this problem. Each has proven effective so far and, as with any "models," is meant to spur thought—and further action.

Los Angeles County's Ritual Abuse Task Force

An organization helping to set the pace is the Los Angeles County Commission for Women (mentioned earlier).

In 1988 therapist Myra Riddell spearheaded a movement to establish a Ritual Abuse Task Force under the umbrella of the Los Angeles County Commission for Women. At the time of this writing, Ms. Riddell is both commissioner of the Commission for Women and chair for the Ritual Abuse Task Force.

For years Ms. Riddell has worked with ritual abuse victims in her practice. Clearly, she said, she saw the need to take this issue to another level of societal awareness.

She rallied enough support so that, on the evening the commission was to vote on the establishment of the task force, more than seventy people from throughout the state showed up for the meeting.

"We had people from as far away as San Diego and Bakersfield come to that meeting," she said. "It was a tremendous response and showed that not only were people concerned about the problem, but they were willing to take action."

The task force was established primarily to research and disseminate information about satanic cult ritual abuse. And one of the priorities was to authorize the drafting of a comprehensive booklet that touched on most every aspect of the problem.

The booklet, *Ritual Abuse*, was first printed in 1989, and at the time of my interview with Ms. Riddell in early 1991, 10,000 copies had already been distributed throughout the United States, Canada, England, Germany, and Holland.

The task force is also in the process of developing ritual abuse education and training programs for mental health workers, teachers, attorneys, and law enforcement officials.

According to Ms. Riddell, the task force has been able to recruit a diverse mix of people, which has helped in getting the message out to as many populations as possible.

There are currently thirty-seven members on the task force. They include therapists, a district attorney, police officers, teachers, a Catholic priest, ritual abuse survivors, and parents of survivors.

Like some of the survivors who are now coming out to tell about the abuse, Ms. Riddell said that she, as a therapist, had seen enough of the devastating effects of ritual abuse and felt it was time to start to fight back.

"For me, it's been taking all the rage about this and turning it into activism," she said with emphasis.

Setting up a Ritual Abuse Task Force

For information about setting up a ritual abuse task force in your area, contact the Los Angeles County Commission for Women at 213/974-1455.

To obtain the *Ritual Abuse* booklet, call that number or write to the Commission for Women, 383 Hall of Administration, 500 W. Temple St., Los Angeles, CA 90012. (A donation of $5.00 is asked for each booklet. If you are ordering quantities of twenty-five or more, they ask for a donation of $3.00 a booklet.)

JUSTUS Unlimited

JUSTUS Unlimited is a nonprofit group formed in Colorado to reach out to help ritual abuse victims across the United States, and maybe eventually, the world.

The organization was the brainchild of three satanic cult ritual abuse survivors who, over the years, have watched in frustration the "injustice" survivors have had to endure at almost every level of society.

"First, these people should never have had to go through the abuse they did. But what's more, then they often have to deal with insensitive and uninformed law enforcement people, attorneys, judges, therapists . . . ," said Faith Donaldson, one of the organization's co-founders. Faith Donaldson, who was mentioned earlier in the book, also writes and speaks publicly on the topic.

Because of the extreme trauma and the often debilitated state of ritual abuse survivors, it is very hard for some to stand up for their rights, to be in a position to pay for adequate help, sometimes just to be able to ask for help.

The three co-founders of the organization already have been through extensive stretches of recovery and each has a good, firsthand grasp of what someone going through the process will need. The significance of the name JUSTUS: victims helping victims.

The intent was to create a multifaceted organization to deal with as many areas of ritual abuse as possible.

JUSTUS, for example, is becoming a "center for information," said Faith Donaldson. As a referral source, they have gathered information on psychiatric hospitals that now provide services for the ritually abused. They have also developed a list of therapists sensitive to the issue, as well as a list of outpatient and Twelve Step support groups, so a victim can make an informed choice.

In addition, JUSTUS is developing a library of books, articles, and tapes on ritual abuse issues.

The organization also wants to be able to provide much-needed financial assistance for victims who need treatment or long-term therapy. They are in the process of developing fund-raising activities, soliciting donations, and obtaining grants.

JUSTUS has developed a fourteen-member advisory board that includes businesspeople, psychiatrists, psychologists, a doctor, and an attorney.

Part of the organization's purpose statement reads: "Mending the emotional damage [from ritual abuse] is complex, painful and expensive. All too often, these expenses are beyond the survivor's means. The final wrong is they are denied treatment, which would free them from the destructive cycle of self-hate and abuse which can be the last legacy of their abuse."

Faith Donaldson said the group is currently in the process of trying to solicit memberships. Members would receive periodic newsletters and other informational releases. She points out that you don't have to be a ritual abuse survivor to join.

She also said people in Ohio and Minnesota are in the process of forming JUSTUS chapters.

Anyone interested in information about membership or starting a chapter, or simply for referrals, may write to JUSTUS, P.O. Box 1121, Parker, Colorado 80134; or call 303/643-8698.

Monarch Resources

In recent years resource organizations, hotlines, and literature for ritual abuse survivors have mushroomed (see Resources).

Monarch Resources is an organization that has been very involved in the evolution of the ritual abuse awareness and recovery movement. The California nonprofit organization, started in 1988, provides referral information pertaining to help with ritual abuse, multiple personality syndrome, childhood sexual abuse, and incest. The organization also offers information for partners, parents, and friends of survivors.

Monarch functions as an informal clearinghouse, providing lists of bibliographies, newsletters, hotline numbers, support group locations, and audiovisual resources. The organization also publishes a calendar of events, listing upcoming conferences and workshops, and offers a speaker's bureau and conference planning service.

Executive Director Maureen Brugh is a ritual abuse survivor herself and believes one of the best ways to fight back against ritual and other forms of abuse is to educate as many people as possible. Based on figures from Monarch, that education process has been increasing in measured increments.

In 1990 Monarch fielded an average of fifteen calls a day. In 1991 Monarch averaged twenty-five calls a day and received approximately thirty-five pieces of daily mail as well. And Ms. Brugh predicts that these figures will continue to increase as more and more abuse survivors move toward recovery and society's acceptance of these issues grows.

As with JUSTUS, Monarch Resources is an outgrowth of personal recovery—in this case, Maureen Brugh's own.

In 1984 Ms. Brugh became involved with ACA meetings to work on codependency issues. About three years later, she began to have incest flashbacks and started to attend a Twelve Step group for incest survivors as well. She supplemented the Twelve Step involvement in these two groups with therapy work and eventually began having flashbacks to satanic ritual abuse in her childhood. Shortly after the ritual abuse memories surfaced, Ms. Brugh went for inpatient treatment at the Cottonwood Center in Los Lunas, New Mexico.

Coming out of Cottonwood's sexual trauma center, Ms. Brugh returned to California and began doing research on therapists and groups that might be sensitive to ritual abuse issues. Although she began this research for her own continued recovery, as time went on she began sharing the information with a few others moving into ritual abuse recovery, then a few more. . . .

She continued to accumulate more referral information and became involved with helping a friend who had developed the RAP line, a nationwide ritual abuse help line. In 1990 RAP fielded almost 2,000 calls. Ms. Brugh developed Monarch Resources in 1988.

One of her philosophies is that it's important for survivors to talk about the abuse as part of the re-empowerment process. And over the past few years, she has given media interviews and talks at national incest survivors conferences and colleges.

Based on what she has seen of the ritual abuse recovery movement, Ms. Brugh said there is good cause for optimism. She cited the ritual abuse survivor support groups as an example. She said when she first started going to the meetings four years ago, a majority of the group members were in their forties, fifties, even sixties. One evening Ms. Brugh asked a sixty-five-year-old ritual abuse survivor what motivated her to deal at her age with all her past pain.

"If I only have one year of peace, it will all be worth it," this woman responded.

Ms. Brugh is now observing that many are coming to the support groups in their thirties, twenties, even late teens.

Many incest survivor organizations are now starting to conduct workshops and entire seminars on ritual abuse issues, she said. Ms. Brugh reported that an overriding theme at the 1991 International Society for Multiple Personality and Dissociation conference was not whether ritual abuse was real or not, but "what are we going to do to help survivors?"

Write to Monarch Resources at P.O. Box 1293, Torrance, CA 90505-0293, or call 310/373-1958.

Minnesota Awareness of Ritual Abuse (MINNARA)

Sgt. Jon Hinchliff has been a member of the Minneapolis Police Department for twenty-three years. In 1987 he was transferred from the Homicide Division to the Special Investigations Unit. This unit deals primarily with long-term criminal investigations and monitoring of extremist groups.

At the time of his transfer, said Hinchliff, ritual abuse was a relatively low priority subject. There were a few isolated reports, and photos of animals found killed, their blood drained, in parks throughout the outer Minneapolis area. And a few reports of people coming upon what appeared to be ritual sites in wooded areas. But there was no long-term focus, and no one specifically assigned to this area.

Hinchliff's curiosity about this topic had been piqued back in 1981, when a woman in the Minneapolis area had been convicted of murder. She had been involved in the Afro-Caribbean practices of Santeria.

Santeria's roots are an actual blending of occult practices with Catholicism. It began in Nigeria, and came to the Western Hemisphere with slaves shipped to Latin America. According to Hinchliff, Santerians generally practice blood sacrifices only with animals.

However, in the Minneapolis case, the woman, who was the victim's grandmother, had driven "blessed stakes" through her grandson's heart because she felt he was possessed by evil spirits.

The case had remained filed in Hinchliff's mind, and when he got to the Special Investigation Division, he was granted permission to do some investigation in the ritual crime area.

He started reading literature on the subject and, at the same time, began searching through old records and contacting other law enforcement officials.

In networking with Park Police throughout the state, he began hearing story after story of police officers coming across the same things: There were mutilated animals, almost all with their blood drained. And there were also numerous reports of the Park Police happening upon groups of people engaged in different types of covert ritual ceremonies.

By contacting the State Bureau of Criminal Apprehension, Hinchliff found that there had been reports of a series of break-ins to churches in rural areas throughout the state. From the evidence, it was surmised that these churches had been used for satanic rituals and sacrifice. To desecrate a Christian church in such a way is considered one of the ultimate forms of worship to satan.

Actually, there had been enough of these reports that one crime analyst in Minnesota was sending out warning correspondence to police departments around the state at the time of satanic holidays such as the Summer Solstice and Halloween, said Hinchliff.

Usually, however, these types of cult reports were discussed in guarded conversations, if at all, said Hinchliff, mostly because of the "bizarre" nature of the topic.

Through enough contacts, Hinchliff formed a network alliance with Park Police throughout the state, initiating a consistent flow of information.

His next step was to do a television spot on the subject.

Shortly after this, he was contacted by the Sexual Assault Center in Minneapolis. There he met twelve people with interests in ritual abuse work who had informally joined the center. These included law enforcement officials, counselors, a college professor, and transgenerational cult survivors.

"In a way, it was actually a relief finding other people who were dealing with this as well at this level," said Hinchliff.

In the winter of 1988, Hinchliff and two counselors decided to form a group called Minnesota Awareness of Ritual Abuse.

They began to schedule regular meetings to network information and formulate goals, and within a couple of years their membership had grown to a list almost two pages long, said Hinchliff. The membership included lawyers, mental health counselors, law enforcement officials, and teachers (a group make-up very similar to that of the L.A. Ritual Abuse Task Force).

Besides providing a forum, one of the group's goals has been to promote as much public awareness of this issue as possible. Hinchliff has done many more television spots and media interviews. Also, in early 1991, the group sponsored a two-day seminar on aspects of ritual abuse.

"We had almost three hundred people attend. Counselors, law enforcement people, the general public," said Hinchliff. He was sure some of the attendees were cult members as well.

"They simply want to know what we know," said the sergeant. Hinchliff and others interviewed throughout this book said cult members want to find out who's involved so sometimes they can begin to mount strategies for harassment campaigns, or strategies to try to undermine publicly a professional's credibility or someone's reputation in general.

Related to his specialized area of investigation, Hinchliff also has developed sources in the occult world. He said that one of the biggest aids to him is that he's been able to gain insight into how cult members think, both from the sources and from reading material.

One of the major obstacles in his field of investigation is the general tendency to just pass the whole thing off as unbelievable, Hinchliff said, because, again, at first glance it appears so bizarre. However, he said, once you understand some of the rationale—and there is rationale for all behavior—then not only does cult activity become more believable, but people are actually able to approach the subject with some objectivity.

An example of this would be treating reports of sacrifice and cannibalism by upper-middle-class suburbanites as pure idiocy. However, when the sacrifice is recognized as being an offering to satan for financial power in business, for example, this puts it in a somewhat more believable context. And what's more, understanding that the drinking of blood and eating of flesh are believed to be conduits for increased spiritual power (in satanism, again, the power isn't in the spirit as it is in Christianity, but in the flesh), puts this practice in another light.

Like many other experts, Hinchliff sees the ritual abuse problem growing.

One of his occult sources told the sergeant recently that the practice of getting involved with the occult specifically searching for personal power, at almost any cost, has been accelerating. And along with this, reports indicate that a lot of people gradually cross over from what would be construed as somewhat benign occult activity to the more covert, "dark side" activities.

As time goes on, Hinchliff said he predicts more groups like MINNARA will start up in other parts of the state, and eventually a centralized group somewhere in the state will coordinate the efforts of local chapters.

Anyone interested in more information about MINNARA can contact either Sgt. Jon Hinchliff at 612/348-4977, or counselor Dorothy Fisker at the Hennepin County Sexual Violence Center, 612/824-5555. Or write 1222 W. Thirty-first St., Minneapolis, MN 55408.

California Ritual Crime Investigators Association (CRCIA)

Another group that has formed to fight back is the California Ritual Crime Investigators Association (CRCIA). The first of its kind in the United States, the association consists of representatives from local, state, and federal law enforcement agencies and associated professionals.

The association's goals are to promote a coordinated relationship among ritual crime investigators; to provide their membership—and other agencies who request it—training on ritual and multidimensional crimes; to serve as a central repository for statistical ritual crime data; and to provide an information library on the subject.

The nucleus of this group was established initially as a branch of the U.S. Attorney General's office Ritual Crime Committee in 1989. In 1990 the group left the auspices of the Attorney General's office and formed a separate organization.

Randy Cerny, the association's northern California coordinator, said, "We didn't want [our affiliation with this office] to preclude our looking into some of the ritual crime areas for some political reason, for instance."

Cerny is a retired member of the Stanislaus County, California, sheriff's department, where one of his responsibilities was as gang intelligence coordinator. He has investigated gang and ritual cases and has testified as an authority in both of these areas at the superior court level.

He said that the California Ritual Crime Investigators Association's board includes a cross-section of law enforcement representatives, including police detectives, an arson investigator, intelligence specialists, and child abuse investigators. The association also provides for associate memberships for educators, therapists, criminal justice system representatives, members of the military, or others dealing with ritual crime abuse in other professional capacities. For information about the CRCIA, write CRCIA, 808 Alamo Drive, Suite 290, Vacaville, CA 95688, or call 209/575-5550.

Ritual Abuse Seminars

One method of responding to the problems of ritual abuse is through informational seminars. Cerny, who has presented ritual abuse seminars in many parts of the country, as well as in Canada and Newfoundland, spoke at a day-long seminar sponsored by the Monterey-County-based group Breaking Out.

Cerny said he sees a marked increased in awareness in law enforcement—as well as in the judicial system—of ritual crime issues, as evidenced in part by increased departmental allocations for ritual crime training.

At the seminar, Cerny defined ritual crime as any prescribed religious ceremony and/or customarily repeated act, or series of acts that are criminal in nature. He said there are four basic motivating factors in ritual crime—psychological, cultural, spiritual, and sexual.

Cerny stressed that ritual crimes are not just inherent to satanism. Among other nontraditional groups sometimes associated with different levels of ritual crime, Cerny cited some Afro-Caribbean cults, some Wiccan groups, some pagan groups, some ethnic and religious supremacist groups. Cerny also said that law enforcement is dealing with self-styled perpetrators (some serial killers, for example) who may borrow from nontraditional philosophies to justify committing crimes.

In spite of the fact that there are—and have been—significant numbers of ritual crimes, he said that over the years some reports of these crimes have been suppressed. Among reasons for this suppression, he said, have been pressures on law enforcement agencies and the media by community leaders to downplay reports of ritual crime activity. In some cases, this may have been an attempt to circumvent damaging a town's development projects or tourist trade.

Responding to Concerns about Youth

Cerny, expressing concern about the growing numbers of youth becoming involved with destructive groups, outlined a list of characteristics in youth that *may* indicate destructive cult involvement at some level:

- Thoughts of suicide, or suicide attempts
- Undue preoccupation with violence (for instance, compulsive interest in videos displaying violent death themes, occult themes)
- Alienation from family, from [established] religion
- Obnoxious antisocial behavior
- Self-mutilating and/or tattooing
- Bizarre displays of cruelty at times
- Fascination with edged weapons, such as knives or spikes
- Substance abuse
- High truancy rate
- Marked decline in grades
- Compulsive interest in fantasy role-playing games and occult literature
- Preoccupation with ["dark side"] heavy metal music

Cerny added that while some, or all, of these characteristics often fit a typical profile of a cult-involved youth, this doesn't mean that a youth with what he referred to as a "GQ *[Gentlemen's Quarterly]* look and straight A's" might not be cult-involved.

Cerny said he believes that, for some youth, listening to heavy metal music not only can be an indication of destructive cult involvement, but that the music actually may incite them to violence toward others. While Cerny said he strongly supports First Amendment rights, he also believes there should be legislation mandating that recording companies and artists issue warnings about lyric content.

According to Cerny, who has debriefed approximately one hundred cult-involved young persons over the years, it is vital that law enforcement representatives have as much training as possible in the ritual crime area because of its increasing prevalence and the high propensity for violence among cult members, youth and adult.

Combatting Violence of Nontraditional Groups

Besides satanists, Cerny named other nontraditional groups that have displayed tendencies to violence, including the Neo-Nazis and Missing Foundation.

Missing Foundation, begun in New York City in the mid-1980s, decries landlords, "yuppies," and police as "the enemy" in their literature. Missing Foundation is reported to have incited riots and is known for improptu stagings of concerts designed not only to glorify violence, but create it. Cerny played a tape of a report produced by Channel 2 News in New York City, which included a home video segment of violence by band members and audience at a concert staged by Missing Foundation.

An emblem of Missing Foundation is an upside-down champagne glass, signifying, "The party's over!" and implying an end to what this group sees as imbalances between classes. Cerny said that graffiti such as this displayed in certain areas of a city is one way of "establishing turf."

Another area for serious concern, Cerny reported, is the proliferation of crime and intimidation by racist supremacist "hate" groups. As an example, he talked about some white supremacists whose open intent is to establish an all-white North American "Aryan Nation." According to a Public Broadcasting documentary, this group is reported to hold a World Aryan Congress in Idaho every year. Many of its chapters are now said to be linked by a computer network. This, according to taped interviews with some of the group's leaders, not only provides up-to-date group news, but features a "hit list" of people (such as politicians, journalists, judges) deemed adversarial to the group's cause.

There are even indications, Cerny said, that some of these groups are sharing techniques of abuse, propaganda, and infiltration—that some of them may be joining forces. As an example of this kind of crossover, Cerny said he was once a clandestine observer at a Ku Klux Klan outdoor ceremony in Stanislaus County, where reportedly known satanists, with reported ties to a "skinhead" group, were in attendance.

According to Cerny, many nontraditional groups apparently groom their youth to become involved in the community— in law enforcement, politics, business, sciences, and the arts. Cerny said there have been indications that some group members have been publicly toning down their extreme beliefs in order to move further into society's mainstream, even to run for important political offices.

To reciprocate, said Cerny, combatting these societal threats will entail a cross-section of people committed to taking a stand and coming together to share information and form alliances to fight ritual crime on every level.

Breaking Out

Among organizations formed in recent years to help people break away from destructive cults is a grassroots group called Breaking Out in Salinas, California.

In 1990, Sheryl Wernick was approached by a woman trying to leave a witches coven she had been involved with in Chicago prior to moving to California. The coven, apparently involved in sexual abuse, emotional abuse, and torture, reportedly threatened to hurt—even kill—members who broke away. In trying to get help for the woman, Sheryl Wernick and her husband, Steve, went to their Baptist church pastor and several other ministers. Because they had little knowledge about destructive cult activities, these clergypersons were unable to help much in inital counseling.

After doing research to learn as much as she could about satanic and other destructive cult beliefs and activities, with her pastor's approval Sheryl Wernick presented a series of seminars on the subject at her church. The series, attended by members of several churches in the area, generated enough interest to initiate the organization of Breaking Out. Breaking Out is a nonprofit, Christian interdenominational group that disseminates information about covert cult activity and ritual crime. It also is set up to provide crisis counseling, resource information, referrals, and access to a safe network for people trying to break away from destructive cults.

In the past year, Sheryl Wernick reported that the organization has fielded many calls from concerned parents. There also have been a significant number of calls from young people who are "dabbling" in occult practices or who have been drawn into destructive cults.

"Some are really scared," said Mrs. Wernick. "They also often don't think they'll be believed—and it is quite a relief for them to find they *are* believed, that there is help."

Breaking Out contracted with a therapist who regularly works with ritual abuse clients to train volunteers in ways to provide initial crisis counseling.

In one case, a Breaking Out member took legal custody of a child who had been ritually abused. In another, the organization was integral in helping the "high priest" of a local satanic cult break away and find safety.

To contact Breaking Out, write to P.O. Box 6782, Salinas, CA 93912-6782.

Christian Ministries

In the case involving the "high priest," Breaking Out contacted the Bob Larson Ministries in Denver, Colorado, to find a "safe house" in some other area of the country for this person. Larson Ministries has an extensive network for people trying to break away from these destructive cults, or who are having flashbacks to ritual abuse. The ministries also produces a nationwide, daily, call-in show, "Talk Back with Bob Larson," that often deals with destructive-cult-related topics.

Warnke Ministries in Burgin, Kentucky, is another Christian organization that offers nationwide referral and crisis counseling for those trying to leave cults or having initial flashbacks of ritual abuse. Warnke Ministries reports they receive fifteen to twenty calls daily just from people beginning to have flashbacks from childhood ritual abuse trauma.

For addresses and phone numbers for these ministries, as well as other resources—Christian and secular—see Resources.

State Legislation

Some states are responding with legislation to the problem of ritual abuse. Among them is the state of Idaho, which in 1990 enacted a newly worded bill pertaining to the ritual abuse of children, referring to specific forms of abuse, such as torture, forced ingestion or injection of drugs, being forced to witness involvement in a mock, unauthorized, unlawful marriage ceremony "with another person or representation of any force or deity, followed by sexual contact with the child."

At the time of this writing, there is also a bill in the California Legislature to define and set parameters around areas of ritual crime.

LOOKING AHEAD

Writing this book has been an amazing experience. Actually a lot has written itself, as if it has taken on a life of its own. Each interview seemed to come serendipitously and sequentially, illuminating a certain area and, at the same time, raising questions about another, for which I would be shortly connected with another authority who had some answers. And so on.

The reality that emerges from all this is scary, extremely alarming. Yet, there is hope.

Given all the corroborative information from victims, therapists, social service and law enforcement people across the country, it's hard to draw any other conclusion but that ritual abuse exists—and exists extensively.

That is, apparently there are growing numbers of "dabbler" satanic cult groups made up primarily of younger people. There is also purported to be a network of highly organized, transgenerational cults that have existed perhaps for centuries. Cults highly sophisticated in psychological brainwashing techniques to ensure cooperation and silence. Cults that engage in orgies, sexual abuse of children, torture, murder, sacrifices.

What's more, and even more insidious, is that this core evil can impact society at its base with a power commensurate with the business and community positions cult members are reported to hold. This evil can manifest itself again, in anything as overt as pandering child pornography to the greed behind corporate crime.

As evidence that ritual abuse is becoming a more visible issue, in Minneapolis during the week of November 5, 1991, KARE-TV channel 11 ran a series of short features, "Dabbling with the Dark Side," which talked about discoveries in Minnesota communities, in rural areas and parks, of rings of rocks, animal carcasses (some skinned), and satanic graffiti.

A man I met in Santa Barbara, California, told me about visiting friends in northern Idaho a couple of years back. At the time he was there, local law enforcement agencies were warning people to be careful. A number of animals had been found cut up, the blood drained, in what appeared to be cult-like sacrifices.

"This stuff must really go on all over, huh?" he said.

"Yeah, I guess," I half-mused, half-winced, thinking about the children still being abused.

Given the accounts of "dark side" supernatural phenomena and possession-like states of some cult members, as reported by survivors and therapists I've talked with—as well as in the writings of other reputable therapists—it would seem apparent that this area should not be discounted, but studied extensively.

It is becoming increasingly apparent through the experiences of therapists that a significant number of people with severe, debilitating mental disorders may, in fact, be ritual abuse survivors. These are people whose lives have been severely disrupted, whether they are in long-term psychiatric units, homeless on the street, barely getting by in what may be termed a "normal" world, or even functioning quite well outwardly while being racked with emotional problems inwardly.

"It is my belief this is the last frontier on the trauma continuum," said therapist Holly Hector. "And as we develop an index for suspecting it, more and more people will get help."

That "index" is starting to develop in a number of areas. For instance, more and more therapists are starting to deal with cult survivors in their practices, and concurrently more seminars on how to carry out the therapeutic work are developing as well. Likewise, psychiatric treatment units that treat people reporting ritual abuse are starting to appear.

Columbine's Dr. Bruce Leonard said it is his opinion that ritual abuse is going on both in major cities and rural areas. "And somewhere, somehow, it is going to start to be documented," he said. And the by-product of this documentation will be that it will become a tangible legal issue as well, which it should be now, he added.

In Twelve Step recovery, ritual abuse is becoming a more highly visible issue that will continue to lead to the formation of more support groups across the country and throughout the world. And it will perhaps provide the missing piece for some people who have been earnestly working recovery programs, yet always seeming to be in the frustrating dilemma—"there seems to be something else, something I'm just not seeing yet."

Also more law enforcement agencies are now taking steps toward getting more involved, as the Minneapolis Police Department has. We'll be in a much better position to stop the kidnapping and the cult activities in the future.

According to Sgt. Jon Hinchliff, one of the biggest factors to overcome is community denial.

"[Satanic abuse] is such a scary, bizarre thing for people to acknowledge," said Hinchliff. "And what's more, once a community really acknowledges it, they then also have to react. They have to do something about it."

Also, Hinchliff adds, as powerful and sophisticated as these satanic groups seem, they are not above the law. And the more people come together to expose them, the more they *will* be exposed. And the more exposure, the more these people will face the consequences, and the less cult activity there will be.

"Satanic cult ritual abuse survivors are the innocent of the innocent, if you think about it," said Ms. Hector. "There are no more traumatized or brutalized people than these survivors. And brutalized by people [family] they should have been able to trust."

Most of the people I interviewed for this book expressed the belief, in one way or another, that society should rally around these survivors as much as possible. Another positive by-product of what seems to be a completely negative phenomenon is that this rallying is already starting to happen. People from all walks of society are coming together to build a community of sorts—based on helping survivors and fighting back. This community includes mental health professionals, teachers, law enforcement people, religious leaders, survivors, family, and friends. Satanic ritual abuse is a multifaceted problem that will necessitate a multifaceted solution.

A solid start has been made, as evidenced by what is already being done by those interviewed for this book and others like them. All of us can take their lead in keeping alive the fight against satanic ritual abuse, as well as increasing our sensitivity to those survivors struggling to recover.

About the Author

Daniel Ryder, a Certified Chemical Dependency Counselor and a Licensed Social Worker, developed one of the first codependency treatment programs in Ohio. Prior to becoming a counselor, he had been a reporter.

He is a victim of satanic ritual abuse and has spent years in therapy and Twelve Step groups recovering from the trauma.

For reasons of Twelve Step anonymity, Daniel Ryder is a pseudonym. The author has published other books under another name.

APPENDIX
PERSONAL STORIES

In the Light of Memories...

The following is a collection of personal stories
about satanic cult abuse across the country.

Maggie Irwin, counselor at the Meadows, Wickenburg, Arizona,
said she believes as more and more of this becomes public, it will
be the courageous abuse victims' stories, not only about what
they survived growing up, but what they have faced in recovery,
that will provide inspiration for many others on whatever recovery journey they're undertaking.

     In regressions, survivors will sometimes find themselves
in the imagery of a tunnel, moving back toward yet another part
of the past they must face. Mrs. Irwin shared this thought from
the "precious inner child" of one of her satanic abuse patients.

     "Know that these children bring you a gift and a message
of grace. If you allow it, they will bring you a lesson of your own
healing. Know that of all creatures, these tiny warriors are God's
most precious children, closest to His heart. When they perceive
themselves in the tunnels, they are simply being held in the silence of God's breath. Love them, yourself, and each other."

—Eterna

FROM HOLLY HECTOR, THERAPIST IN COLORADO

"Pits. I hear a lot of stories of victims being put in all kinds of pits," said Ms. Hector.

One of the most poignant and surely almost incomprehensible victim memories Ms. Hector recounted was that of an alter, Jean, who was raised in the Denver area. (This was an alter whose task was to be present when a lot of the most horrendous abuse was going on during the ceremonies.)

One particular day, when the girl was about six years old, she was taken to some woods by the cult. A pit about five or six feet deep had been dug, and she was placed in it. The pit was crawling with snakes.

For what seemed like hours, the snakes crawled over her, around her. Cult members, periodically, would tell her she'd be taken back to the pit and left there forever if she ever talked about the cult. Ever.

After a time, she was taken out and allowed to play with a baby goat that had been brought along—they even let her name it.

Later they threw the little girl in another pit. This one was filled with the limbs and insides of dead animals. There was blood everywhere.

Then, the baby goat was extended out over her. One of the cult members cut its legs off, one by one, then slit its throat, the blood dripping down over the girl.

They then cut the eyes out of the goat and inserted them in her vagina. "This way we will use the eyes to always see what you're doing," they told her.

But even this wasn't the end of the abuse.

They took her out of the pit again, and this time let her play with a young boy who had been brought along. She had never seen the boy.

"Where did you come from?" she asked, at one point.

"They took me away from my mom and dad," he related. (He had been kidnapped.) The boy was scared.

The girl tried to comfort him. "Don't cry," she said. "Just be good— they won't hurt you." The cult members assured the child nothing would happen to the boy.

A short while later, they abruptly grabbed the boy and hung him over yet another pit filled with some type of liquid (apparently acid). Slowly, they lowered the boy, making the young girl watch.

As they continued to lower the boy, the girl heard a sizzling sound, then some more. The boy was screaming terrible screams. And they kept lowering, and lowering.

When they raised him, his skin was gone.

They told her it had been her fault he was killed, because she had at one point talked to him about the goat.

She was overcome with guilt, shame.

"This is going to happen to everyone you love, if you ever tell," another said. "And you will be responsible for it."

Then she was hung over the acid pit for several hours before being taken home.

JANE

A thirty-year-old satanic cult survivor, Jane, who grew up in a suburb of Cleveland, Ohio, recently ended up in a psychiatric unit. She had been in therapy for several years working through the cult memories, but hadn't had all the memories yet.

As Jane was flipping through TV channels one morning she came across an ABC affiliate talk show doing a segment with two satanic cult survivors.

At one point in the interview, one of the survivors began to talk about the practice of cannibalism within the cult. Jane became extremely nauseous and began to retch. Shortly afterward, she had a flashback to being forced, as a child, to eat the flesh of a baby who had been sacrificed during a ceremony.

"For the next couple days, I couldn't eat anything. The thought of food repulsed me," said Jane. "I then started to get suicidal and decided to check myself into the psych unit for a while."

While this experience was absolutely horrible for her, she also said she was grateful it happened. Because it provided her with another piece of her past, and did bring up more of the feelings that were buried—moving her closer to being emotionally free.

PAM

The memory had just come for a woman in Ohio. She'd been involved in a Twelve Step ritual abuse group for about a year.

She was six years old, maybe seven. She and some other neighborhood kids had been taken to the woods, again, for another ceremony.

Shortly after arriving there, some chains were brought out. Pam remembered the fear welling inside. (Whenever they brought the chains out, someone was going to get hurt.)

They picked out David, one of Pam's school friends. David was seven too. As his legs were being chained to the trees, the other children were told that David had betrayed the cult. He had told one of the neighbors he had seen his mother have sex with a dog. (This particular cult would sometimes practice bestiality during the orgies.)

The children were told to watch closely, because what was about to happen to David would happen to them if they ever talked about the cult.

And, as the young child screamed in terror, his father approached him, and taking a knife, savagely cut his son's tongue out. The boy was then slowly skinned alive while the rest of the kids were forced to watch.

Satanic cult ritual abuse doesn't just happen within the family, or just within teen cults. It doesn't just happen late at night in attics, out in the woods, in secluded, or not so secluded, churches. It happens in day-care settings. And it happens in schools.

It happened to the author of the next piece in a rural school. And although it went on only for about a year, it left scars that will last a lifetime.

213

VICTORIA LIGHT

There were symptoms of her abuse growing up. But at the time, her parents couldn't read them right, nor could the medical professionals. So, she had to live with the pain and the nightmares, until later in life, when she finally sought help.

We can hope that Victoria's story will save other children years of the same kind of "isolated" pain. Victoria Light is a pseudonym.

Accepting the reality of ritual abuse is like walking from the light into a dark theater. At first it blinds you, but if you stand long enough in the darkness you begin to make out figures and are able to move about.

I am an adult survivor of childhood ritual abuse. I wasn't raised in a cult, but was abused by members of a highly organized satanic cult operating in a rural elementary school (population of the town was 10,000). The abuse took place over approximately a one-year period when I was five-and-a-half to six-and-a-half years old. Then we moved. I was lucky. Many who suffer years of ritual abuse become multiple personalities. I didn't become a multiple, although I blocked out the abuse, "dissociated," as my therapist calls it.

Despite the move and memory loss, the abuse left fingerprints. I suffered frequent nightmares—my parents thought they were "night terrors." In truth, I had repetitive dreams of body mutilation but I couldn't attach words to the feelings nor find an appropriate context.

Throughout the first year after we moved, I would go up to ten hours without urinating. My mother dismissed it as a power struggle. Frequently on school nights, I had stomachaches. In the spring of third grade, a peak cult holiday season punctuated by Easter, the spring equinox, and my birthday, I was hospitalized for abdominal pain and vomiting. My appendix was removed unnecessarily.

At school, I hid behind the student in the desk in front of me and cried. On my papers, I changed my name at least fifteen times. At recess I ran away. Despite a genius IQ, I couldn't learn to spell.

The abuse compromised my relationship with my family. I lived, as if alone, quarantined to a tent outside my home. I transferred the distrust to my mother. Mom was the same height, carried the same weight, and her hair matched the hair color of my primary female perpetrator. Even when I was sick and Mom tried to comfort me, I was filled with a mixture of terror and sexual arousal. Nervously I jiggled my foot throughout the night.

Our school doctor was the leader of the cult. My father became a doctor, adding further ambiguity.

Throughout my late teens and early adulthood, my family of origin became increasingly dysfunctional due to parental alcoholism. In my late twenties, I married and joined a Twelve Step recovery program for codependency. My parents went through treatment and maintained sobriety. I persisted in therapy and ACA [Adult Children of Alcoholics fellowship].

Although not chemically dependent, I was addicted to thinking. I was a chronic worrier, an overachiever, a perfectionist. I lived at a frenetic pace, passing from activity to activity. Anxiety and depression were smeared all over my life. I was the recipient of random panic attacks. I was hypervigilant, living each day as if driving on glare ice. I set up a death watch. I believed if I thought about death all the time it wouldn't catch me off guard. The cult glorified death. Life was a funeral procession.

Physically I never felt well. Every night after I got into bed, I got up to urinate five or six times. (This was a re-enactment. I was forced to urinate before being drugged and abused.) I couldn't relax enough to fall into a deep sleep. I suffered chronic fatigue, body aches, and nausea. Every spring and fall I was treated for gastritis. I developed chronic back pain for no apparent reason.

My recall was triggered by an alleged act of medical malpractice committed against a member of my family. At night I awoke feeling as if I were being suffocated. A voice inside of me kept asking, "Isn't this ever going to end?" My anxiety escalated. In my child's classroom, I hyperventilated and had to be helped to my car. Upon recommendation from my therapist, I joined a support group specifically for adult survivors of sexual abuse. Within weeks, I was flooded with memories.

I invited my mother into therapy for a reality check. I had unearthed a few relics from childhood. I knew I was orgasmic in kindergarten, and had masturbated compulsively. I retained a memory of going to a doctor for a "urethra" problem regularly, albeit I could never remember my parents discussing this with me. Finally I remembered a woman with black hair giving me a pill, "to make that funny feeling [sexual arousal] go away."

Mom said that she had never taken me to a doctor for a urethral problem, nor had she given me pills. Furthermore, I learned that at a preschool physical, my hymen was clipped. Mom was too shocked and embarrassed to tell anyone what the doctor had done.

A week later I had a vivid flashback of being penetrated with a wooden wand while lying restrained upon a table in the school medical office. My therapist advised my mother and me to make a return appointment. Subsequently I underwent age regression hypnosis and recovered the memory of a satanic ritual. For the next two years, the memories of being ritually abused returned spontaneously.

This was not a group of people dabbling in the occult, but an established cult that employed torture, programming, along with animal and human sacrifice. Besides being taken to the school medical office for rituals, I was taken out of the school to the doctor's home, to the local mortuary, or to the local cemetery. And yes, they dug up bodies and dismembered them. The cemetery was in a wooded area outside of town. A member of the local police was involved. The town was infested.

Cults feed children visions for which they have no words. I became mute. One night at 2:00 a.m., I shot up in bed, praying, fearing I was near death. I was in the middle of a flashback. One of my teachers had my coat. (Our class was co-taught.) We were going to the cemetery again. The next day I wrote a poem about the mock burial ritual. I was stripped naked, smeared with excrement, and put in a box with bugs. Over me cult members chanted to satan (the anti-Christ). I chanted to survive.

Mock Burial

The bloated wind sucks the blood from the
corpses that refuse to move, frozen in the ground.

It is winter. I see the vault, golden
in the little brick building.
They are going to bury me above ground in the
little brick building, at the end of the dirt road.

"Mama. Mama. Isn't anybody here?
Mama. Mama. Isn't anybody here?"

Hope dies in the stench of excrement
smeared until I can no longer breathe.
"God, where are you?"
My thin cheeks are sucked inward, to catch
what they will take from me.

The inner wall of terror stands tall.
Fearing the burial of the child inside, she crawls
into the casket. Fear Keeps You Alive,
clinging to terror. A metamorphosis occurs.
In a white cocoon, my spirit rises, my essence;
a fraction of light.

"Am I dead yet?"
Her heart flutters.
"If I give up the fluttering heart will I die?"

Chant!
"Jesus Christ, Son of God, heaven and earth are
filled with your glory.
Jesus Christ, Son of God, heaven and earth are
filled with your glory.
Oh God of Light I live in constant fear,
fear of death,
fear of death."
Like a black fly it bites and eats my flesh and I am
served on a platter before Christ. Before Christ?
Christ, how did you get into this?
Can you get me out?
Out of the box that contains my breath
Tucked deep inside?
They cannot kill me.
In terror I survived.

I emerge.
It's over.

"Good job, good job," they applaud.
But I am hollow, a porcelain doll, waxed in terror,
my lips painted shut with their secret
if I want to breathe.

GINA

In chapter 11, "Threats," a partial account of the plight of a woman trying to break away from a satanic cult in Oklahoma is given. This was a highly orga-nized cult that included "section homes" (a living complex in which all residents were cult members), breeders of infants for sacrifice (including this woman), and abuse so systematic and so heinous that it is best told by the woman herself.

I was born in Colorado. I had four parents and thought everybody had four parents until I got old enough to hear other kids talking about having only one mom and one dad. One of my families lived a more normal life than the other, although I now know it was, and still is, a very dysfunctional family. My other family was part of a satanic cult.

From the best I've been able to figure out, I was passed back and forth from one family to the other from the day I was born. At my birth (to the "more normal" mother), I was to given to the cult in return for a bad drug deal.

My earliest memory goes back to when I was six. I was at home alone with my father in the more normal family. My mother and two half-sisters (who I thought then were my full sisters) had gone somewhere. I had always been made to kiss both parents goodnight and my dad started putting his tongue in my mouth when I kissed him. On this night we were sitting in the living room and he called me to come get in his lap. I told him I didn't want to, but he told me I would get a spanking if I didn't. So I hung my head, walked over, and he pulled me up on his lap. He put his hand inside my panties and fingered me while he licked my ear. He picked me up and carried me down the hall, telling me it was time to learn about love. He would teach me. He sat me on his bed and pulled off my gown. Then he laid me back on the bed and took off my panties. He put a part of his body in between my legs and it hurt. He licked me, made me lick him, and then he touched me some more, which made me tingle. I didn't like it, but it also felt good. (I now know that a normal six-year-old would not have felt a sexual response like I did, which years later became a clue for me that I had been sexually abused in the cult—and maybe in this family too—since my infancy.)

That was the year I started to school. I hated going to school. I had never been anywhere without one set of parents or the other before. I learned how different I was. I seemed to be the only one who came to school with bruises. I didn't know how to play the games the others knew how to play. I didn't know how to talk to them. I didn't know how to make friends.

I remember one day when we were to give a report about our families in class. I stood up and told about my four parents. The kids laughed. Then the teacher took me outside and told me that I had only one mother and father. She asked if my parents were divorced. I didn't know what that meant, so I told her that all four of my parents got along and that I lived with all of them. The teacher called my parents (not the cult ones) and I got in a lot of trouble.

This family went to the Baptist church, and going to church was my happiest time. We put on a happy face there. At church, my mother gave me hugs, pats, or smiles. It was the only time she touched me without sexually hurt-ing me. She was a Sunday school teacher and missions leader. Later she became

Sunday school superintendent.

One day when I was eight and at school, three little girls were reading a book on the playground. I listened to them and liked the story. When we all came inside, we were to put up our things, go get a drink, and go to the restroom. I didn't go, but stayed in the classroom and stole the book. I kept it hidden at home until the next weekend. It would be years before I would understand the significance of the book.

On weekends and in the summer I lived with the cult. I had a little sister in my cult family, and I shared the book with her. I couldn't read very well, but I tried to tell it to her from what I had heard and from the pictures. The book was Cinderella. We loved it and hid it, getting it out whenever we were alone. It gave us hope that there would be a better life than we had. We certainly knew a lot of people like the wicked stepmother, and we began to believe that maybe some-day we would get a fairy godmother to help us live happily ever after.

In the cult, we lived in what was called a "section home." Section homes were large houses of fifteen to twenty families. Most were built way out in the country where they were difficult to find. The cult bought the land and built the houses themselves. They were large, with basements and attics and many people slept in one room. If strangers did come by, they didn't realize how many lived there. Each group had a cult bride and a cult leader. My cult parents were bride and leader when I was eight or nine.

I had no choices when I was at the section home. This included food. The food we ate in the section home was either half-raw or not cooked at all. We ate hamburger meat, eggs, and occasionally steak, which was bought at a store. The rest of the meat was raised at the section home—goat meat, chicken meat, horse meat, and cat meat. We ate snake meat. We fished and ate a lot of raw fish. Satanists believe that eating animal or human flesh gives them more power and dominion. Drinking blood is believed to do the same thing. Most of it made me sick. When I got sick, I got in trouble. If I was eating and had to go throw up, I still had to come back and finish what was on my plate. Sometimes when I knew I was going to throw up, I would hurry to gulp it down before I threw up so I wouldn't have to come back and finish.

I had no choice about who I slept with and no choice about participat-ing in rituals. I very seldom slept in the same bed, in the same room, or with the same persons. I usually began the night in a bed with other children. Later in the night I was sometimes taken to be with another set of children and we were forced to touch each other sexually. Other times I was taken to the bed of an adult or adults who sexually abused me, but they called it "touching." I had to touch them too. They put gels on me and licked it off and forced me to do the same. Sometimes they put objects in me. Sometimes they made me drink water until my bladder was full and then they made me urinate on them. If I ever cried or objected, I was hit in the face, punched in the stomach, or kicked. As I got older, they got rougher sexually. When I cried they called me a baby and told me that I was never going to be a lady if I couldn't handle it.

One day my cult sister and I were playing and our mother called me out to "touch" me. When she was finished, she came for my sister. I told her I would go again to take it for my sister, but my mother wouldn't let me. She then took my sister out, who went kicking and screaming all the way. When they got her into my mother's room, my sister kicked her. Mother finished with her sexually and then ordered an axe to be brought in. She chopped off my sister's foot. A physician in the cult treated the foot because my mother didn't want her to bleed to death but to remember that she should never disobey. About a year later, my sister drowned because she fell out of a boat and couldn't swim. She had been born without one arm and now with no foot, she didn't have a chance.

There were rituals every Friday and Saturday night, as well as several during the week. They usually began with everyone wearing black robes, holding candles, and chanting. Chanting was talking in another language, which I couldn't understand. (I now know that, just as some Christians "speak in tongues" to get closer to God, they spoke in a satanic language to get closer to satan.) We sang songs, also in the strange language, and then they killed a goat as they shouted, "Hail Satan, Hail Satan, Hail the Beloved One." After that they would kill cats, dogs, or children. Some of the animals had been picked up off the street, but most had been raised at the section home. More often than not, the leader and two or three others then had sex with the bride while the others watched. The first one to make the bride bleed without using objects got to spend the rest of the night with her after licking the blood off. After that, the entire group got stoned and everybody had sex with everybody until they passed out or went to sleep.

Some women in the cult were breeders, whose primary job was to have children for sacrifice. They were kept pregnant all the time. Their infants were usually killed within two or three days of their birth.

The cult made a living by selling some of the babies (through attorneys), animals, and drugs. Some had real jobs. There were doctors, policemen, lawyers, salesmen, who left in the morning to go to work and then returned in the evening. Others lived in the community but participated in cult activities on the weekend. Many of the women prostituted and dealt drugs, and then turned the money over to the leader. If they kept money, stole money, or failed to pull off the expected drug deal in the process, they were "given" to the cheated person in exchange for the money or drugs. That was enough to keep most of us honest and determined to complete our jobs. Nothing happened to the men if they made bad deals, only to the women and children.

Leaders and brides changed every year. The new leader's first job was to put the spirit of satan into the bride through a sexually brutal ritual. If she survived, she was satan's bride on earth. If she died, she was satan's bride in hell. The leader trained other cult members, was responsible for the killings during rituals, and was generally in charge. The bride committed herself sexually to the leader and to anyone he ordered her to be sexual with, including other men, women, children, and animals. She was responsible for keeping the section home spotless, seeing that all the laundry was done, and that meals were prepared. This was a nonstop responsibility for twelve to fifteen families within one section home. It was impossible to stay on top of it all because of so many interruptions, such as sex with numerous partners every day as ordered by the leader. If the jobs weren't complete, however, she was beaten and then forced to finish the work, regardless of the hour when she finished.

My periods started at school one day when I was almost eleven, and it scared me. I had bled there many times before but only from being "touched." I was staying with my "somewhat normal" family during the week and no one had hurt me for several days. From that point on, I was kept pregnant much of the time. I only went to school off and on around pregnancies. The schools were told that we were moving, that I was sick, that there had been a death in the family, or any other excuse my parents could think of.

I had a miscarriage when I was eleven and then a birth at twelve. It was a little boy. He was born in the section home. I held him a few hours, but couldn't get him to stop crying. They told me how to breastfeed him. My mother showed me how. I fed him and then my mother told me to lay him on a table near the bed. She, my father, and the leader then sexually abused me. The baby started crying again. They handed him back to me and told me to nurse him again, but he wouldn't eat. I knew he was scared. They kept yelling at us and telling me to make him stop crying, but I couldn't. My father took him back to the table and told me to get up. He got a knife. He put the knife in my hand and then put his hand over mine. He made me stab my baby, then he cut off his penis. I don't know where they took him after that. Usually the sacrifices were chopped up and burned or buried in many places. They were careful to be sure no bodies were discovered.

The next year I had twins, and they were born in the section home too. The first one was a boy and he was born dead. The little girl was born alive and cried. My mother threw her up against the wall until she stopped crying.

After that it seemed like I had babies about every year. They were all sacrificed. The one I got to keep the longest was a little boy. I was forced to kill him when he was about three and a half. It was just before my twentieth birthday. I had spent the day back with the "somewhat normal" family. My mother and I argued because she wanted me to let her fondle him and I hadn't let her. I overheard her calling my cult mother and telling her that she wanted me punished when I returned to the section home. When I got there, my cult mother called me back to the dark room, beat me, and "touched" me. Then she took me to the slaughter room and made me fondle him and bite the end of his penis off. He was bleeding real bad and I was trying to get it stopped. She called the leader and another man, and they stripped me and chained me to the wall. She smeared his blood on me and made me hang there and watch until he bled to death.

My cult mother committed suicide shortly after that.

I can't write too much about my twenties, because I'm just now uncovering the memories. I do know I was designated "Johnny's woman" somewhere in my early twenties. He was several years older than I was and had been in the cult as long as I could remember. My fleeting memories of those years include alcohol and other drug abuse, prostitution, rituals, and every kind of abuse imaginable. My flashbacks include times both within the cult and with the "other" family. I fear that uncovering these memories will be excruciatingly painful.

I got married when I was twenty-nine. My selected husband was a drug dealer for the cult and operated around Oklahoma City. He probably didn't know he was dealing with a satanic cult. I married him because Johnny had made a bad drug deal with him and I was the payback. I didn't mind because I saw it as a possible way to get out. Maybe the cult thought I would draw him in, which would be good for their drug business. I became pregnant immediately and I am very proud to say that our child, a little girl, is still alive. Because she was fathered by someone outside the cult, they pretty much left her alone. Her death would be noted. She is now four years old.

The marriage was strange and short-lived. My new husband knew he got me through a drug deal, but he didn't realize that the cult was still very tied to me. He did know Johnny, and he knew that Johnny was a mean man. When he realized that Johnny still considered me his woman, he wanted no part of it. The cult had no intention of releasing me just because I had married someone outside. Shortly after my little girl was born, I became pregnant again, but with Johnny's child. I moved back into the cult with my daughter.

I suppose if my husband had known what my life was really like, he would have tried to get custody of our daughter. But he only knew bits and pieces, and he knew that his way of life would not please a judge either. He has been a good father though. He pays child support very faithfully and has visitation with our daughter one week a month. He has straightened his life out now and has remarried.

Johnny's baby was born, a little girl. I tried my best to protect both the girls and begged to take any abuse that had been selected for them. They seemed to have little interest in my one-year-old, but they constantly reminded me that the new baby was satan's child. They abused her often.

I knew then that I had to find some way to get out to save the girls' lives. I couldn't be sure they would leave my older daughter alone. It became more and more clear to me that the girls were all I had. I kept remembering the Cinderella book.

My growing commitment to escape was complicated by a very big hurdle, however. Johnny became leader and I became bride the Halloween after our baby was born in June 1988. It would be very difficult to escape under those circumstances. Those who managed to escape were always pursued until they were caught, even if it took years. They were then brought back and severely punished or killed. To escape during my year as bride would enrage Johnny no end. I knew they would plot to kill me as well as the girls. Yet, I knew it was our only hope because we were all doomed to an eternity of hell on earth if we didn't get away.

The memory of my bride ritual also motivated me to try to leave. I had suffered abuses of every kind, but nothing so brutal as that. I knew I didn't want my daughters to have to endure anything like it. During the day on that Halloween 1988, cult members chanted around me and poured oils over me. That night, a goat meat dinner was prepared, after which I had sex with the outgoing leader to break his reign. Then Johnny and I were brought into a room together. He and others wore black robes and held candles. I was stripped. They put me on a table and surrounded me. The previous leader was at my head with a candle. The others blew out their candles while his remained lit. Johnny then shouted, "Hail Satan, Hail Satan!" and the ritual began. He got on top of me. They called the spirit of satan into him, and injected my arm and my vagina with drugs. I kept going in and out of consciousness. He very painfully raped me, unlike any other sexual experience I have ever had. I can't imagine any way it could have caused that much pain except that the spirit of satan was really in him. After that, I heard a loud scream, raised my head up off the table, and saw a broom handle being rammed into my vagina. I returned to consciousness only from time to time. One time when I did, a man holding my hand said, "We've got to get her some help." Johnny responded, "No, she's satan's now. Whether she lives or dies is up to him."

I was taken somewhere for treatment, though, as I remember waking up in a room which looked like a hospital. Usually, all medical treatment was given by a physician in the section home, so I'm not sure to this day where I was. If it was a real hospital, I'd love to see my record, but chances are it has been destroyed. Cult doctors seem to have ways of getting into medical records of legitimate institutions when records need to be destroyed.

This awful experience further convinced me that the girls and I had to leave. I thought about stealing Johnny's billfold because he usually had a thousand or more dollars in it. I thought about leaving through a window either at night or during a ritual when I might not be detected. Every idea I came up with had pros and cons. It would not be easy and I knew that to do so would be to risk our lives.

I was sick of the killings. I was sick of all the screaming at night. I was sick of it all. Finally, another horrifying experience convinced me that I had no choice but to get out. After a ritual, the group was doing drugs and having sex with each other. A twenty-one-year-old man had been heavy into acid and heroin. He really tripped out, ran into the kitchen, grabbed a knife, and started shouting that he was an orange. He started "peeling" his left arm with the knife. As several of us tried to stop him, he slashed at us with the knife. We couldn't get close enough to him to try to restrain him. There was skin and blood everywhere. On this particular night, no medical people were in the section home. We thought (briefly) about calling an ambulance, but there was no way we could quickly conceal all the drugs, the sacrificed cat, and the blood. Several people were passed out naked on the floor, and we wouldn't be able to get them up, dressed, and coherent. So, he bled to death. His body was destroyed.

Three days later, on a Friday night in spring 1989, I left. A young woman in the cult had become something of a friend and we sometimes talked secretly about leaving. When I told her I was really going to try it, she said she was willing to help me, but too afraid to try to leave herself. I wonder why I was willing to trust her, but I did, and it turned out okay. She arranged to get a car for me, from whom I don't know. We both knew I would not return it. Late in the day of my planned escape, someone brought the car and parked it about an eighth of a mile down the road from the section house. My friend gave me the key. I packed and hid a few clothes for me and the girls.

I took over seven hundred dollars from Johnny's billfold while he was in the shower that night and we waited until everyone was stoned out after the ritual, probably around 3 A.M. I had put the girls to sleep in an upstairs room. A downstairs room had the fewest people in it—two women and a man—so my friend and I planned the escape through a window in that room. I went upstairs and was horrified to see that Johnny had gone to sleep in the room with the girls. I knew if they woke up and cried, we wouldn't make it. I carried my oldest daughter downstairs, my heart in my throat, crept into the room, stepped over the two people sleeping near the window, and handed her to my friend. She woke up a little as I passed her over, so I told her we were playing a game and she needed to be very quiet. I told her I would go to get Sissy and be right back. It worked.

I then went back upstairs for the baby. As my final defiant act toward Johnny, I noticed a blanket lying on the floor, folded it exactly the way he had always required me to, and laid it beside him. To me it said, "I got my babies. I got out, and you didn't stop me!" That felt great!

I carried the baby downstairs, stepped over the people, and crawled out the window with her. I rushed to the car and put her in it. She didn't wake up. Then I ran back to the house for my older daughter. As my friend handed her to me through the window, I thanked her, said good-bye, and wished her good luck.

Once in the car, I was both excited and scared. It was the first time I had ever left the section home alone. No one was ever allowed to leave alone for fear of their running away, not even brides and leaders. The car had been parked at the top of a hill so it could roll down the other side before I had to start it. It rolled perfectly when I took off the brake, then I started it and took off. It suddenly dawned on me that, while I had so carefully planned the escape, I didn't know where to go. I drove for several hours, then stopped at a motel about dawn.

Johnny had an apartment of his own where he stayed when he wasn't living in the section home. We both stayed there sometimes. Weekends, however, were always spent at the section home, and it was now Saturday. My friend took the apartment key I had given her, picked up the person who had gotten the car for me, and they retrieved some more of my things from the apartment and put them in storage before the weekend was over. One was the waterbed I had brought from my marriage. As we had arranged, I met my friend and her contact person who had gotten the car the following Monday in Shawnee, Oklahoma. They were to tell me where my things had been stored. That was the last time I ever saw them. Her friend must have been in the cult too or she would never have been allowed to leave with him. Maybe they wanted me to have a car they could find. I never did figure it out. But at least temporarily, it seemed that everything was okay.

After a week or so of traveling around, I was lonely and unsure of what to do, so I decided to re-establish contact with my "more normal" family. We visited them a couple of weeks and I then rented a low-income housing apartment in Madill. I got on food stamps and AFDC and felt some assurance that we would survive. I was naive. It wasn't long before I began getting obscene phone calls and notes left on my door saying things like, "I know where you are and I'm gonna get you." I couldn't figure out how they had found me, so I decided that the family had told them. I left again, less than a month after I had moved in and told no one.

I rented another apartment in Ardmore. The same thing happened there, but I had had no contact with my family. I guess the cult people simply followed me. (Looking back on it, I can see how they did it, because I stayed within a radius of a hundred miles or so from the section home. But I had no concept of geography or distance and assumed that I was far away from them.)

In early June 1989, I went back to Madill and rented a little house. I loved it! I cleaned it, painted it inside and out, shampooed the carpets, and felt that, for the first time in my life, I had something that was mine.

I started attending a little Assembly of God church with a friend I had met in the apartment complex in Ardmore. I hadn't told her about my past, but she could see I was pretty fragile, I guess, so she wanted me to go to church. It frightened me, especially the speaking in tongues, but it also seemed a little like the Baptist church I had spent some time in as a child with the "somewhat normal" family. I also figured out that if there was a God, I had better learn about him if I was ever going to be free of the satan stuff. It was a small church. People seemed to care about me, and I trusted them. They helped me get some things for my house and were there when I needed them.

It wasn't long, though, before the same old stuff started happening again —notes, phone calls, and eventually the puppy I had given my baby for her birthday was killed and put on our porch.

While out shopping one day, I ran into another woman from the cult. I wonder now if she had been following me, but then I thought it was a coincidence. She told me that she and her family had also escaped and that I needed to be careful because she had heard that the cult knew where I was. That, of course, was no surprise to me. She wanted my address and phone number, but I was reluctant to give them to her. I did, however, agree to meet her again.

We met a couple of times after that. She told me that she and her husband had a cabin in Colorado, and that, if I wanted, I and the girls could go there with them. She said they had set it up as a hideaway if they were discovered and that it had everything anyone would need, including a car. I told her I was living on very limited income, but she told me not to worry. They would help me out. So I began to plan to run again.

She bought airplane tickets for my daughter and me and took us to the airport early one morning. She told me her husband would pick us up at the Denver airport, which he did. He drove us up in the mountains outside Buena Vista to the cabin. It was a typical L-shaped log cabin with a swing on the front porch. It was immaculately clean and had two bedrooms. He told me they would check back with me in a few days and that I was welcome to use the food in the pantry, the washer and dryer, and the car in front. He gave me some money and showed me where other money was hidden in the cabinet. He hugged me, told me to be careful, and left around noon.

I fed the girls and realized I was both relieved and scared about being there. I felt safe, fortunate to have found someone to help me, and yet a little antsy about being in a place where I knew no one. But I blew that off and played with the girls. We took a little walk and enjoyed the rest of the day. The next day was much the same.

The second night I made a big pallet on the floor in front of the fireplace and the girls fell asleep, one in each of my arms. I felt warmth and love from them on both sides of me and I remember feeling a strong urge to cling to them. It was as if I wanted to hold onto those feelings...and to them...forever. I savored the fact that we were free at last and I trusted that all our days would be as good as this one had been.

The next morning we ate, took another walk, came back to the cabin, and took a bath since we had gotten a little sweaty. After lunch we played some more and my older daughter began to get fussy. She fell asleep in my arms, so I took her to one of the beds. The baby was playing happily but noisily, so I took her out on the porch so she wouldn't wake up her sister. It was misty, but not really raining, so I let her wander out into the front yard.

I was watching her from the porch as she toddled toward a big tree several feet from the path we had driven in on. I was thinking I would go get her when I heard tires screeching down the path. I jumped up because I had to look around the L-shaped wall of the cabin to see where the car was coming from. The car sped around the corner, jumped the ditch between the path and the yard, and hit the baby. She was pinned between the car and the tree.

I screamed as a man jumped out of the car, dropped a liquor bottle, and ran off into the woods. I froze, but came to my senses after a few seconds. I jumped off the porch and ran out to the tree. Blood was running out of my baby's mouth and oozing out of her ears and nose. Her eyes were open, so I thought that she was alive. I tried to push the car off of her but couldn't. Another car then sped up, stopped, and Johnny, the couple who had helped me get to Colorado, and another cult leader named Calvin got out of the car.

My "friend" took me back up on the porch and tried to calm me down while the men stayed out near the cars. I guess I was in too much shock to realize yet that I had been betrayed. Johnny got in the car and backed it off the baby. I was still screaming, begging them to try to save her.

Calvin then came up to the house and took me in the bedroom. He tore my clothes off, telling me to shut up, and saying over and over that it had been a long time. He raped me.

When he was finished, Johnny brought the baby into the room and kept trying to make her sit up on the bed. When she would fall over, he would hit her. Then he propped her up on a pillow, took his clothes off, and raped me. I continued to cry and begged him to stop and try to save the baby. I guess I still hadn't grasped that she was dead. While raping me, he would occasionally look over at the baby and say something like, "Your mother thought she was so clever, but she wasn't." At one point he picked her up, threw her on top of me, and said, "Does it look like she's okay?" He ordered me to nurse her, and of course she couldn't. He kept hitting me, telling me to put my "tit" in her mouth. When she wouldn't take it, he screamed at her and slapped her.

Then he took her bloody playclothes off and told me it had been all my fault that he had to kill her. He told me that she now truly belonged to satan. He put his finger in her blood, and licked it. Then he made me do it. He fondled her body and eventually raped her body too. I started screaming again, which woke up my other daughter. She was crying, but Johnny wouldn't let me go to her. I could hear the woman trying to calm her. Johnny went in there and told her to do something with that "damn kid." While he was gone, I looked at the baby and saw tears coming out of her eyes. I now know that's a normal part of head injury, but then it upset me so much. I though she was still crying silently. I heard the door slam, so I presume the woman took my daughter outside, so Johnny wouldn't hear her crying.

Johnny came back in, told me I was dirty and that the baby was dirty, so he made us go take a bath. The first thing I always wanted after a rape was to take a bath, so I was eager to. I wanted to get the baby clean too, even though I now knew she was dead. (I still have flashbacks of the blood in the tub nearly every time I take a bath. Therefore I usually shower.)

He stayed with us in the bathroom until I was finished and dressed, and then he started a burial ritual. He poured oils on her, chanted over her, made me carry her out behind the cabin and told me to start digging a hole. I was still crying and there was just no fight left in me. So I laid her down on the ground and started digging. Johnny told me he was going to bury us both. After a while, he got mad because I was crying too hard and was too overwhelmed to dig, so he slapped me, grabbed the shovel, and finished the hole. Then he pushed me down in it and threw the baby in on top of me. He shoveled dirt in on us. I tried to put my hand over my nose so I could breathe, but I was getting dirt in my mouth. He threw enough in to cover us but not enough to suffocate me. He was chanting, laughing, and saying again that I thought I was so clever, but that I would never be able to get away from him. He yelled at me to dig my way out of the hole. Somehow I managed to do so.

After I crawled out, he made me carry the baby back in the house and ordered me to take another bath with her. After that, Johnny, Calvin, the woman, and her husband all fondled me and raped me yet another time. I could once again hear my living child crying in the other room. A part of me wanted Johnny to go ahead and kill me, because I thought that was what they were going to do eventually anyhow. On the other hand, her cries made me want to live. The woman eventually went to get her and took her outside, as she had done before. I could still hear her crying for me, and the woman telling her I was okay. Johnny told the woman that, for the rest of the night, her job was to keep my daughter quiet.

They took us into the kitchen, and laid the baby on the table, and made me sit in a chair at the head of the table. Then Johnny ordered me to pick up a knife. He told me to stab the baby in the heart, and, while I did it, I was to tell her that it was my fault that she had been killed and that I was stupid for believing we would ever be safe. He reminded me again that he had told me he would kill her, and he had done it.

I told Johnny that I wouldn't do it, but he told me that he would kill me if I didn't. I didn't care. So I told him to go ahead. He backhanded me, knocked me out of the chair, grabbed the knife away from me, and stabbed her over and over again. He cut her heart out and praised satan for giving him the power to fulfill his mission. He took a bite of her heart and said that he would then be one forever with this child.

I went into hysterics again, so they shot me up with drugs. I don't remember what happened after that until the next morning.

They stayed for two more days and kept me in a room programming me that I was still satan's and that, even though I had tried to escape, I never would because I had been crucified as the bride of satan. I am not sure if they programmed me to forget what happened or if I was so traumatized that I split the memories off, but the memory of this has only come back in bits and pieces over the past two years.

By the third day, their food, alcohol, and drug supply were running low, so the men went into town. The woman stayed with me, so I was allowed to see my daughter again for the first time since the baby had been killed. I decided to try to talk to the woman a little bit. I wanted to know how she could do this to me. She said she had done nothing to me, but that I had done it to myself. She then shot up and tried to get me to. I refused, but she kept on until she eventually passed out. When she did, I grabbed my daughter, and ran to the car that had been parked there since my arrival.

Fortunately I remembered where the keys were. There was only one path out and I was afraid I would meet the men as they returned home. On the other hand, I quickly realized that it was our only chance of escape, and that they would probably eventually kill us if we stayed. Even if they caught us, it would be no worse than waiting for them to kill us in the cabin.

I drove as fast as I could toward Buena Vista and got off the path before they returned. I stopped at the first church I saw. My limited background in church had taught me that churches sometimes help people in need, and I thought maybe they would help us. I knew I couldn't tell the real story, so I told the minister that my mother was dying back in Oklahoma and that I needed to go but had no money. For some reason, he didn't check it out. He could probably see that I had been traumatized, as the tears were still flowing easily. He asked about my bruises, so I told him that my husband had beaten me up. I guess it was easy to see that we were truly in need, so he bought us tickets and took us to the airport. He gave me a little pocket change.

When we got back to the airport, we used the money to take a bus to Durant, and then a cab back to Madill. I was finally home and had to try to figure out how to get through the days. My little girl was terribly upset that we had left "Sissy" behind, and I didn't know what to tell her. At first I told her that she was with a friend, because that was all I could think of. But later I began to tell her that Sissy had gone away to another place where we couldn't go.

We weren't home more than a week until the notes and phone calls started up again, and yet another dead dog was left on our porch. Johnny found us, broke into the house, and nearly cut off my right breast with a knife. He said he wasn't going to kill me yet because he took so much pleasure in torturing me.

I knew I had to get help, but I had no idea where to go. I spent most of the time watching television and began to be aware of various 800 numbers that offered help. No matter if it was a number for rape, child abuse, spouse abuse, or any other kind of abuse, I realized I had been a victim of it. So I called several, telling each telephone counselor the portion of my life that fit their services. However, my own fear and distrust wouldn't allow me to be totally open. They wanted to know my address and I was afraid to tell them. They wondered why I hadn't called the police, but I knew if I told them all that had happened, they would be overwhelmed.

During this time, I also realized that I was missing gaps in time and now believe that I split off into multiple personalities for a while, or at least fragments of personalities. A police investigator evidently tapped my phone and tells me that I made calls to some 800 numbers which I don't remember. She also says I upset some of them by telling a very convincing story but not helping them find me. For any distress I caused any of those people during that time, I am truly sorry. I would never have intended to be a burden to anyone. Yet I know I was absolutely desperate.

One day on television, I saw the 800 number for Mothers Against Drunk Driving. It dawned on me that my baby had been killed by a man who was drunk and/or on drugs when he crashed his car into her. So I called MADD.

I spoke with a couple of phone counselors, who were attentive and concerned but sounded confused. I didn't want to tell them about my cult involvement, so I told them my baby had been killed near Fort Worth. The rest was pretty much the truth—that I had gone "there" to visit a friend, and while I was there, a drunk driver drove up into the yard and ran over my baby. I didn't know an address. Of course they checked with the Fort Worth Police Department and the Sheriff's Department for crime reports from July 11, the day she had been killed. No record. When they related this to me, I figured they would give up on me. I was pretty depressed and even suicidal by this time, so they referred me to their supervisor, Janice Lord.

She talked with me time and time again, always assuring me that I could call anytime day or night. Somehow I felt a connection with her and began to share a little more of my story. I was amazed that she seemed to believe me. I thoroughly assumed that she would think I was crazy and send the police to pick me up, but she didn't. However, as I told her more, I became frightened that she wasn't really from MADD, but was perhaps linked up with the cult herself. I had to find out.

I told her I wanted to meet her. She said that was fine, gave me directions for the drive to Texas, and told me to go to a particular motel where she would prepay for a room. I was to meet her at her office the following morning. Again, I was amazed. Why would anyone do that for me? Could I trust her, or was I being naive again? I didn't know, but, as I had felt so many times before, I had nothing to lose. I took my daughter to stay with one of the ladies from the Assembly of God church, and headed for Texas.

The next two years of my physical, emotional, mental, and spiritual healing would take another book to write. Janice Lord's husband turned out to be a minister and she was a professional counselor. They insisted that they could help me get away. Familiar story. I loved my little house in Madill, but didn't love what seemed to be never-ending trauma. Again, it seemed I had no other choice, so I agreed to let them help me move.

Janice's husband, Dick, and a young woman who worked with her at MADD and her husband came to Madill to move us. My daughter and I stayed in the battered women's shelter until I could get on low-income housing. During this time, I met with Janice or her colleague from her work almost daily. I eventually got an apartment, but sure enough, I had been followed again and was raped and assaulted one night as I carried out my trash. I didn't know the man who did it, but he said he had been sent by Johnny. After leaving the hospital that night, I stayed with the Lords. They and their daughter became my new family and they still are.

The past two years have not been easy, but for the first time I've been able to see first-hand what a Christian home is like. I was astounded that Dick never hurt his wife or daughter. I had never known anyone with patience and love to give like Janice had for me. I had never experienced the joy of having a sister who stood with me no matter what. Women who work at MADD with Janice have helped me and prayed for me. I now have a new grandma, a woman my "mom" (Janice) had known a long time through her work.

Her children were murdered in Indiana about twelve years ago (it was not cult-related—or at least they don't think so), so she has no children now and is very willing to have me as a granddaughter. Some very wonderful women in our church have worked as a team with Janice to take care of me and my daughter. A Sunday night Bible study group prays for us regularly. Only a few people in the church have rejected me.

Janice and Dick continue to learn all they can about satanic ritualistic abuse and multiple personality disorder. Janice has functioned both as my "mom" and my therapist, which must have been incredibly tough at times. I know it was—and is. She has stayed up hours with me as I struggled with memories and re- enactments during the long nights. Then she gets up and goes to work, where she has a very important and sometimes draining job.

Dick and Janice have also worked with me spiritually. While Dick is my "dad," he is also my pastor. He's a wonderful preacher and walks what he talks. When Janice realized I was demon-possessed (that's another book all on its own), she got guidance from an Episcopal priest and deacon who were experienced in exorcism work. They did the first deliverance on me, along with Janice, Dick, and Janice's colleague from work. "Mom" has continued the exorcism of many demons since then. She had never done anything like that before—or even believed in it—but quickly learned.

Although Dick said one time that he felt like his job was somewhat like Joseph's (biblical)—leading the donkey—he has played a very big part in my recovery. Most important, he has supported "Mom" every minute. He knew my fear and distrust of men, so gave me plenty of space until I could open up to him. Through these past two years, he has kept my car running, and within the past few months helped me get my own apartment and a new car. He gave me lots of encouragement to go to beauty school to become a manicurist. He bought me a beautiful purse and perfume for Christmas all on his own. After my last assault, he brought "Mom" a dozen roses and a bouquet of pretty flowers for me. He bought a flowering tree and a marker so we could have a memorial place at the church for my baby. I have no idea how much money this family has spent on me, but it's been a lot.

I wish I could tell you that the Cinderella story came true, but it hasn't, and I guess it never totally will. Johnny, or someone he sends, continues to track me down. Phone calls and notes continue, but now the police department has the notes and recordings of the phone calls. We report every assault. As a matter of fact, there's a wonderful young policewoman on the force who will come when I need her day or night. More than any other police officer, she has treated me with dignity and respect. She has allowed me hours to tell what happened and arranged to take photos herself because the usual police photographers are male.

Every month or so, just when I let my defenses down a little bit, Johnny or someone he sends gets me again. They apparently follow me when I'm alone. They've used many tactics, but the most recent is typical. I had just moved into my own apartment and went into a Homefront store to pick up a few things for it. A young woman was in the store carrying a baby and seemed to be near where I was much of the time, but I paid little attention. When I moved to the check-out stand, she came behind me with a large purchase, some pillows, I think. She asked if I would mind waiting on her and helping her to her car with the big bag and the baby. I told her I was happy to, so we walked to her car, which was out near the street of the large parking lot. A van was parked next to her car, and after she got in and I handed her bag to her, the van door slid open, two men grabbed me, and pulled me in before I knew what was going on. One of them paid her, and she left. I don't know where they took me, but I was assaulted again, severely beaten on the head with num-chucks (a bar with steel balls on strings on each end). I was diagnosed with a head injury and stayed in the hospital overnight. I had short-term memory loss for a while, but am better now.

Most of the attacks have also included vaginal and anal rapes, and sometimes branding with a branding iron. Last Easter, they branded my stomach with the symbol of a traitor—an upside-down cross in a broken circle. I'm still in and out of emergency rooms and have constant headaches from concussions.

These people know what they're doing. They make sure there are no witnesses, they use gloves, they use different vehicles every time, and they send different people to do the jobs. I am always told that Johnny is taking great delight in this torture and probably won't actually kill me for a long time. The good part of this story, though, is that, as my therapy has "worked" and as my spiritual life as a Christian has grown, I believe that I am somehow protected. I know I have guardian angels, and I know the cult will not destroy me. Too many people know about us and have cared about us during the past two years for our absence to go unnoticed. My new family has never been touched, nor has our church. I know that satanic cultists are very frightened of Christians and Christian churches. As a matter of fact, this is about the only thing they are afraid of.

I'm also more and more careful as time goes on. I can't tell you how I pray that they will eventually leave me alone, and sometimes I pretend I'm truly free. But I know I'm not, so I will probably have to spend the rest of my days having to be on guard. On the other hand, I am more free all the time. As I've worked on the memories, relived them, and gone through memory healing, they no longer have such an emotional hold on me. The Arlington Police Department is just waiting for the right time to intervene.

I've found some wonderful friends, who were also satanic abuse victims and found their way into our lives. We have a support group together once a week. And, most of all, I know that, no matter what happens, I will be victorious. I now understand that Jesus Christ died to pay for my sin—all of it. It took me a very long time to grasp that, and I'm not sure I still fully do. But I understand and accept enough of it to be assured that I and all my babies are heavenbound. That's not where Johnny is bound. He lives in hell on earth and he will live in hell eternally if he doesn't change his ways.

As I've grown, I'm now able to reach out to others. "Mom" and I have worked with several others during the past year who were ritualistically abused. Those of us in the support group help each other out when we're in trouble. One of them is in therapy, but "Mom" and I help with her spiritual issues. My mother from the "more normal" family is now trying to get away and I have minimal contact with her. She is getting counseling and spiritual help, and I think maybe I can have a relationship with her again in time. I have told her, though, that she hurt me and allowed others to hurt me too much for me to be able to forgive and forget. She will have to get into therapy and prove a lot of things to me before that can happen.

I believe with all my heart that recovery from ritualistic abuse has three parts: good therapy, spiritual work, and new families where people like me can learn how to live. I thank God every day for the life I have, for my daughter's life, for our new family, and for our future.

And I thank God that I found that Cinderella book because without it I might never have dreamed of another life. Please pray for others like me who have no one to pray for them.

I have used no names in this writing except for Johnny and Calvin, who I believe should be named because of their evil (although they change their names all the time), and Dick and Janice Lord, who should be named because of their good. They are open in their commitment to Christ and to other victims who may need them, and I have used their names with their permission.

Jo G.

This chapter is dedicated to all those who have helped me trust and to all the healers in my life, especially Annie, who, from the start of my journey, helped me to understand what being loved really means and helped return to me the gift of believing in myself.

Plea Bargain

I yearn to live
without fear of punishment
without the rush of red anger pushing through
or self-mutilation

I yearn to live
without scars that reveal
the me no one knows

I yearn to live
without running away from myself and others
because of the "us" they forced me to become

I yearn to live
without the memories of flesh—
dismembered—
of infants' innocence slaughtered
of darkness and deep woods
of fire and smoke

I yearn to live
without the programming of them
without the mockery of Christ

I yearn to live

Please

help me walk from darkness to
light

Do you hear my cry?

© Copyright Jo G. 1991. Used by permission.

All children ever want and need is to be loved. It is what I longed and hoped for as a child, but what I am today only beginning to understand.

For many years I could not discern truth from lies, for instilled in my brain was the reverse of everything that was true. Down was up, inside was outside, destruction of life was empowering, and God was nothing. Every one of my potential boundaries—physical, emotional and spiritual—had been crossed and invaded.

I had been incested and ritually abused by my uncle, cousin, aunt, mother, and multiple perpetrators whose names I cannot remember but whose faces which reflected the lustful power and evil within their hearts will remain forever etched in my mind. When my memories of incest began, they were first seen as if through a veil of fog. I could not discern all that was in the pictures that entered my head. But I never realized that those memories were only the beginning of the alarmingly clear portrait being painted of my descent into hell.

I can't see! Something is burning my eyes. I'm blind. No—something is covering my eyes. I struggled. I could hear only low humming, almost groaning noises being repeated. I wish they would stop. My ears feel as though they are going to burst. The noises kept getting louder. Where am I? Why can't I see? Please. I screamed. No, I couldn't look. I was too afraid. But I could still move. I tried moving my arms and legs. No, please. I was laid down on something cold and hard. The humming and groaning noises continued. Something was now being placed around both of my tiny wrists and pulled tightly. I knew my struggle was hopeless.

It is difficult for people to believe that evil exists in the world to the extent of torturing, harming, and killing the innocent in the name of satan. Clergy tend to think of Satan as a "spirit form" representing evil. Artists have given the world a stereotypical rendition of Satan that portrays him in a red suit with horns on his head, a pointed tail, and pitchfork in hand. This portrayal is naive compared with who Satan really is, for he takes on many forms. I have met Satan, and he is a real entity. He is more than a spirit form. He is more than the man in the red suit. He is the prince of deceit who attacks the young and those who feel powerless. He is a heinous entity. And he is alive.

I still couldn't see. Something heavy was placed on top of me now. I couldn't breathe very well. What was it? It didn't smell good either. I think I'm going to be sick. I started to scream but stopped. Suddenly there was a gentle hand comforting me and stroking my forehead over and over. I started to feel relieved. Someone will help me now, I thought. Now I will be safe. But I still couldn't breathe. The smell was so bad from the thing on top of me that I was starting to choke. Someone took the covering off my eyes. When I first tried to open them, everything was blurry. I was having a hard time opening them. It felt like my eyes were glued together. The person with the gentle hand kept stroking my brow saying, "You are pleasing to him. You are chosen." "Please help me," I said. Her voice was soft and gentle. She wiped my eyes, and I opened them widely. It felt good for them not to be burning, and I would finally be able to see. But as I opened them, I screamed. I finally saw what lay on top of me.

Recovery from Satanic ritual abuse takes many years. I never realized that fact when I started my path to recovery eight years ago. I only knew that all my life I believed that I was not meant to be in this world. I didn't belong. I had to be destroyed. I believed that I could vanish into nothingness, as if my ever being here would have made a difference.

Today I understand the origin of these programmed messages of destruction and nothingness. All survivors of Satanic ritual abuse have had their lives threatened at one time or have been programmed to suicide if they do not return to the cult or if they reveal information. Most of us have been afraid to talk. To reveal anything about the cult is to die, or worse, to be tortured to death. Because death never comes quickly to a betrayer of Satan and his followers.

On top of me was a boy—a dead body of a child. I think it was a boy, but the skin was sloughing off so I couldn't tell. I don't know how long he had been dead. He was black in parts. He smelled bad—like when you accidentally burn your hair or you leave something around that spoils. I tried to move, but my hands and feet were still tied. I could see the woman who had been stroking my forehead and who had spoken to me gently. Her face was extremely beautiful. But I saw that she had on a black hood trimmed in red. She had bright, dark red lips. Again I said to her, "Please help me." But now she started laughing and her beautiful face became hideous. Then she started humming that low sounding noise with the other people. I couldn't see all of their faces clearly. They were in a circle around me. The humming and groaning kept getting faster and faster, louder and louder. I still couldn't breathe. I wanted the dead body off of me so that I could breathe. I tried to start moving again. Just when I did, the little boy's arm fell off.

Cult ritual abuse always involves promised empowerment to individual cult members if they carry out specific acts—usually torture in the name of Satan—on the victim(s). The victims are often animals, but for various solstices and Good Friday, human sacrifices to Satan are absolutely required. The promised power is "specialness to Satan" and increased ability to summon demons.

For a child forced into acts of perpetration and death, there is no hope, only despair. There seems no way out of the cult, only death by destruction or torture. It is often—as it was for me and other survivors—a choice of continuing as ordered to choose the next child to be killed or to yourself become the next victim of Satan's slaughter.

Constantly programmed into believing that your soul and life belong to king Satan makes it difficult as a survivor to make any decision about spirituality. Christianity is undermined totally by Satanists. For me, spirituality became one of the most frightening issues to confront as a survivor. Yet, ironically its confrontation and resolution became one of the greatest sources of my healing. I have chosen Christianity as my belief system, because it is what *I believe to be true!* No one forced me, brainwashed me, or programmed me. Today, I believe that the hope for healing takes place when a survivor decides to resolve spiritual issues from ritual abuse, *not when someone else decides what their spirituality should be.*

A huge man in a hooded white satin robe came forward and got up on the table where I was tied. They finally took the boy's body off of me. The woman who stroked my brow looked at me as the body was removed and said, "We never want you to forget who you belong to." The man straddled his legs over me, pulled out something, and put it in my mouth. It was hard. He kept jamming it in my mouth while everyone else kept humming, and groaning louder and louder. At the same time he wiped some stuff on me that smelled putrid. I felt sick again. I couldn't see his face. I started to look around the room. I could not move my head, but I turned my eyes to the side. It was dark, but there was a reflection of flickering lights on the wall, which outlined the figures of the people around me. As I looked through the occasionally opened spaces between the people moving faster and faster around me, I could see that there were birds and animals hanging on the wall. There was also the outline of an inverted cross. I started to choke. I looked at him. He took the hard thing out of my mouth. I still hadn't seen his face.

The incest had begun at age less than one year. I was brought to the cult when I was about age two or three. My father worked night shift much of the time. My uncle, involved heavily in the cult, would pick up my mother and me late at night. At first, I was too sleepy from the drugs my mother forced me to take to care where we were going in the car. But after I realized what awaited me, I welcomed the drugs to blacken out the horror that I knew was inevitable each time my uncle drove to that place.

The huge man now stood at my feet. Two people in dark robes stood on either side of my head. They untied my hands, and forced me to sit up so quickly that I felt dizzy. Then the woman who stroked my brow came forward, and said to me, "Look to the one who has chosen you as his own. Look to him who has anointed you into his kingdom forever." She lifted my chin up and charged me to look at the huge man at the end of the table. I didn't want to look. I tried to keep my eyes closed, but the people in the robes forced them open. Then I saw his face. It was my uncle. But then it suddenly changed into my aunt's face and then my mother's. He never spoke. Only a guttural, gasping, hissing groan came forth from his mouth. The face began to melt, and where there were once eyes, two demon spirits came out with screeching sounds. Each was translucent. One was green with a lizard-like appearance, the other black with a small body but the large head of a snake. When it opened its mouth, blood came forth. Satan commanded them to enter me, and then he was gone. At that moment, I felt a searing pain in my chest. It is all that I remember of that evening with Satan.

I have struggled in my recovery to deprogram the many years of brainwashing instilled in my head that to tell means death, to remain silent means staying alive. I have lived, only through God's grace, through torture both then and in the present flashbacks which brought the feelings and facts of yesterday into today's reality.

I have struggled through multiple suicide attempts. I believed that the pain buried from the past, but which had resurfaced, would never end, and so I wanted to end the pain. When I cut myself and saw the blood flowing, there was a feeling of relief. As I placed the plastic sheeting over my head and tied it around my neck, I felt a sense of place and of peace. But today I am beginning to understand what true peace is and what my true place is among the living.

The fear that once enveloped me as a victim of Satanic ritual abuse has been dissipated. Through the many years of self-mutilation and struggling to stay alive, to learn the truth, and to finally become fully human, fully a survivor, I have learned that there is hope. And I know that God—Whom I could not previously acknowledge as a part of my healing—gives us His light to illuminate and guide us on the road ahead, not the path behind. When I look back on my path of recovery, I cannot see the steps where the journey began.

There are many kinds of survivors. Although common threads weave together the fabric of survivors, each has a unique spirit. Survivors of Satanic ritual abuse experienced during childhood have emerged nationally from their bed of silence—often at risk to their own lives.

I have decided that the hope for my healing lies not in my silence but in my speaking out. For if I remain silent today, it allows those who controlled me in my past to thrive. If I remain silent, it allows them to continue to target innocent children and to build Satan's army. If I do not speak, it allows Satan to win the battle. My silence today means death and destruction of myself.

But most importantly, I choose to no longer remain silent for others, those who have died at the hands of torture, and those who have died at their own hands believing that there is no hope. I choose to no longer remain silent so that others may know and believe that they are not alone, that if they were strong enough and courageous enough to survive the abuse, they can survive the healing, and that through our mutual brokenness, we can be made whole through bringing hope and healing to others.

DAN

Dan is what's considered a "high functioning" satanic ritual abuse survivor. He's owned lucrative businesses, raised a family, and has been actively involved in civic and church activities.

However, all his life there's been another side to Dan, the one plagued by inexplicable fears, inexplicable episodes of manic and depressive states, and inexplicable blanks in his memory. That is, this was all inexplicable until he got into therapy and Twelve Step recovery several years ago and started winding his way back into his past. Ultimately, all the way back to a secluded basement of a small-town bar in the Midwest where some of the most heinous things imaginable went on.

As I sit to write my story, a flood of painful feelings overwhelms me. Scary as it seems, my recovery has taught me to embrace this pain, since it is part of me and through it I am made whole.

The feeling of fear is more manageable and diminished now at age fifty-four than at any time since age four, when I experienced the first of many abuses that were either done to me or that I watched in unbelieving horror as they were done to someone else. This particular experience at age four was a gang rape and a bloody beating that may have left the girl dead.

Fear is even an old friend, who helps me integrate my feelings rather than be the enemy who drove me to twenty years of psychiatric and psychological treatment, as well as being sentenced to taking medication for the rest of my life to maintain some semblance of normalcy. As I was told over and over again by doctors and therapists, I should get used to taking the medication, as I would need it for the rest of my life.

But, at last my life makes sense rather than making me feel crazy, depressed, and permanently defective. I understand myself and can accept myself more each day. I have more and more days of joy, peace, and serenity. No longer do I fear God and how He will see me as unworthy, therefore dealing me lots of earned emotional pain and failure in every aspect of my life.

I am the oldest of three sons born to an upper-middle-class family. We lived on a gentleman's farm with animals to care for, a beautiful southern colonial home set a half mile off the road, a swimming pool, and what appeared to the world as the ideal family. My father, the perpetrator of my abuse, was extremely handsome and headed a small business that has been owned by our family for five generations. My mother was unbelievably beautiful, a homemaker, artist, and active in various women's organizations—all in spite of increasing bouts with paranoid schizophrenia.

As a child, I was always an adult. Experiencing the degree of abuse I did—and having to caretake my mother, as her surrogate husband, as well as my brothers during the "craziness" we lived in—left little carefree play time. As I grew up, I became a people-pleaser and caretaker for everyone, since I didn't think I would be wanted for just myself.

I was seemingly popular and socially very active. But I never felt good about myself or that I belonged anywhere I went. I felt that somehow I was defective. I had a lot of body shame and could not join in sports or normal adolescent male activities.

Dating was okay, since I felt more comfortable with women than with men—less threatened somehow. I was very reserved around girls and had, by the time I graduated from college, only one serious relationship. All other relationships amounted to three or four dates at the most, before I found a "good reason" to date someone else.

Fear of everything was my constant companion and created unbelievable pain. It mostly centered around my own feelings of inadequacy—I was less than everyone and everything else. I was sure others would find out about me, since I had a whole string of imagined flaws that would drive them away and somehow destroy me.

While in graduate school, I had terrible bouts with manic depression and sought psychiatric help. After two years of weekly therapy and constant medication, I still had frozen feelings—only good, bad, and okay. I couldn't distinguish feelings such as love, hate, anger, or joy. My therapist decided to give me truth serum treatments to unlock the reason for my frozen feelings.

While the prognosis for this type of treatment is mixed, it "blew my feeling jets," unlocked some disjointed forgotten horrors of my childhood, and over the course of a few weeks I became "normal."

For three months after the treatment, the memories continued to be released to me and became so bizarre that I could not handle them. In a few minutes one day, my subconscious rescued me from a morass of pain and fear and reclaimed my secrets. It would not release them again for another twenty-five years. The normalcy began to decline rapidly after two or three years, and five years afterward I was emotionally ill again.

[The memories were abbreviated flashes to things like standing naked with his father as a young boy in the shower and feeling extreme panic, to flashes of blood, to sounds of people chanting, to what seemed like sex orgies.]

During my "normal" period, I married. We ultimately had four children and I became very successful in my work. Most of my existence was an act; I wore a mask at all times. I couldn't let anyone know the real me since I would be "found out" and would be abandoned by everyone. I had no redeeming qualities, I thought.

As with my family of origin, I had the perfect family for the world to see. But something was wrong—dreadfully wrong. My relationship with my wife was abusive of me as I slipped more deeply into my people-pleaser/caretaker role. I didn't trust my wife, with some justification, or anyone else for that matter. Gradually I slipped further and further into depression, feeling defective and filled with fear.

The only thing that held me together was my relationship with God. I felt his hand on and in my life always, for some strange reason. This, in spite of all my fears of his wrath and retribution. There was a faith and relationship with God that had always been there. I could not understand the tie—there was something more to it than I could fathom, but what? It seemed to defy reason and everything I knew.

In spite of this, my addictive personality carried me rapidly into all sorts of ways to kill the horrible, unexplainable pain I was feeling. Working night and day to get ahead, I began to drink more and more. Drinking led to drugs, and drugs led to sexual escapades. Soon I had a second personality—I couldn't understand where it came from. How did I know to do those things, go to those places, and be with those people? By day I was an Eagle Scout, perfect husband, perfect father, regular churchgoer, and perfect community leader. But, at night, after a few drinks, I was someone I didn't know.

I had sought therapy again, another fifteen years of it, but nothing helped, not hypnotherapy, not group therapy, not any kind of therapy. Nor did any of the prescription drugs help permanently—and I had them all. The therapists all said I needed medication for the rest of my life. None of it could get me to feel! I was back where I started, only with a whole host of active addictions dragging along with me.

I hated the medication because it was a tangible sign that I was defective—crazy. I felt that I was never to overcome my bleak situation. It was hopeless. I resigned myself to that fact. I was permanently flawed!

And then my fake life began to fall apart. The company was sold, and I lost my job. I had achieved a good measure of financial success, but several bad investments and a bad economy at the wrong time wiped out almost all of my wealth. The blow was staggering. I had told myself that I couldn't be too defective because of my job status and wealth, and now it was all gone. And on top of it all, I realized my family situation gave me no peace or solace. There was nowhere to go with my pain but to fall back increasingly on my addictions.

Fortunately, I started my own business and, after a few hard years, was able to begin re-establishing my financial strength.

By December 1988, I was a disaster—and so was my life. My marriage was falling apart, my finances were destroyed again, my emotional pain was beyond belief, and I was barely able to function part-time with constant therapy and medication. I was fifty-two years old and saw no way out of my messy life.

I was now drunk two to five nights a week. After my family went to sleep, I stole out of the house and sought relief in alcohol, drugs, and sex. I suffered blackouts and often when I came out of it at 4:00 or 5:00 a.m., I had little or no recollection of where I had been or, worse, what I had done. The brief wisps of memories I did have filled me with horror and shame.

In my pain, I picked up Melody Beattie's book *Codependent No More*, which my therapist had given me. For the first time in my life, I read about myself. The relief was beyond description. I cried. I wasn't alone for the first time in my life. Maybe if I could learn about the codependent stuff, I'd be better.

My therapist switched my therapy to learning about codependency, got me into a codependency therapy group, and helped me find two Codependents Anonymous (CODA) groups. I met people just like me from all different life situations and ages.

Gradually, as I met the people from the meetings for coffee afterward, I began to trust them enough to share my story, such as I knew it, and all of the pain in my life. I became more comfortable with myself and felt better generally.

But then a strange phenomenon began to happen as I grew more relaxed with myself. I was sleeping less and less. I would awaken more often at night. Finally, I was sleeping only fifteen to thirty minutes at a time. I became aware of being wide awake and angry when I awoke, ten to fifteen times a night. Having seen anger work done in a group therapy setting, I decided to go to the recreation room in the middle of the night and beat on the sofa. This allowed me to dissipate most of the anger and to finally fall asleep.

Gradually words of anger and hate began to come out of my mouth in these sessions. I screamed them into the sofa, "Don't touch me! I hate you! Get away from me you filthy_____!" I had no idea where they were coming from or what they meant.

Then I began having a vision of my hands in a certain position before my face. This vision persisted, and finally one afternoon, while alone in the house, I put my hands up before my face as I saw them in my mind's eye. It was as if I had been hit on the head with a sledgehammer. I knew instantly that I had been severely sexually abused—and had no conscious memory of it till then, I thought. I fell to the floor, sobbing uncontrollably.

The few sketchy memories that I experienced had no logic and were too painful at first to think about. Gradually I was able to recall many memories in a logical order and progression. *[As an example, the scene with him and his father in the shower came back again. Later he remembered being forced to have oral sex with the father, and later yet he remembered being forced into anal intercourse.]*

The memories would cause a new experience in my life— spontaneous age regression that was almost impossible for me to control at first. My body seemed to have a mind of its own: I would shake; my muscles would spasm uncontrollably; I would fall on the floor or sofa drawn up in a fetal position; I couldn't talk at times—with only air being forced out of my mouth; I would experience various other scary exhibitions that I couldn't control. The more I tried to get control of myself, the less I could. It took one and a half years of therapy and hard work to learn to walk through the pain of the sexual abuse. It was nothing short of hell on earth. I wanted to avoid these physical manifestations like the plague, but my therapist encouraged and sometimes pushed me into reliving each experience, each secret, until it lost its power to control me in the "here and now."

Most important, particularly during the first month, was to have safe people I could go to when I became overwhelmed and scared—unbelievably scared. My best friend spent hours daily with me for the first three weeks. I could sob forever it seemed, spontaneously regress in age, draw up into a childish position and be unable to talk even though I tried. The love and patience he gave me was probably the greatest blessing in my recovery. A close second was my priest, who lives God's will in an unbelievable way. He would drop anything, often on no notice, to be there for me time and again. Without these two touchstones, I would have lost my mind, I think.

A Trap Door to Hell

A plummet into the bowels of hell; that is how I describe what happened to me on that Monday afternoon when I put my hands up before my face. An instant flash of a sexual encounter with my father in the shower when he used to bathe me was my first recollection. It turned my stomach and stunned me.

In a flash, I realized that all of my emotional agony, over forty-five years of it, was caused by being sexually abused. In some vague way, I knew there was more, much more to be remembered. It terrified me, and all I could think of was to run—run away from the sofa, only to collapse in a heap on the floor. I experienced my first of many spontaneous age regressions.

When I was finally able to control myself, I began pounding on the floor and crying uncontrollably for a long time. I then forced myself to deny what I had seen in my mind. And from that I later learned the extent we go to in order to deny painful truths.

I had a group meeting that evening with my therapist and afterward asked to see him alone. I started to tell him of my experience and suffered the second bout of spontaneous age regression. Unable to speak, I gasped for air and tried to force sound out. He finished my story. "You found that you were sexually abused as a child." How did he know? I regained my voice and protested. All he said was, "Look at you—I've suspected for a long time but wanted you to remember on your own."

With that I was washed with a wave of anger like I have never known. I began screaming in anger and pain and started to destroy his office. He put me in an arm lock to restrain me from hurting myself as well as his office. In his calming voice he spoke words of hope: "Now you will begin becoming free and being made whole in a way you have never known. You now have the key." I left his office in a stupor which was to be my state of existence for much of the next eight or nine months.

Sense out of Nonsense

"Whole in a way you have never known" was what he said, but that wasn't true. I had been whole after the truth serum treatments. I often had thought about that period in my life and how I had lost the feeling of wholeness, the ability to feel joy in a wonderful way, and most of all, the ability to feel all together, not apart from myself.

I couldn't remember what transpired during the actual treatments, so I attempted to figure out logically what had happened. Since my mother had mental problems and had kept me very close to her as I grew up, I thought that I had gotten rid of the poison of her mental problems, which she had dealt me. But in the back of my mind, I remembered dealing with my father and discussing him at great length with the psychiatrist after the treatments. It had never occurred to me that Dad was the main issue.

As I later was to learn, I was bonded to my perpetrator, and my mind would not accept the truth. This is a common phenomenon and was only revealed to me in a series of dreams later in my recovery.

With that door to a "quick fix" closed, I began in earnest my walk through hell. They say that the only way to get whole is to walk through the pain of remembering, and my recovery is a testimony to that.

All of my life, I remembered Uncle Jimmy coming one sunny afternoon to take me for an ice cream cone and my being terrified to go with him. My mother thought I was just being a difficult four-year-old and forced me to go with a man who had previously been one of my favorite people.

I also remember running away from home as a four- and five- year-old. I would get up before anyone and carry my clothes over to my grandmother's around the corner early in the morning to have her get me dressed. I then began running away during the day. After two different fences wouldn't hold me, they put a harness around me and tied me to the garage next to the dog. I can still remember running away with Popeye, my imaginary friend, who was strong and wouldn't let anyone hurt me. As my own children were growing up, I would often think of how I ran away and couldn't visualize them doing the same thing at ages four and five.

And now I know. The memories never came in a logical progression. I would get bits and pieces at a time. Sometimes they would come during a business meeting, sometimes while I was alone thinking about the abuse, and sometimes while I was talking to a friend or giving a talk to a Twelve Step group. The first memory came while I was alone. I had a memory of peering over the front seat of our car and seeing my father performing oral sex on a woman lying across the seat and my uncle Jimmy forcing her to perform oral sex on him. The recollection was devastating. I suffered a major age regression. It took days before I could look at the incident again and get another piece of the puzzle.

The second piece was a memory of riding in our car with my father and Uncle Jimmy on a sunny afternoon. I can still see the girl walking along the sidewalk and Uncle Jimmy trying to talk her into the car. She kept joking with him and acting very friendly. I thought it was a great game and yelled out the window too. My father grabbed my arm and told me to let Uncle Jimmy talk to the girl. Suddenly, my uncle opened the car door and scooped the giggling girl into the seat between him and Dad.

The next memory was of the girl sitting in the middle of the front seat and crying, "Just take me home, just take me home, please." My father was raging at her to shut up. He began to beat her. I hid on the floor of the back seat in terror.

It took several weeks for all the parts of this story to come into my mind. When I had it all, I saw my father beat the girl bloody and drag her body into the weeds of the field where we were parked. Before he did, he was in such a rage that he grabbed me from the back seat. As I remembered grabbing the seat belt (hey, what seat belt? There were no seat belts then)...I desperately clutched on to this word as evidence that I was making all this up. This kind of thinking would reoccur often; I would have things come back to my mind and my denial system was so well entrenched that I could barely force myself to accept truth. Later, as my therapist, Jim, age-regressed me to the incident, I recalled grabbing the hand strap that all cars had then and clinging for my life, as I thought I was in mortal danger.

In any event, my father pulled me clear of the car and began shouting to look at the cheap _____ . As I looked at her bloody body, I "checked out" [dissociated]. The sight was so horrible that I could not handle it; I went inside myself and couldn't see what was happening. Dad finally threw me on the girl and I somehow got into the back seat again. I think Uncle Jimmy put me there. Dad hurled her out of the car and they took off. They then began to talk about me and what I had seen and what I would do. They told me not to tell anyone, and I think they said they would kill me if I told. While I only think this was said as an idle threat, I took it seriously. And so, when Uncle Jimmy, who worked for my father, turned up on an afternoon when Dad was still at work, I thought they had decided to do just that.

It is funny how our minds work to protect us when we are in overload. For me, the first thing my mind would do was "check out"—in other words, I would just not be there. The second thing it would do is erase from my conscious memory all recollection of an incident. This forgetfulness was assured by two things—the threats of harm if I told and a bond that is created between me as the victim and the perpetrator of the abuse, a state I had no conscious control over.

And so I know why I was always trying to run away from home. The fear I felt was so overwhelming that I had only one thing to do as a four-year-old: run away from the pain. What a relief to understand another part of my life!

Many memories of abuse came back to me, usually of sexual abuse. They all unfolded in bits and pieces, and when I had enough of the story, I found so many parts of my life would make sense. It would explain a recurring memory I had all my life that made no sense but was disturbing for some unknown reason. Or it would explain some act or behavior that I couldn't explain.

A Premonition of Death

God had told me that I would be killed or die in some fashion in connection with a bridge. This I believed, to the point that whenever I went over, under, or near a bridge, I would wonder if this was the time. It would be worse at times. And if I got stopped on a high level bridge for some reason, it was all I could do to remain in the car and not throw open the door and run screaming off the bridge.

In addition, I would often see the face of satan in my mind as I was near a bridge. I would think about this face, but not be able to tie it to anything. It would make me shudder and I would force it out of my mind. The complete story behind this face would not be clear until much later in my recovery, but after this next recollection, I thought it was explained.

One afternoon I was grieving over the pain of my past and working on some of the anger that was always with me, when all of a sudden I felt a hand on my back. I jumped up from my seat and looked at the wall behind the chair I was sitting in. There was no one there. And stranger yet, I still felt the hand on my back. It wouldn't leave. A major age regression overtook me. As I was lying on the floor, the hand was still there. How did I know it was a hand? I couldn't fathom it. After a few hours, I seemed to get used to feeling it there and it left, only to return from time to time for no apparent reason.

A few days later I was in the city downtown area going to a business meeting. As I walked along the street, I suddenly felt as if I had a bad case of diarrhea that was running down my leg. I was filled with the expected shock and embarrassment and ran for the nearest restroom. The sensation was so vivid and so real that there was no way that the mess would not be visible to anyone looking at me from behind. I was dumbfounded to discover that I was completely dry—not a trace of mess. Having become somewhat accustomed to these episodes, I proceeded to my meeting, wondering what was coming next.

I didn't have to wonder long. Later that evening, I was alone in my home office and I had the same sensation again. I didn't have time to remember the afternoon's experience as I ran to the bathroom. Nothing again! As I stood in the bathroom, it all fell together—the hand on my back, the messy pants, satan, and the premonition of my death involving a bridge.

I was about seven years old and had been asked by my father to take a walk with him alone. I was excited to do this as he never paid any attention to me. As we walked a couple of miles from home into a field, I saw him. He was walking towards us and I remember his face and especially his eyes. All of my life I was to remember this face as the face of satan. I was terrified as I saw it the first time in that field. I tried to run, but Dad caught my arm and told me not to worry.

They took me under a nearby bridge and the man exposed himself. He asked me to perform oral sex on him. This was not in itself uncommon, but unlike other occasions, I was terrified and wouldn't comply. (By this time in my life I had been so badly abused that nothing of this nature was different than many, many other incidents.)

The man, however, became very angry and my father attempted to placate him by encouraging him to try to excite me first, which was the normal approach. To do this, they would rub my genitals and speak in loving, reassuring tones. All of this was to no avail on this occasion for some reason.

Finally, my father in total frustration for not being able to please this man, grabbed me around the waist, turned me around, bent me over and exposed my anus to the stranger. They proceeded to put some lubrication on me and the man had intercourse with me. During this, my father held my shirt up on my back with his hand, the hand that I felt from nowhere on my back forty-five years later. The diarrhea sensation was from afterwards when we were walking home. As I walked down the street, semen and the lubrication kept running out of my anus. I kept telling my dad about it but he didn't care and further, proceeded to get angry with me, telling me to forget it, there wasn't anything there. At this point I was numb.

As I said before, the magnitude of this memory was not to be totally understood by me until much later when more of my past came together. But what was clear was that I was terrified of the stranger and the experience, thinking for some reason that I was going to be killed. My only tie to life—to a feeling that I might not die—was my father's hand on my back, and I apparently concentrated so intensely on it that it had the power to give me one of the most startling body memories that I have had to date.

The good news was that after getting this memory back, I lost all fear of being near a bridge. For the first time in my adult life, I drove over and under bridges without fear or having to face the prospect of my impending death. It was exhilarating. I actually looked for bridges to drive over.

What Freedom! Bridge to the Truth Serum

As I gloried in the newfound freedom from fear of bridges, I would think of the phenomenon of the body memories. Again my therapist age-regressed me to free me of all the power of this secret. As I was remembering the hand on my back, I got a flash of a discussion I had had twenty-seven years before with the psychiatrist who performed the truth serum treatments on me. It had to do with the importance of my father's hand on my back during the sodomy. I remember him telling me that I had feared for my life and the only hope I had that I would survive was that my dad was there.

In my victim's mind, I thought of my father as my savior and that he wouldn't let anything happen to me. It never occurred to me on a feeling level that he had caused the abuse and put me in these dangerous situations. It also was the desperate attempt of a child to find love where there was none. It was a fantasy and a sad one at that.

With this revelation, however, the truth serum treatments began to fall into place. It would take many weeks to put it all together. But at last I understood why I had the nagging feeling that, even though I blamed Mother for my emotional illness, it had something to do with my father.

To this day, other than the discussion of the hand incident, the only recollection I have of the involvement of my father in the truth serum treatments is several sessions with the psychiatrist wherein he kept emphasizing that I didn't have to be like my father. Dad's life was his and mine was mine and I could be my own vision of a man. It was so very hard for me to get this idea on a gut level, but once I did, I was 99 percent free and whole. Unfortunately, recalling the discussions and the great effect it had on me did not bring the same response through simply remembering it. As with most abuse survivors, I keep going into my head to try to think things out logically. It rarely works. In the case of my getting well after talking about my father during the truth serum treatment, I only knew in my gut that this was the key issue— this was the part that had brought healing to me. I really always knew this on a feeling level but discounted it. Since I couldn't "logic it out"—remember all of the specifics that led in a logical progression toward healing—I didn't trust my instincts.

Trusting my instincts is another part of my healing that has paid dividends. Most abuse survivors have trouble knowing what a feeling is, let alone knowing what they feel about a particular matter. For instance, I was told by my father that I didn't have anything wrong with my backside as semen and lubrication were running out. This happened many times over and over again to me. In other words, I didn't see what I saw and I didn't feel what I felt. It doesn't take much of this for a child to learn to not trust their instincts or their feelings.

The final vivid memory I have of the truth serum treatments is my response to the psychiatrist's question about sexual relations I had with women. I remember covering my face with my hands and being filled with fear. He kept coaxing me to remove my hands from my face, but I wouldn't. I told him that I was afraid that I would see the face of my mother. I had seen this in an article somewhere and was afraid of having experienced it. It took a couple of sessions before I finally lifted a finger to peek. Why holding my hands over my face could keep me from remembering, I don't understand. But it did. When I lifted the finger to see, I told the therapist that I saw all the laughing faces. It took a few minutes for me to put it all together.

Actually, I had the memory return at age fifty-two of being abused at a sex orgy where my father had taken me. I recalled having to perform various sex acts with many women and ultimately have intercourse with them, such as a child of six seven or eight might. And I remember the women always were laughing about the situation, which I had interpreted as them laughing at me. It was a terrible experience for me. But as I struggled through the memory's pain in order to get it to lose its power over me, I recalled my experience in the truth serum treatments. This was further evidence that I had come across the truth of my background during the treatments.

Another part of the story I could remember is that the memories kept coming back more and more after the treatments. It nearly blew my mind, and I remember crying and crying. I tried to use denial and thought I was making them up or was making them worse than they really were. Denial would force them from my mind for a short time, but they would only return to haunt me later.

I also remember approaching my father one night as he was working alone in his home workshop. Crying uncontrollably, I told him, "I want you to know that I remember all those things from when I was little." His back had been to me and he turned around and looked at me for a few seconds. He seemed to be searching for a response and finally said, in a voice filled with disdain, "Oh grow up!" and turned back to his work.

Finally, as I said earlier, the memories that kept flooding back were more than I could handle. My subconscious reclaimed all the history of my abuse and I didn't have to deal with the pain any longer. I had retreated into denial and held on to my secret again. The consequences were devastating for my life.

A Child Alone

I had no one, nowhere to turn. I remember coming home with Dad after one of the escapades and standing in the landing to our back door. I can still "feel" seeing my mother in the kitchen. She was looking at me, not at my father, with this inquisitive expression that also said she knew something funny was going on. She asked if we had a good time. I remember drawing the conclusion right there that she knew but wouldn't help me. Why didn't she intervene? She had to know something strange was happening. I can still feel the sick feeling of loneliness. Where could I turn? I did the only things I knew how to do at the ages four through nine.

The first thing I was proficient at doing was checking out when the situation got too bizarre and/or fearful. I knew I did this, but didn't understand it until during a therapeutic session of age regression. As the situation I was experiencing in my memory got so horrible, I went inside myself and it all went blank. It felt like a trance state, but whatever it was, it protected me from overload. I was able to remain a functioning human being when I otherwise might have just gone crazy.

The second thing that I did was forget. Somehow, I made no conscious decision to achieve this. My subconscious simply took over and made a secret of my experiences. To this day it still holds experiences that are too horrible to remember. I now trust my subconscious to know best when to release its secrets. God is gentle, and I believe He has a plan for these matters in my life. All things work for good in this case. Time and again I have experienced this.

A major part of the healing process is to grieve over the lost childhood and horrible experiences I lived through. I can tap into the pain of my abuse almost instantly by remembering what it was like to be all alone. I had no one to turn to. There was nobody to help me. I muddled through as best I could. As I remember myself as a child and the pain, I often cry for long periods of time. The experience of grieving is so healing. When I get depressed or down in spirit, I often get by myself and think of being alone in this mess.

Writing this account started to become somewhat difficult for Dan as he approached writing about the specific satanic cult abuse memories. Instead of proceeding on his own, a mutual decision was reached to finish the story by switching to an interview.

About this time in recovery, Dan went to a week-long inpatient recovery treatment center in Ohio to deal with both abuse issues and spiritual issues. It was recommended there that he begin attending a Twelve Step incest group.

Shortly afterward, he began attending a men's Twelve Step incest group in Cleveland.

"All of a sudden there were people I could really talk to about all this," he said. "That was somewhat difficult to do [talk explicitly about the incest] in the CODA meetings."

As he continued with the incest meetings, more sexual abuse memories came. Then, oddly, the memories took on yet another dimension.

The first of these even more bizarre memories was Dan, as a young child, standing terrified in front of a man dressed in a black robe.

Through more age regression with his therapist, memories of a basement in a bar started to come, then memories of black curtains over the windows in this room.

Then, gradually, full memories of a string of satanic cult ceremonies came back.

In one, Dan remembered a young man of about nineteen being stabbed to death by several cult members. The victim was then laid on a makeshift altar, and Dan had to first watch the head being cut off, then the genitals, then, finally, the heart being cut out.

These were then placed on some sort of tray with a bowl of blood, and Dan was made to hold the tray as each cult member came by, dipping their fingers in the blood, then licking them. The rest of the blood was then poured over the boy's head.

By this point, Dan remembers people worked up into a sexual frenzy and going off into another room. One of the woman cult members was left with the boy and would occasionally stroke his head and tell him what a good job he had done.

"I know this sounds strange," Dan said in a perplexed, somber tone, "but I think this was the only type of what seemed like love I felt growing up. Can you imagine how hard it was for me to trust later in life?"

Another memory was of another ceremony in this basement room of the bar. A girl of about five was brought into the room. She appeared drugged. Her eyes were glazed. The cult members stripped her and put her on the makeshift altar. Dan recalls being about seven years old at the time.

They stripped him as well and began fondling his genitals until he had an erection. They then placed him on top of the girl and forced him to have intercourse with her.

"They kept chanting 'POWER POWER POWER' . . . as if they were trying to imbue me with some sort of sexual power—to use me later in some way, I guess," he said.

Then they took the girl into the other room and killed her.

Dan recounted these incidents with his hands shaking visibly and his breathing rapid and labored. As these memories were coming, Dan began attending a Twelve Step ritual abuse group that had recently started in Cleveland.

"When I started to hear the same types of stories, it really made me feel relieved. Relieved I wasn't crazy," Dan said.

As he felt the increased support of these group members, even more of the memories started to come. And what's more, he was able to reconcile more with his past.

For instance, during one of the Twelve Step ritual abuse groups, one of the other group members designed a kind of requiem ceremony for the victims who had been killed.

"This was extremely timely for me," said Dan. "Because I had this tremendous need inside to do something for those two people I had remembered, so far, being killed. I sobbed throughout the whole meeting and felt reconciled afterward."

As time went on, more memories came, more repressed feelings surfaced. Concurrently, other areas of Dan's life continued to change. His fear of authority, fear of rejection, and other similar fears were significantly diminishing. In addition, his periods of depression came less often, and when they did come, the level of intensity was nowhere near what it had been before.

At this time, Dan continues with the Twelve Step meetings and therapy. And while he feels that at some point he will finish with dredging up the feelings and the memories, he will be going to Twelve Step meetings and working the Program, one day at a time, the rest of his life.

The meetings and working the Steps will serve as emotional "maintenance" for him, and will also give him the opportunity to help other victims—just as others have been there to help him, he said.

Faith E. Donaldson

The following drawings were done in therapy by a child alter, Gigi, of Faith E. Donaldson, a ritual abuse survivor who speaks publicly on the subject.

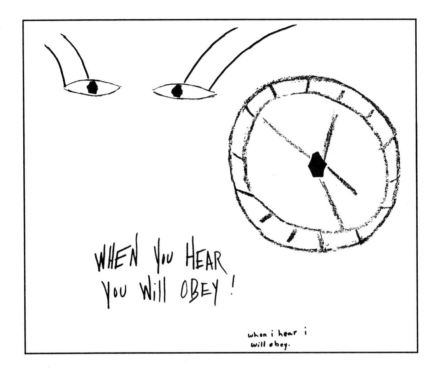

WHEN You HEAR You Will OBEY !

when i hear i will obey.

I began to tell a memory, and I couldn't speak. I was frozen with terror. In my head I could hear, "Don't speak. Do as I say. When I give you the message to die, you will obey." My therapist handed me some paper and this is what I drew. The high priest's voice saying, "When you hear, you will obey!" And the child's help-less reply, "when i hear i will obey." My drawing was a way of speaking, and two hours later, my memory was pouring out. I was the victor once again.

This was a large, ceremonial gathering. The naked woman was a high priestess. The high priest stood with me as we cut the still-warm heart from a recent human sacrifice into six pieces. We then each took a bite of the heart and drank the blood from the cup, representing communion in a Black Mass. I dissociated into a tree and sat calmly looking down at what my body was doing. This is why I drew this scene in this way.

A woman killed this infant in a ritual and then as part of the ceremony walked among the participants with the child placed on the sword, blood dripping down. The child was later dismembered and eaten by all. The infant was brought to the cult meeting by inducing premature labor in one of the women.

This was most likely the high priest, who re-enacted the demon and then raped me publicly . . . acknowledging his possession of me before everyone.

[This is] a Halloween memory when I, a nine-year-old child, encountered five demons that were summoned to participate in the night's ritual. I was painted, the death sign on my chest over my heart, inverted pentagrams on my knees to keep me from fleeing, and the red circle on my forehead to control the mind. The picture depicts one of the five demons I encountered that night.

The final fifth demon took me away. I literally remember my soul being pulled from my body. The high priest is telling me, "He will call!," knowing that when that happened, I would go. As I did. First into darkness, then into a terrifying place, where I encountered the fifth demon. As you can see by the tree, it is late fall, October 31.

My inner child drew this at a point when she felt safe from the evils of her past. This was years into my therapy, but it was the first sign of hope that the programming of my past was coming undone. The rainbow, God's promise, was now protecting me.

The Twelve Steps of Alcoholics Anonymous

1. We admitted we were powerless over alcohol—that our lives had become unmanageable.

2. Came to believe that a Power greater than ourselves could restore us to sanity.

3. Made a decision to turn our will and our lives over to the care of God, as we understood Him.

4. Made a searching and fearless moral inventory of ourselves.

5. Admitted to God, to ourselves, and to another human being the exact nature of our wrongs.

6. Were entirely ready to have God remove all these defects of character.

7. Humbly asked Him to remove our shortcomings.

8. Made a list of all persons we had harmed, and became willing to make amends to them all.

9. Made direct amends to such people wherever possible, except when to do so would injure them or others.

10. Continued to take personal inventory and when we were wrong, promptly admitted it.

11. Sought through prayer and meditation to improve our conscious contact with God, as we understood Him, praying only for knowledge of His will for us and the power to carry that out.

12. Having had a spiritual awakening as the result of these steps, we tried to carry this message to alcoholics, and to practice these principles in all our affairs.

The Twelve Traditions of Alcoholics Anonymous

1. Our common welfare should come first; personal recovery depends on AA unity.

2. For our group purpose there is but one ultimate authority—a loving God as He may express Himself in our group conscience. Our leaders are but trusted servants; they do not govern.

3. The only requirement for AA membership is a desire to stop drinking.

4. Each group should be autonomous except in matters affecting other groups of AA as a whole.

5. Each group has but one primary purpose—to carry its message to the alcoholic who still suffers.

6. An AA group ought never endorse, finance, or lend the AA name to any related facility or outside enterprise, lest problems of money, property and prestige divert us from our primary purpose.

7. Every AA group ought to be fully self-supporting, declining outside contributions.

8. Alcoholics Anonymous should remain forever non-professional, but our service centers may employ special workers.

9. AA, as such, ought never be organized; but we may create service boards or committees directly responsible to those they serve.

10. Alcoholics Anonymous has no opinion on outside issues; hence the AA name ought never be drawn into public controversy.

11. Our public relations policy is based on attraction rather than promotion; we need always maintain personal anonymity at the level of the press, radio and films.

12. Anonymity is the spiritual foundation of all our traditions, ever reminding us to place principles before personalties.

The Promises of Alcoholics Anonymous

We are going to know a new freedom and a new happiness.

We will not regret the past nor wish to shut the door on it.

We will comprehend the word serenity and we will know peace.

No matter how far down the scale we have gone, we will see how our experience can benefit others.

That feeling of uselessness and self-pity will disappear.

We will lose interest in selfish things and gain interest in our fellows.

Self-seeking will slip away.

Our whole attitude and outlook upon life will change.

Fear of people and of economic insecurity will leave us.

We will intuitively know how to handle situations which used to baffle us.

We will suddenly realize that God is doing for us what we could not do for ourselves.

Adapted and reprinted from *Alcoholics Anonymous,* AA's "Big Book." Copyright 1939, 1955, 1976 by Alcoholics Anonymous World Service, Inc. Third edition, 1976, pages 83 and 84. Used by permission.

The Twelve Steps
for Ritual Abuse Survivors

1. We admitted we were powerless over the effects of ritual abuse, that our lives had become unmanageable.

2. Came to believe that a power greater than ourselves could restore us to sanity.

3. Made a decision to turn our will and our lives over to the care of God as we understood Him.

4. Made a searching and fearless moral inventory of ourselves.

5. Admitted to God, to ourselves, and to another human being, the exact nature of our wrongs.

6. Were entirely ready to have God remove all these defects of character.

7. Humbly asked Him to remove our shortcomings.

8. Made a list of all the persons we had harmed and became willing to make amends to them all.

9. Made direct amends to such people wherever possible, except when to do so would injure them or others.

10. Continued to take personal inventory and when we were wrong, promptly admitted it.

11. Sought through prayer and meditation to improve our conscious contact with God as we understood Him, praying only for the knowledge of His will for us, and the power to carry that out.

12. Having had a spiritual awakening as a result of these steps, we tried to carry this message to other ritual abuse survivors, and to practice these principles in all our affairs.

Adapted from the Alcoholics Anonymous Twelve Steps and used by permission.

Since there is no unified Twelve Step ritual abuse movement as yet, the Twelve Traditions of AA will be used, changing the terminology as needed.

RESOURCES

Organizations

American Family Foundation
P.O. Box 2265
Bonita Springs, FL 33959
212/249-7693
(information packet, books, bibliography)

Beyond Survival Foundation
M. K. Gustinella, MS., MFCC., President
1278 Glenneyre No. 3
Laguna Beach, CA 92651

Beyond Survival Magazine
Craig Lockwood, Editor
P.O. Box 20063
Fountain Valley, CA 92728
714/563-6330
(articles for all areas of abuse, individual and group counseling)

Bob Larson Ministries
P.O. Box 360
Denver, CO 80236
303/985-HOPE
(crisis counseling, referrals)

Breaking Out
P.O. Box 6782
Salinas, CA 93912-6782
(information, crisis counseling, referrals)

CARA (Churches Against Ritual Abuse)
P.O. Box 584
Pasadena, CA 91102

CARAC (Committee Against Ritual Abuse of Children)
P.O. Box 74
Saskatoon, Saskatchewan
Canada S7K 3K1

Child Help U.S.A.
P.O. Box 630
Hollywood, CA 90028
800/422-4453
(for survivors and therapists)

CRCIA (California Ritual Crime Investigatators Association)
808 Alamo Dr., Suite 290
Vacaville, CA 95688
209/575-5550

Cult Awareness Network
2421 W. Pratt Blvd., Suite 1173
Chicago, IL 60645
312/267-7777

Cult Hotline/Crisis Clinic, Jewish Board of Family and Children's Services
120 W. 57th St.
New York, NY 10019
212/632-4640
(counseling)

FOCOS (Families of Crimes of Silence)
P.O. Box 2338
Canoga Park, CA 91306
805/298-8768

Healing Hearts Project
357 MacArthur Blvd.
Oakland, CA 94610
510/465-3890
(sponsored by Bay Area Women Against Rape)

International Cult Education Program
P.O. Box 1232
Gracie Station
New York, NY 10028
212/439-1550
(a resource list including general and law enforcement information, counselors and treatment, support groups, and research agencies)

Jewish Family Services of Los Angeles Cult Clinic
6505 Wilshire Blvd.
Los Angeles, CA 90048
213/852-1234

JUSTUS Unlimited
P.O. Box 1121
Parker, CO 80134
303/643-8698

MINNARA (Minnesota Awareness of Ritual Abuse)
Hennepin County Sexual Violence Center
1222 W. 31st St.
Minneapolis, MN 55408
612/348-4977

Monarch Resources
P.O. Box 1293
Torrance, CA 90505-0293
310/373-1958
(information, publications, counseling ritual abuse survivors)

Real Active Survivors
> P.O. Box 1894
> Canyon Country, CA 91386-0894
> 805/252-6437
> (offers multiple personality disorder workshops, anger workshops, retreats, a listening-line service, and consulting)

Survivor Newsletter (supported by the California Consortium Against Child Abuse)
> 3181 Mission St., No. 139
> San Francisco, CA 94110
> 415/334-5979
> (newsletter is devoted specifically to ritual abuse and recovery)

Task Force on Ritual Abuse, Los Angeles County Commission for Women
> 383 Hall of Administration
> 500 W. Temple St.
> Los Angeles, CA 90012
> 213/974-1455

Victims' Hotline (Texas)
> 713/779-7979

VOICES (Victims of Incest Can Emerge Survivors)
> P.O. Box 14309
> Chicago, IL 60614
> 312/327-1500
> (VOICES support groups all over the United States)

Warnke Ministries
> P.O. Box 472
> Burgin, KY 40310
> 800/345-0045
> (crisis counseling, referrals)

Treatment

The following are examples of centers currently set up to treat people reporting ritual abuse in their backgrounds. For other treatment resources that may be available in your part of the country, contact JUSTUS at 303/643-8698, Monarch Resources at 310/373-1958, or International Cult Education Program at 212/439-1550, or other resources listed.

Centennial Peaks Hospital Post-Traumatic Stress and Dissociative Disorders Center
2255 S. 88th St.
Louisville, CO 80027
303/673-9990

Center for the Treatment of Ritualistic Deviance
Hartgrove Hospital
520 N. Ridgeway Ave.
Chicago, IL 60624
312/722-3113
(adolescent inpatient treatment)

Child and Adolescent Service, Langley Porter Psychiatric Institute
University of California
401 Parnassus Ave.
San Francisco, CA 94143-0984
415/472-7231
(inpatient treatment for children)

College Hospital Dissociative Disorders Program
10802 College Pl.
Cerritos, CA 90701
310/924-9581

Columbine Psychiatric Center Dissociative Disorders Program
8565 S. Poplar Way
Littleton, CO 80126
303/470-9500

Cottonwood
P.O. Box 1270
Los Lunas, NM 87031
505/865-3345

Four Winds Hospital
Cross River Rd.
Katoneh, NY 10536
914/763-8151
(twenty-bed treatment unit)

The Meadows
P.O. Box 97
Wickenburg, AZ 85358
800/621-4062
(addictions, compulsions, and post-traumatic stress syndrome)

BIBLIOGRAPHY

Bass, Ellen, and Laura Davis. *The Courage to Heal.* New York: Harper and Row, 1988.

Bradshaw, John. *Healing the Shame that Binds You.* Deerfield Beach, Fla.: Health Communications, 1988.

Braun, B. G. *The Treatment of Multiple Personality Disorder.* Washington, D.C.: American Psychiatric Press, 1986.

Callaghan, Linda. *Inrage: Healing the Hidden Rage of Child Sexual Abuse.* Traverse City, Mich.: Neahtawanta Press, 1991.

Crewdson, John. *By Silence Betrayed: Sexual Abuse of Children in America.* Boston: Little, Brown and Co., 1988.

Detling, Lynda. *Checklist of Signs and Symptoms of Adult Survivors of Ritual Abuse.* (Available from Los Angeles County Commission for Women, Ritual Abuse Task Force.)

Finklehor, David. *Nursery Crimes: Sexual Abuse in Day Care.* Sage Press, 1988.

Friesen, James G. *Uncovering the Mystery of MPD.* San Bernadino: Here's Life Publishers, 1991.

Gould, Catherine. *Signs and Symptoms of Ritualistic Child Abuse.* 1988. (Included in Los Angeles County Commission for Women, *Ritual Abuse: Definitions, Glossary, the Use of Mind Control,* see below.)

Hector, Holly. *Satanic Ritual Abuse and Multiple Personality Disorder: Understanding and Treating the Survivor,* 1991. (303/430-7100.)

Hollingsworth, Jan. *Unspeakable Acts.* New York: Congdon and Weed, 1986.

Hudson, Pamela S. *Ritual Child Abuse: Discovery, Diagnosis and Treatment.* Saratoga, Calif.: R and E Publishers, 1991. (408/866-6303.)

Kahaner, Larry. *Cults That Kill.* New York: Warner Books, 1988.

Kluft, Richard. *The Childhood Antecedents of Multiple Personality.* Washington, D.C.: American Psychiatric Press, 1985.

Koch, Kurt. *Christian Counseling and Occultism.* Grand Rapids: Kregel Publications, 1972.

Los Angeles County Commission for Women. Report of the Ritual Abuse Task Force, *Ritual Abuse: Definitions, Glossary, the Use of Mind Control,* 1991. (213/974-1455.)

Peck, Scott, M.D. *People of the Lie.* New York: Simon and Schuster, 1983.

Peretti, Frank E. *This Present Darkness.* Wheaton, Ill.: Good News, 1990.

S., Joe. *Out of Hell Again*. Lakewood, Ohio: State of the Art Publishing, 1991. (800/735-1929.)

Smith, Michelle, and Laurence Pazder. *Michelle Remembers*. New York: Pocket Books, 1981.

Spencer, Judith. *Suffer the Child*. New York: Pocket Books, 1989.

Terry, Maury. *The Ultimate Evil*. New York: Doubleday, 1987.

Wagner, C. Peter, and F. Douglas Pennoyer, eds. *Wrestling with Dark Angels*. Ventura, Calif.: Regal Books, 1990.

Warnke, Mike. *The Satan Seller*. South Plainfield, N.J.: Bridge Publishing, 1972.

White, Thomas R.A. *A Believer's Guide to Spiritual Warfare: Wising Up to Satan's Influences in Your World*. Ann Arbor: Vine Books, 1990.